BRITISH WEST FLORIDA

1763-1783

CANADA

ILLINOIS COUNTRY

River

Ohio R.

Mississippi

Yazoo R.

LOUISIANA

WEST FLORIDA

Pensacola

New Orleans

GULF OF MEXICO

GULF OF CAMPECHE

Vera Cruz

Campeche

Espiritu Santo Bay

CROWN

Ft. Pitt

line of 1763

Wazzard

GEORGIA

Augusta

Charles Town

EAST FLORIDA

St. Augustine

NEW YORK

N. H.

MASS.

CONN.

Boston

PENN.

New York

Philadelphia

MARYLAND

DEL.

VIRGINIA

Williamsburg

NORTH CAROLINA

New Berne

SOUTH CAROLINA

ATLANTIC OCEAN

BERMUDA IS.

New Providence

BAHAMA ISLANDS

Nassau

Havana

CUBA

SANTO DOMINGO

PORTO RICO

JAMAICA

Kingston

CARIBBEAN SEA

WEST FLORIDA

AS IT RELATED TO
OTHER PARTS OF THE COLONIAL WORLD

SCALE OF MILES

0   500

Lucia Porcher Johnson '42

PORTO RICO

LEEWARD IS.

Guadaloupe

Dominica

Martinique

St. Lucia

St. Vincent

Barbados

Grenada

CARIBBEAN SEA

WINDWARD IS.

SOUTH AMERICA

BRITISH
WEST FLORIDA
1763–1783

BY

CECIL JOHNSON

ARCHON BOOKS

1971

Printed in the United States of America

To

CHARLES McLEAN ANDREWS

PREFACE

THERE has been a tendency among those interested in American History to stress the importance of the "original" Thirteen Colonies and to slight or ignore the remaining twenty-odd which were parts of the British Empire in the New World. While the thirteen are deservedly of greatest interest, the others also were a part of the colonial picture. Some of them were of sufficient significance to the empire, to other colonies, and to subsequent history to warrant careful study. The province of West Florida, created by the Royal Proclamation of October 7, 1763, affords a good example. This colony was an integral part of the British plan for administering the new territory which had been acquired as a result of the French and Indian War. Adjacent to Louisiana, it had a military importance from the standpoint of defense and offense and was a convenient base from which the activity of the Spanish in New Orleans could be observed. Two West Florida towns, Pensacola and Mobile, were scenes of major Indian congresses, and the latter place was a center for those engaged in the Indian trade. The colony offers an engaging study in colonial administration and in land, as regards both distribution and speculation. It was a part of the western movement with immigrants from all of the older colonies. The Spanish conquest of the province is an interesting but neglected aspect of the American Revolution. Though West Florida was ceded to Spain at the conclusion of this war, all the territory that it embraced was eventually included in the states of Louisiana, Mississippi, Alabama, or Florida. To tell the story of this British province, from its origin in 1763 until its surrender to the romantic young governor of New Orleans in 1781, is the purpose of this volume.

Citations made in this study to manuscripts from the

British Public Record Office are, unless otherwise indicated, to photostats or transcripts in the Library of Congress. Citations to Minutes of Council or to Assembly Minutes are to transcripts or originals in the Library of Congress. Spelling, capitalization, and punctuation, save in a few obvious instances, have been modernized.

Chapters V and VI have in slightly different form appeared in the *Louisiana Historical Quarterly* and the *Mississippi Valley Historical Review*, respectively. I am indebted to the editors of these publications for permission to use them here.

It would be impracticable to mention all the individuals and institutions that have helped in the preparation of this study. The assistance of some, however, has been such that specific acknowledgment should be made. I am appreciative of aid rendered by Mr. Howard Peckham of the William L. Clements Library, Dr. Hunter D. Farish of Colonial Williamsburg, Incorporated, Miss Ellen M. Fitz-Simons of the Charleston Library Society, Miss Georgia Faison of the University of North Carolina Library, the late Dr. Dunbar Rowland and Dr. W. D. McCain, both of the Mississippi Department of Archives and History, the late Dr. James Alexander Robertson of the Florida State Historical Society, and by attendants and officials of the Alabama Department of Archives and History, the Howard Memorial Library, the New York Public Library, the Yale University Library, and the Manuscripts Division of the Library of Congress. The Smith Fund of the University of North Carolina, through timely grants-in-aid, has helped to make possible the continuing research embodied in this work. The late Professor Ulrich B. Phillips out of the fullness of his experience gave discerning suggestions. Dr. C. C. Crittenden at one stage in the preparation of this study read the entire manuscript critically, and Dr. Hugh T. Lefler read and made suggestions on the first two chapters. Miss Porter Cowles of the University of North Carolina Press has not only typed the final draft of the manuscript but has made numerous suggestions regarding stylistic changes. Invaluable have been the guidance and encouragement of Professor Charles M. Andrews, under whom this study in an earlier form was prepared and presented as a doctoral dissertation at Yale University, and Professor Leonard Woods Labaree, under whose direction it has been revised and prepared for the press. Lucia Porcher Johnson has made the maps and has rendered additional aid of a less tangible but nonetheless essential character.

C. J.

Chapel Hill, North Carolina,
  September 12, 1942.

CONTENTS

MAPS

BRITISH WEST FLORIDA, 1763-1783

I

BACKGROUND AND BEGINNINGS

THE Seven Years' War, coming to a close with the Treaty of Paris in 1763, brought to a climax the epic struggle of England and France for European leadership and for political and commercial supremacy in India and North America. By this treaty France, for the time being, gave up her ambitions for a colonial empire. To England she ceded all of her territorial claims in North America east of the Mississippi, except the Isle of Orleans and two unimportant islands in the St. Lawrence, which she kept for fishery purposes. She also yielded to England Grenada and the Grenadines on the southeastern edge of the Caribbean, and agreed to an arrangement which gave England possession of the neighboring islands of St. Vincent, Dominica, and Tobago. Spain ceded Florida to England and in return received Cuba, which had been seized during the latter part of the war. At the same time, by an agreement which had been negotiated secretly, France ceded her ally, Spain, all the territory that she possessed west of the Mississippi, together with the Isle of Orleans. The continent was thus divided between England and Spain with the Mississippi as the principal boundary. In this way England came into undisputed possession of settlements in Canada, Florida, and eastern Louisiana, and a huge unsettled strip west of her original settlements, for which provision must be made. These arrangements—particularly the decisions to take Canada rather than the rich West Indian islands from France, and Florida from Spain—indicate the ascendancy in British colonial affairs of the imperialists, the group which held that the needs of the growing empire should receive paramount consideration even when they conflicted with the time-honored tenets of mercantilism.

The conclusion of the war and the acquisition of so much additional territory brought the British ministry face to face with several important problems.[1] In early May, 1763, the Earl of Egremont, secretary of state for the Southern Department, put before the Board of Trade a number of general and specific questions which were to be considered and reported upon. Among these were the following: By what regulations might the most extensive commercial advantages be derived from the recent cessions? How might those advantages be rendered more permanent and secure to his Majesty's trading subjects? What information could be furnished in regard to the climate, soil, produce, and harbors of Florida? What new governments should be established, what form should they take, and where should the capitals be located? What military establishments should be sufficient? By what means, least burdensome and most palatable to the colonists, could they contribute to the expense which must attend these civil and military establishments? Directly related to the question of military establishments was that of Indian tranquillity. In this connection, Egremont mentioned that the governors of the Carolinas and Virginia, as well as the Indian agent for the southern district of North America, had already been instructed to "adopt the more eligible method of conciliating the minds of the Indians by the mildness of His [Majesty's] government, by protecting their persons and property, and securing to them all the possessions, rights and privileges which they have hitherto enjoyed."[2]

1. The classic treatment of British policies in the West just prior to the Revolution is Charles W. Alvord, *The Mississippi Valley in British Politics.*

2. Earl of Egremont to the Board of Trade, May 5, 1763, Adam Shortt and A. G. Doughty (eds.), *Documents relating to the Constitutional History of Canada, 1759–1791* (second and revised edition), pp. 127–131. Hereafter cited as Shortt and Doughty, *Documents.*

In a lengthy representation, the Board of Trade attempted to answer the questions which Egremont had propounded. The most obvious advantages which might be derived from the recent cessions were: those arising from the fishery rights in Canada; the supplying of all Indian tribes with European commodities immediately through English traders; the possibility of settling the coast, from the mouth of the Mississippi to the Hudson Bay settlements, and of obtaining the great variety of produce which it was possible to raise in that immense tract of seacoast, peopled either by foreign emigrants or by the overflow of population from the older colonies; the additional supply of naval stores; and the increase in the trade of sugar, coffee, cotton, and other products by the speedy settlement of the newly acquired islands. These advantages might best be secured by the adoption of a number of suggested measures. New regular governments should be established in Canada, Grenada and East and West Florida; the form of each of these governments, because they were infant settlements, should be that of a governor and council. The large tract of land bounded by the Floridas on the south, by the Mississippi on the west, by Canada on the north, and by the older colonies on the east should be reserved to the Indians, and governors should be strictly prohibited from making any new grants of land beyond certain points. The Indian trade in this tract should be open to all English subjects under certain regulations. The board regretted that lack of information prevented a report on Florida, recommendations regarding military establishments, and the "mode of revenue least burdensome to the colonists." [3]

In reply to this representation, Egremont stated that the king had, for the most part, approved the board's suggestions and that James Murray, Francis Grant, and George Johnstone had been selected as governors of Canada, East Florida, and West Florida, respectively. The board was asked to prepare drafts of commissions and in-

3. Representation of the Board of Trade, June 8, 1763, *ibid.*, pp. 132–147.

structions for these appointees and was in addition instructed to report on the most reasonable and frugal methods for peopling the new colonies with useful and industrious inhabitants, either from such of his Majesty's colonies as might be overstocked or from foreign parts.[4]

Meanwhile the Indian situation had been brought to a crisis by the outbreak of Pontiac's conspiracy, an insurrection caused by resentment of the natives over the continual encroachment on their lands. News of the trouble reached England in late July or early August. Some action to pacify the Indians was necessary at once. On August 5, 1763, the Board of Trade suggested that an immediate proclamation be issued setting forward the determination of the king to prevent further encroachment on Indian lands, and his intention to open East and West Florida for settlement under conditions especially favorable to those who had so faithfully and bravely distinguished themselves in the late war.[5]

The Earl of Halifax, who succeeded Egremont as secretary of state for the Southern Department, notified the board that the king had approved its suggestion of an immediate proclamation, but that his Majesty was of the opinion that several other subjects of great concern should be provided for at the same time. The board was requested, therefore, to prepare a proclamation covering, in addition to the matters of the Indian reservation and the opening of new lands to settlers, the question of boundaries and constitutions for the new governments, a prohibition on private purchase of land from the Indians, a statement of the right of all Englishmen to participate in trade with the Indians, and a provision for the return of all criminals who might flee to the reserved lands.[6] Two weeks later, the board sent the draft of the proclamation to Halifax with the explanation that on further thought they had decided

4. Egremont to the Board of Trade, July 14, 1763, *ibid.*, pp. 147–150.
5. Representation of the Board of Trade, Aug. 5, 1763, *ibid.*, pp. 151–153.
6. Halifax to the Board of Trade, Sept. 17, 1763, *ibid.*, pp. 153–155.

that it was expedient for his Majesty's service to give confidence and encouragement to prospective settlers by an immediate and public declaration of the plan of summoning assemblies, and that the proclamation had been drawn in accordance with this opinion.[7]

The resulting proclamation of October 7, 1763, is one of the most important documents in later colonial history. Its primary purpose was to reassure the Indians by reserving for their exclusive use the lands, roughly speaking, between the Allegheny Mountains and the Mississippi, south of Canada and north of Florida, and by forbidding private purchase of lands from the Indians. Prior to this time the private purchase of Indian lands had frequently been accompanied by frauds, with resultant misunderstandings and ill-feeling. The secondary purpose of the proclamation was to provide for colonial expansion in a manner at the same time attractive to the colonists and satisfactory to the Indians. Because of overpopulation and speculation desirable lands in the Atlantic colonies were becoming scarce, the colonists were growing land-hungry and were not likely to view with equanimity their exclusion from the broad and fertile area specifically reserved for the Indians. Therefore, three new continental colonies—Quebec and East and West Florida—were established in which land was to be granted on very favorable terms. The island of Grenada with the Grenadines and Dominica, St. Vincent, and Tobago were erected into the government of Grenada. In order to encourage settlers the usual type of royal government by an appointed governor and council and an elected assembly was promised for the new provinces. The coast of Labrador between St. John River and Hudson Straits, with adjacent islands, was added to Newfoundland; the islands of St. John's and Cape Breton were annexed to Nóva Scotia; and the land between the Altamaha and the St. Mary's was given to Georgia. The Indian trade, subject to certain regulations which were to be drawn up later, was opened to all Eng-

7. The Board of Trade to Halifax, Oct. 4, 1763, *ibid.*, pp. 156–157.

lishmen who took out licenses from the provincial governors.[8]

Such were the international events, the political exigencies, and the economic considerations which brought the colony of West Florida into existence as a royal province. The boundaries, according to the proclamation, were to be the Gulf of Mexico on the south (including all islands within six leagues of the coast), Lakes Pontchartrain and Maurepas and the Mississippi as far north as the thirty-first parallel on the west, this same parallel on the north, and the Chattahoochee and Apalachicola rivers on the east. Governor Johnstone reported to the Board of Trade that the colony thus constituted did not include certain considerable settlements on the Mississippi, or even Mobile and adjacent territory. Consequently, on a recommendation from the board, a supplementary commission was issued to Johnstone in 1764 which moved the northern boundary to a line drawn due east from the confluence of the Yazoo and Mississippi rivers. This increased the size of the colony,[9] which now embraced the former Spanish territory including and adjacent to Pensacola; former French territory including and adjacent to Mobile, Biloxi, and Natchez; and certain land that might have been claimed by Georgia under the Charter of 1732. Free navigation of the Mississippi had been granted to the English by the seventh article of the Treaty of Paris.

The colony as laid out was composed of the southern

8. This proclamation may be found in *ibid.*, pp. 163–168; *Michigan Pioneer and Historical Collections,* XXXVI, 14–19; the *South Carolina Gazette,* Dec. 31, 1763; *Annual Register* (1763), pp. 208–213; and in many other places. A thoughtful analysis of the background of the proclamation is Charles W. Alvord, "The Genesis of the Proclamation of 1763," in *Michigan Pioneer and Historical Collections,* XXXVI, 20–52. There is an excellent account of the events leading to the establishment of West Florida in C. E. Carter, "Beginnings of British West Florida," in *Mississippi Valley Historical Review,* IV, 314–341.

9. *Acts of the Privy Council, Colonial Series,* IV, 668. A copy of the commission is in a manuscript volume of West Florida commissions in the Library of Congress. It is printed by James A. Padgett in *Louisiana Historical Quarterly,* XXI, 1034–1035.

halves of the present states of Mississippi and Alabama and the southeastern and northwestern fractions of Louisiana and Florida, respectively. It was roughly rectangular in shape, approximately 150 miles in width, north to south, and 375 in length. Pensacola, the seat of government, was 180 miles east of New Orleans, and 750 miles northeast of the Spanish settlements on Campeche Bay; it was 600 and 1050 miles northwest of Havana and Jamaica, respectively. Augusta, in Georgia, lay 400 miles northeast of Pensacola and Charles Town was a hundred miles farther in the same direction.

The soil of the province was of varying degrees of fertility. Along the gulf coast it was very sandy and without many possibilities for cultivation. Some of the lowlands were suitable for rice, but this commodity was never produced in large quantities. Although the coastal lands were not particularly suited to cultivation, they did furnish excellent pasturage, and several travelers in the region commented on the herds of black cattle near Mobile and Biloxi. As one went north from the coast the land became increasingly fertile, but this was held by Indians—Choctaws, Chickasaws, and Creeks—who were slow to make valuable cessions, notwithstanding their fondness for congresses with the accompanying free victuals and presents. Especially fertile and desirable land was to be found on the Mississippi between Manchac (at the mouth or beginning of the Iberville) and Natchez. Since the Indian danger was not great in this section, numerous grants were made to settlers and speculators, particularly after 1768.

The territory is without mountains and the district around the Gulf—the coastal plain—is almost flat. All the streams flow southerly or southwesterly and empty into the Gulf, the lakes, or the Mississippi River. The principal rivers are the Escambia, emptying into Pensacola Bay; the Perdido, formerly separating Spanish Florida and French Louisiana; the Alabama and Tombigbee, converging just above Mobile Bay; the Pascagoula, with its mouth near Biloxi; and the Pearl, emptying into the Gulf outlet of Lake Pontchartrain. The Iberville was an effluent of the Mississippi when that stream became swollen from spring floods, but during the rest of the year it was a stagnant bayou or, in some places, completely dry.[10] It connected with the Amite, which finally reaches the sea by way of Lakes Maurepas and Pontchartrain.

The climate of the new province was, on the whole, not considered very salubrious. Although the weather in spring and autumn was very mild, in summer it became excessively hot unless tempered by Gulf breezes. In winter, especially along the Mississippi, temperatures fell so low as to cause discomfort. Garrisons, particularly those at Mobile, suffered periodically from plagues and epidemics which would doubtless be called malaria and yellow fever today.

The transfer from Spanish and French to English dominion was accomplished in the late summer and early fall of 1763 when military forces took possession of the ceded territory.[11] On July 3, Major General William Keppel, acting in accordance with the twentieth article of the Treaty of Paris, ordered Lieutenant Colonel Augustin Prevost, with the third batallion of the Royal American Regiment, to occupy Pensacola and all dependencies.[12] Prevost left Havana in early July and, after a voyage hindered by contrary winds, arrived at Pensacola on August 6, and received the surrender of the post on that day. The Spaniards, delayed by lack of transports and by the

10. Bayou Iberville no longer has a contact with the Mississippi. It is said locally that Jackson closed this waterway just before the Battle of New Orleans to prevent the British from using it in a flanking maneuver.

11. C. N. Howard has two articles: "The Military Occupation of British West Florida, 1763," in *Florida Historical Quarterly*, XVII, 181–199; and "The Interval of Military Government in West Florida," *Louisiana Historical Quarterly*, XXII, 18–30. Howard quotes copiously from contemporary letters. He has not used the unpublished Gage Papers. There is an article by W. H. Siebert, "How Spain Evacuated Pensacola in 1763," in *Florida Historical Quarterly*, XI, 48–57.

12. Keppel to Prevost, Dunbar Rowland (ed.), *Mississippi Provincial Archives*, English Dominion, I, 130–131. Hereafter cited as *Miss. Prov. Arch.*

necessity of loading numerous stores, did not actually leave until a month later.

The accounts which Prevost and other officers gave of Pensacola were far from flattering. The town consisted of about one hundred huts. According to Prevost, "The country from the insuperable laziness of the Spaniards remains still uncultivated, the woods are close to the village, and a few hawltry [paltry] gardens show the only improvements. The climate is not healthy, the soil around the village though sandy is able to produce vegetables; further back the country is good and capable of improvement—but years and a number of industrious settlers can only make a change on the face of the colony. Stock they have none, being entirely supplied from Mobile. . . . Game is extremely plenty in the woods and the sea supplies quantities of fish of different sorts and kinds." [13] Major William Forbes, who arrived with the 35th Regiment on November 30, commented on the dilapidation of the fort, the inadequacy of barracks composed of "bark huts without any sort of fire places or windows, void of every necessary utensil," and the sterile and sandy nature of the soil.[14] Both officers spoke feelingly of the unpleasant necessity under which they labored of supplying visiting Indians with food and presents.

Major Robert Farmar, with the 22nd and 34th regiments, also under orders from General Keppel, went by way of Jamaica and Pensacola to Mobile,[15] and on October 20, 1763, took possession of that town and Fort Conde. An Indian congress was in session at the time and the French officials suggested that the English commander delay the debarkation of his troops until the meeting had adjourned. Farmar, however, urged the necessity of landing his troops immediately, since they had been on board

13. Prevost to the secretary at war, Sept. 7, 1763, *ibid.*, pp. 136–137.
14. Report of Major Forbes, evidently to the secretary at war, Jan. 30, 1764, *ibid.*, pp. 112–115.
15. General Keppel to Major Farmar, on board the *Conquistador*, July 19, 1763, *ibid.*, pp. 128–129.

for quite a long time, and he carried his point.[16] On taking possession of the town he issued a manifesto which substituted English for French law, assured the inhabitants of protection and invited their friendly coöperation, forbade all sale of land and other real property until titles had been recorded and verified, commanded all who intended to remain in the colony to repair within three months to Mobile and take the oath of allegiance, and promised safe transportation for the movable property of those who possessed an inclination to withdraw from that section of the country. Orders were issued for the proclamation to be read in the church of each parish for four consecutive Sundays and to be posted in public places.[17] A month after the occupation of Mobile, a force of thirty men under the command of a subaltern took possession of Fort Tombigbee.[18] Because of lack of men no effort was made to occupy Fort Toulouse.

Since Major Farmar had arrived and insisted on landing in the midst of an Indian congress, he was confronted with the immediate problem of formulating Indian policy, a subject upon which he had no instructions whatever. The French policy of extending lavish hospitality and numerous presents to powerful chiefs was characterized by the major as "a vile custom," sacrificing every thought of social enjoyment. The idea of keeping his "house constantly open to them, giving them victuals whenever they ask it, and the government making them annually considerable presents" was extremely distasteful to him. However, the weakness of the force under his command, the large number of Indians living in or adjacent to the province, and the desire not to antagonize them at the outset, made it expedient for him to follow the French procedure. In his report to the secretary at war he said: "The most disagreeable custom the French have introduced amongst the Indians, is that of constantly giving them

16. Major Farmar to the secretary at war, Jan. 24, 1764, *ibid.*, pp. 7–17. This letter carries a full account of the occupation of Mobile.
17. *Ibid.*, pp. 60–63.
18. Farmar to Egremont, Jan. 24, 1764, *ibid.*, pp. 137–139.

victuals and drink, and which I have been under the necessity of adopting. I have had five hundred a day during the congress to entertain in this manner, and now that the main body is gone, I have twenty or thirty that dine every day in the house and must have Indian corn to carry to their camp for their children."[19] The items in his contingent account for entertainment of Indians, totalling more than £319, excluding numerous presents, speak eloquently of the expense of such a policy.[20]

For the purpose of quieting the Indians, Farmar and the French authorities drew up an agreement in regard to Indian affairs, and at a council with the eastern part of the Choctaw nation, held at Mobile in November, they issued a joint address. This speech announced the transfer from French to English dominion (the change, one would be led to believe from the language of the paper, was made largely for the benefit of the savages) and explained that in the future the Indians living on the eastern side of the Great River should look to the English for presents and trade. If a red man killed a white man, the head of the red man would be required; but the head of a white man who had killed an Indian would be turned over to the family of the slain man. The Indians were urged to pay what they owed the French, and it was promised that the French chief in New Orleans would require Frenchmen who owed Indians to pay their debts. The Indians were asked to deliver to the English any Frenchmen who came into their land without permission from the commander at Mobile.[21] Similar harangues were made to the Creeks and the Alabamas on their visits to Mobile.[22] Farmar's instructions to officers directed that especial attention be given to the protection of Indians against the dishonesty of traders.[23]

19. Farmar to the secretary at war, Jan. 24, 1764, *ibid.*, pp. 7–17.
20. Farmar's contingent account is printed in *ibid.*, pp. 65–74. The items for Indian entertainment include 10 barrels of sweet potatoes, 56 barrels of Indian corn, 8,374 pounds of beef, 3,586 loaves of bread, and one firkin of butter.
21. Agreement and address printed in *ibid.*, pp. 83–91.
22. Printed in *ibid.*, pp. 80–83 (no dates).
23. Printed in *ibid.*, pp. 92–94.

The population of Mobile was estimated at about 350 when Farmar arrived.[24] Though the Treaty of Paris provided that the French Catholics should not be disturbed in the exercise of their religion, the inhabitants of Mobile were rather slow in taking the prescribed oath of allegiance and it was generally expected that most of them would remove to the territory around New Orleans and west of the Mississippi, which region would presumably remain in French hands. By April, 1764, only eight persons had taken the oath.[25] The transfer of Louisiana to Spain, however, was not popular with the French and by the following October over a hundred additional residents had sworn allegiance to the English king. Farmar stated that he was "in constant expectation of numbers from New Orleans as the cession of that city to the Spaniards was made public last week." [26] Throughout this period the English authorities in West Florida, in order to encourage emigration from Lousiana, tried to take advantage of this dissatisfaction of the French with Spanish rule, but their efforts were not generally successful.

Farmar found the fort at Mobile (as Prevost and Forbes had found the fort at Pensacola) in a very dilapidated condition. The townsmen, he complained, claimed most of the property that was necessary for the proper support of a military post. "I have reason to believe," he wrote the secretary at war, "that the officers and French inhabitants have endeavored to . . . [claim] everything without the works that belonged to His Most Christian Majesty, as they do not allow that he had anything without the works; the hospital and magazine with all the buildings belonging thereto (except one store house) they pretend was private property, although they allow that most of them have been built at the king's expense, and assert that the king paid rent for them." Major Farmar

24. "State of the Revenue of Louisiana, . . ." enclosed with Farmar's letter of Jan. 24, 1764, to the secretary at war, *ibid.*, p. 30.
25. Farmar to the secretary at war, April 7, 1764, *ibid.*, pp. 116–117.
26. Same to same, with enclosures, Oct. 2, 1764, *ibid.*, pp. 120–122.

interpreted the treaty as meaning that all the property of the French government in Mobile should be turned over to the English. Monsieur D'Abbadie, the ranking French officer in Louisiana, thought otherwise. A compromise was finally reached by taking an inventory of the goods under dispute and submitting the question to the respective courts.[27]

The year of military government, preceding the arrival of Governor Johnstone, was marked by much sickness, especially at Mobile. In the early fall of 1764, Farmar reported the death of two officers and added, "this place is at this season so dreadfully sickly, that I am greatly afraid for many others." [28] A few days later he stated that "the raging fever still continues both amongst officers and men . . . and we have no other hopes than that the approaching cold season will effectually stop it." [29] Captain Robert McKinen, in a report from Pensacola, mentioned the evil consequences to the regiment of "inveterate scurvys which terminate in mortifications and death." He was afraid the condition would grow worse, since there was a total lack of vegetables and since the bedding of the soldiers was very bad.[30] Mobile retained its bad reputation for sickness, though Pensacola soon came to be considered a place of great healthfulness.

The interval before a civil government was established witnessed one situation interesting both in itself and in its relation to the future welfare of the colony. A Spanish vessel from Campeche with a large amount of coined silver, a cargo of logwood, and other tropical produce was seized at Pensacola by an officer of the royal navy. The vessel was released when it was found that she had not broken bulk or attempted to trade. Major Forbes reported the incident to General Thomas Gage, military commander for North America, insisting that unless trade of this kind

27. Same to same, Jan. 24, 1764, ibid., pp. 7–17.
28. Same to same, Sept. 15, 1764, ibid., p. 120.
29. Same to same, Oct. 2, 1764, ibid., pp. 120–121.
30. Oct. 30, 1764, ibid., p. 123.

were allowed, Florida would be of little value to the British.[31] There will be occasion later to comment more fully on the efforts that were made to develop commerce with the Spanish ports in the Gulf of Mexico.

Before discussing the inauguration of the civil régime in West Florida it is desirable to examine the form of government which was prescribed by the proclamation of October 7, 1763, and the commission and instructions to the first royal governor, George Johnstone.[32] These documents have been aptly characterized as the constitution of West Florida.[33] The proclamation, as already noted, created the province, established its boundaries, and outlined in a general way the form of administration. The commission, a formal document couched in legal terms, appointed Johnstone captain-general and governor-in-chief of West Florida with full authority to exercise the powers mentioned therein. The instructions, composed of seventy-nine articles, were more informal in character and gave specific directions as to the ways in which the powers mentioned in the commission were to be exercised. The commission was to be published immediately after the governor's arrival in the colony, but the instructions were primarily for his personal guidance. The latter were not to be made public generally, but those relating to the council were to be revealed to the councillors, and those setting forth the conditions

31. Forbes to Gage, May 20, 1764, Gage Papers, William L. Clements Library of the University of Michigan.
32. Commission and instructions may be found in the Public Record Office, Colonial Office 5: 201. Hereafter cited as C.O.5. The reference here, and in other cases where these papers are cited (except when otherwise noted), is to transcripts or photostats in the Library of Congress. The Department of Archives and History, Jackson, Mississippi, also has transcripts of C.O.5: 582-597. Johnstone's regular and supplementary commissions and his vice-admiralty commission have been published by James A. Padgett in *Louisiana Historical Quarterly*, XXI, 1020–1068. A convenient work of reference is *Royal Instructions to British Colonial Governors, 1670–1776*, collated and edited by L. W. Labaree.
33. C. E. Carter, "Some Aspects of British Administration in West Florida," *Mississippi Valley Historical Review*, I, 364–375.

under which land should be granted were to be recorded
in the grants.

The type of government provided was that of the usual
royal province, a form which varied only slightly throughout the brief history of the colony. The administration, of
course, centered in the governor, who was the local representative of the royal prerogative. This official was to be
assisted by a council of twelve men, among whom were to
be the chief justice of the colony and the surveyor general
of the customs for the southern district of North America.[34] The other members were to be selected by the governor from the most prominent inhabitants or persons of
property, and their names were to be sent to the Board of
Trade to be laid before the king in council for approval.[35]
Councillors were usually named in the instructions, but the
fact that civil government was just being instituted in
West Florida made this procedure impracticable in the
case of Johnstone. The governor was directed to submit a
list of ten additional men from which names might be substituted in case any of the original appointees were not approved. A quorum of the council was set at five. When a
vacancy occurred the governor was to notify the Board of
Trade immediately and to submit a list of three or more
men whom he thought fitted for the office; but whenever the
number of those resident in the colony fell below seven, he
was authorized to bring the number up to seven by temporary appointments. The governor, upon a careful examination of the charges made, and with the advice of a
majority of the council, might suspend a councillor, but
in such instances the minutes of the council were to be submitted to the Board of Trade in order that the Privy
Council might pass finally on the case. Councillors who
absented themselves from the province for six months with-

34. John Stuart, superintendent of Indian affairs for the southern
district of North America, was later made an *ex-officio* member of the
council in West Florida and in all the other colonies under his supervision. Stuart to General Thomas Gage, May 24, 1772, Gage Papers.
   35. Instructions 2 and 4.

out the governor's permission or for twelve months without the king's leave were to forfeit their places. The governor was to summon the council as he saw fit and was to allow freedom of debate in matters of public concern.[36]

In case of the absence or death of the governor when no designated successor was at hand, the eldest or senior councillor was authorized to assume the government with full powers, but he was instructed to take no actions, except those necessary for the peace and welfare of the province, without a particular order. The governor was forbidden to leave the colony to go to Europe except by permission from England. In case of sickness, however, he might go to New York or some other northern colony for the interval necessary for the recovery of his health. When he was absent from the province half of the salary and perquisites of his office were to go to the acting governor.[37]

Until an assembly was convened, the governor, with the advice and consent of the council, was charged with the making of the ordinances necessary for peace and order, but acts affecting the life, limb, and liberty of the subjects and those levying taxes or duties were forbidden.[38] Regulations necessary for improving trade were to be similarly made, but the governor by assenting to any laws for setting up manufactures and carrying on trades, which would be hurtful and prejudicial to Great Britain, would incur the pain of the king's highest displeasure. He was commanded to discourage to the utmost any attempts to set up manufactures or to establish such trades.[39]

The governor, with the advice of the council, was empowered to summon an assembly when he thought expedient, and to determine districts and apportion representatives. The assembly, together with the council acting in a legislative capacity, formed a bicameral legislature whose

36. Instructions 2, 6, 7, 8, and 10.
37. Instructions 76–78.
38. Instruction 11.
39. Instruction 60.

acts, unless containing suspending clauses,[40] should become laws when approved by the governor. A number of restrictions, found advisable largely by experience in the other colonies, were placed on this legislature. The style of enacting was prescribed, "by Governor, Council and Assembly." Each matter was to be in a separate act, no clause foreign to the title should be inserted, and no perpetual clause should be part of a temporary act. No law respecting private property should be passed without a suspending clause and unless it had been read in the parish churches for three Sundays before its passage. All laws for levying taxes or imposing fines, forfeitures, or penalties should expressly mention the fact that the proceeds were granted to the king for the public use of the province and the support of the government thereof, as therein directed. Such laws should provide for the auditing of the funds by the auditor general of the plantation revenues or his deputy. No law was to be passed which in any way affected commerce or shipping, or related to the prerogatives of the crown, or the property of the subjects, or which should be found in any way unusual or extraordinary, until a draft of it had been approved by the Privy Council or unless it had a suspending clause. To prevent a practice, in vogue in several of the other colonies, of enacting a law for a brief period in order to escape the royal disallowance, the governor was ordered to assent to no law, except in case of imminent necessity or temporary expediency, which had been enacted for a space of less than two years; nor should he agree to any law reënacting a disallowed act or repealing legislation which had been confirmed unless it contained a suspending clause. All laws, with reasons for their passage and full information concerning them, together with fair copies of the journals of both houses, should be sent to the Board of Trade within three months of their enactment.[41] This body would send

40. An act containing a suspending clause did not go into effect until it had been approved by the Privy Council.
41. Instructions 11–15.

them to the Privy Council with recommendations for approval or disallowance.[42]

Johnstone was instructed to establish, with the advice of his council, courts patterned after those already in operation in the other colonies, and more particularly in Georgia. Judges and justices of the peace were to be appointed with the advice of the council to serve during pleasure; but neither they nor any other officers were to be removed except for good and sufficient reasons, which should be immediately transmitted to the Board of Trade. The governor was forbidden to exercise any of the judicial offices either directly or through deputy. Appeals from the provincial courts, in civil causes, to the governor in council and thence to the Privy Council were to be allowed, with the procedure in such cases governed as nearly as possible by the regulations prescribed for such processes in the instructions to the governor of Georgia.[43] Copies of all commissions establishing courts and jurisdictions were to be submitted to the Board of Trade for royal approval. The governor was reminded of the frequent complaints that had come from other plantations of delays and undue proceedings in the courts. He was admonished to see that justice was promptly and impartially administered in the province under his care.[44]

Some of the provincial officers were appointed directly from England with commissions under the great seal or

42. See Chap. IV for an account of the assembly in session and a discussion of the laws enacted.

43. These provided that appeals might be made from the common-law courts to the governor in council, provided the amount involved exceeded £300 and the appellant posted security to guarantee payment of the judgment and costs in case the verdict was confirmed. Councillors who had acted as judges in such cases should not be allowed to sit with the council though they might appear and offer reasons for their verdicts. A case might be appealed from the council to the Privy Council provided that the amount involved exceeded £500, that appeal was made within fourteen days, and that security was posted as before. Any case to which the king was a party might be appealed to the Privy Council regardless of the amount involved. These regulations had become fairly uniform in all of the crown colonies by this time.

44. Instructions 16–23.

sign manual. The governor was instructed to see that these men or their deputies performed their duties acceptably. He was authorized to suspend officers for misbehavior and to fill the places thus made vacant by temporary appointments until the king's pleasure should be known. In case of a vacancy caused by the death of a deputy, a temporary appointment was to be made until the will of the patentee was ascertained.[45]

Johnstone was directed to abide by the clause of the Treaty of Paris which provided that Catholics be allowed freedom to exercise their religion as far as the laws of England permitted. Those professing the faith of the Roman Church were to give, from time to time and under oath, an account of the arms and ammunition in their possession. The governor was to send to the Board of Trade as soon as possible an exact account of the religious communities of this church, with a statement of its property, claims, and revenues, together with the number of its priests. All residents of the province were to be summoned to take the oath of allegiance and to subscribe to the declaration of abjuration. Any Frenchmen who refused to do this were to depart forthwith.[46]

Governor Johnstone, according to the usual procedure, received a vice-admiralty commission and was instructed to put into execution the powers authorized thereby. Pirates were to be tried for the time being in Georgia, and all diligence was to be exercised in apprehending these marauders and in obtaining evidence necessary for convicting them. Without special permission no letters of marque and reprisal were to be granted against any prince or country at peace with England.[47] In case a situation vital to the interest of the province and not covered by instructions developed, the governor might act with the advice of the council, but full particulars were to be sent to the Board of Trade at once so that the matter might be laid

45. Instruction 24.
46. Instructions 28–31.
47. Instructions 63, 64, and 66.

before the Privy Council for approval; under no color, however, was the governor to declare or commence war without the knowledge and consent of the home government.[48] The usual correspondence was to be with the Board of Trade; but in affairs requiring immediate attention, and in those where the royal orders had been transmitted directly by one of the principal secretaries of state, correspondence was to be with them only. Instructions concerning the granting of land will be discussed specifically later. Trade instructions, some twenty-six in number and in a separate document, enumerated the different acts of trade and navigation with their main provisions and urged the governor to enforce these with great diligence.[49]

From this summary it is evident that the government of West Florida was definitely patterned after that of the typical royal province. In one very important particular, however, West Florida differed from nearly all the older royal colonies. The civil establishment was supported by an annual grant from parliament. This appropriation was made necessary by the needs of the frontier province, the sparsity of population, and the absence of wealth. It was doubtless intended as a temporary expedient, but was continued throughout the period of English control and was of great constitutional importance since it made the governor independent of the assembly. For instance, Governor Chester did not summon the legislative body from 1772 until 1778. This financial independence did not prevent the struggle between executive and legislature which was so characteristic of royal colonies, but in West Florida the disagreements were largely over writs of election and

48. Instruction 74. It is interesting to note that a violation of this instruction resulted in Johnstone's recall. Shelburne to Johnstone, Feb. 19, 1767, Mississippi Transcripts, vol. X. (This is a volume of miscellaneous transcripts from the Public Records Office in the Department of Archives and History, Jackson, Mississippi.) Hereafter cited as Miss. Trans. Also, General Gage to Colonel William Tayler, April 30, 1767, Gage Papers.

49. These have been published by James A. Padgett in *Louisiana Historical Quarterly*, XXI, 1044–1067.

privileges of the assembly rather than over provincial finances.

The annual support fund varied from £3,900 to £7,200. Certain items were fairly constant in appearance and in amount,[50] but there were interesting variations. Estimates during the early years contained a bounty fund of £50 to be used for the encouragement of the culture of silk, grapes, and other agricultural products, but in 1767 this bounty was omitted since it had not been used.[51] Appropriations totalling £2,500 were made from 1771 to 1773 to pay for the construction of a house for Governor Chester,[52] a building unhappily never completed and eventually taken over by the military. In 1773, and for several years thereafter, an allowance of £50 was made "to Mr. Romans for his care and skill in the collection of rare and useful productions in physic and botany." [53] In 1777, after Romans had left the colony and was reportedly in

50. The estimates for 1768–69 may be taken as typical.

Salaries
Governor	£1,200
Chief Justice	500
Attorney General	150
Provincial Secretary and Clerk of Council	150
Register	100
Surveyor	120
Assistant surveyor	30
Agent (residing in London)	200
Minister at Pensacola	100
Minister at Mobile	100
Schoolmaster at Pensacola	25
Schoolmaster at Mobile	25
Provost Marshal	100
Contingent Fund	1,000
Indian Expenses	1,000
Total	£4,800

C.O.5: 586, pp. 45–52, Miss. Trans.

51. Shelburne to the governor of West Florida, April 11, 1767, Miss. Trans., vol. X.

52. John Pownall to Governor Chester, Feb. 12, 1771, *ibid.*

53. William Knox to the governor of West Florida, March 3, 1773, *ibid.* This was Captain Bernard Romans whose *A Concise Natural History of East and West Florida* is a valuable source.

the service of the Americans, the item was discontinued.[54] Beginning in 1776, £100 was included for the receiver general.[55] Appropriations amounting to more than £2,500 were made in the period from 1771 to 1775 to Engineer Campbell and Lieutenant Governor Durnford for surveys and fortifications in the province.[56] In 1777, the sum of £1,000 was added to the contingent fund in order that the governor might aid the distressed loyalists who came to West Florida from the rebelling colonies.[57]

The contingent fund was used by the governor to meet the unexpected expenses of the government and to pay those provincial officers not provided for in the parliamentary grant.[58] The Indian fund provided the entertainment and presents necessary for retaining the good will of the savages. It was doubtless a source of peculation. Governor Chester and his versatile secretary, Philip Livingston, Junior, were said to have outfitted their slaves from the Indian supplies. The Indian superintendent for the southern district, of course, had a separate fund, and during the last two years of the colony's history his department had charge of all distribution of presents to the Indians. When it is realized that the military establishment in the colony was perhaps more expensive than the civil, it will be seen

54. Knox to Governor Chester, March 5, 1777, Miss. Trans., vol. X.
55. Knox to the governor of West Florida, March 24, 1776, *ibid.*
56. Pownall to Governor Chester, Feb. 12, 1771; Knox to the governor of West Florida, enclosing civil list, March 3, 1773; Pownall to Governor Chester, enclosing civil list, March 3, 1775, all in *ibid.*
57. Knox to Governor Chester, enclosing civil list, March 5, 1777, *ibid.*
58. When Johnstone left the colony in 1767, he submitted to Lieutenant Governor Browne the following list of annual salaries:

Clerk of the Crown	£30
Clerk of the Court of Requests	20
Clerk of the Court of Common Pleas	10
Messenger of the Council	20
Deputy Provost Marshal at Mobile	20
Negro Jailer at Mobile	18:5
Jailer at Pensacola	20
Clerk of Court of Requests at Mobile	20
The Coroner	a guinea an inquest

C.O.5: 585, pp. 255–256, Miss. Trans.

that West Florida was a costly part of the imperialists' plan.[59]

This review of the circumstances that led to the erection of West Florida, together with the examination of the topography of the province and the form of government which was prescribed for it, has set the stage for the entrance of the colony's first civil governor and most colorful character, George Johnstone.

59. Nova Scotia, Georgia, and East Florida also had parliamentary support funds.

II

THE ADMINISTRATION OF GOVERNOR JOHNSTONE

GOVERNOR Johnstone[1] arrived at Pensacola on October 21, 1764, eleven months after his appointment. Not much is known of the motley group which was on hand to greet him in the crude capital of the new province. The Spaniards, it seems, had departed almost to a man leaving doubtful claims to their real property in the hands of a few speculators. The military composed the largest single element in the population and we may be assured that it lent some starch and for-

---

1. George Johnstone was born in Dumfries, Scotland, in 1730. He was the fourth son of a baronet of Dumfriesshire. He entered the navy at an early age and became a post captain in 1762. His record, though marked by a number of acts of gallantry, was marred by disputes and duels. On November 20, 1763, he was appointed governor of West Florida, probably through the influence of his fellow countryman, Lord Bute, who was at that time an influential member of the ministry. The report of his appointment to West Florida and of James Grant's to East Florida gave occasion for an attack on Scots in the sixty-second number of *The North Briton,* a scurrilous sheet especially opposing the participation of the Scots in government. As a result of this article Johnstone assaulted the supposed author. On his return to England after his recall from West Florida, Johnstone was elected to Parliament and served for many years, being regarded as an authority on American affairs. In 1778 he was with Carlisle on the commission to conciliate the colonies, but because of indiscreet negotiations with individual members of Congress, his usefulness to the commission was destroyed and he withdrew after Congress had adopted a caustic declaration refusing to deal further with him. After additional parliamentary and naval service he died in 1787. The otherwise excellent sketch of Johnstone by J. K. Laughton in the *Dictionary of National Biography* ignores, except by implication, his administration of West Florida. See also *Appleton's Encyclopaedia; Miss. Prov. Arch.,* I, xiii-xxi; *Journals of Continental Congress,* XI, 770–773; indexes of *Scots Magazine* and *The Gentleman's Magazine;* W. E. H. Lecky, *History of England in the 18th Century,* IV, 84–85; C. M. Andrews, *The Colonial Background of the American Revolution,* p. 157; S. F. Bemis, *The Hussey-Cumberland Mission and American Independence.*

mality to a society which would otherwise have been informal in the extreme. There were a few merchants engaged in furnishing the troops with supplies and interested in the possibilities of the Indian trade and commerce with Spanish ports in Mexico and Central America. There were no doubt the usual adventurers and riffraff who congregate in frontier towns and around army posts. Probably there were not yet many who had come for the purpose of clearing ground and establishing plantations, since the real influx of settlers of this type did not reach appreciable proportions until several years later. An occasional indentured servant, a rare slave, and a few wandering Indians begging bread or trinkets would perhaps complete the picture.

Several problems demanded the governor's immediate attention. It was necessary to organize civil government and to replace the military rule which had been in operation for a year. Pensacola was in such wretched repair that it was advisable to lay it out anew and to devise some plan for the distribution of town lots. The lack of favor with which the French inhabitants regarded the transfer of Louisiana to Spain made it probable that judicious soliciting might attract to the province valuable settlers from across the Mississippi. Several powerful tribes of Indians lived in, or adjacent to, the colony and it was highly desirable that friendly relations be established with them. Johnstone attacked these problems with characteristic energy and enthusiasm.

The first meeting of the council was held on November 24. On this occasion the governor took the oaths required by his instructions and administered those prescribed to the members of the council. Present, in order of seniority, were James McPherson, John Stuart, Robert Mackinen, James Bruce, and William Struthers, all of whom had been appointed by the governor.[2] McPherson,

2. Minutes of Council, Nov. 24, 1764, C.O.5: 632. The reference here and in other citations to Minutes of Council followed by British Public Record Office serial numbers are to transcripts or photostats in the

by authority of a warrant issued under the royal sign manual, had been commissioned by Johnstone on November 2 as provincial secretary and clerk of the council.[3] As one of the privileges of his patent, McPherson appointed Alexander Fraser deputy clerk of the council. Stuart was the superintendent of Indian Affairs for the southern district of North America, and no British official in the southern colonies was to play a more important rôle than he in the period which followed. Mackinen, commander of the local garrison, soon had disagreements with the governor and resigned his place, according to council minutes, on account of ill health.[4] Bruce later became collector of customs at Pensacola, while Struthers was particularly interested in the trade with the Indians. On November 27, Elias Durnford was admitted to the council.[5] As surveyor and engineer of the province, and later as lieutenant governor, he played an important part in many phases of West Florida activity. Inasmuch as some official business was transacted at Mobile, it seemed advisable for some members of the body to be residents of this town. Consequently, in a council held at Mobile in December, Jacob Blackwell, Francis Morcier, and Robert Crook were admitted.[6] Blackwell was collector of customs at that port, and later the agent designated for the distribution of stamps under the law of 1765; but little is heard of Morcier and Crook.

On November 27, 1764, a blanket commission was issued appointing as justices of the peace all members of the council and nineteen other residents. These officers were empowered to bind persons over by bond or imprisonment to keep the peace. Two of them acting together, one of whom must belong to a select group known as the

Library of Congress. Where no serial numbers are used, the reference is to originals in the same institution, unless otherwise indicated.

3. Record of His Majesty's Sign Manuals, Patents, Commissions, and Other Papers Passed under the Broad Seal of His Majesty's Province of West Florida, pp. 1–4. This is a manuscript volume in the Library of Congress and will be cited hereafter as West Florida Commissions.

4. Minutes of Council, Jan. 30, 1765, C.O.5: 632.

5. *Ibid.*, Nov. 27, 1764.

6. *Ibid.*, Dec. 11, 1764.

"quorum," might try offenses against the laws of England and the province; but where the life of a man was involved the case was to be referred to the "judges of the supreme courts of judicature" for determination.[7] Edmund Rush Wegg, later described by Johnstone as a beardless youth of twenty, presented a warrant under the sign manual ordering the governor to appoint him attorney general.[8] By authority of a similar warrant, William Clifton, formerly attorney general of Georgia, was commissioned chief justice, with the right of holding supreme courts of judicature.[9] Both of these officials were to serve during the king's pleasure and were to have all rights and privileges enjoyed by similar officers in any province in North America. On January 22, 1765, a commission was issued under the seal of the province establishing the general court of pleas with criminal and civil jurisdiction. This court was to be held at Pensacola on the second Tuesday in January, April, July, and October, according to the laws of Great Britain and such laws as might thereafter be enacted in the province. Appeals were to be allowed according to the governor's instructions and procedure was to be modelled after that in English courts.[10] Governor Johnstone established a vice-admiralty court in February, 1765, with his appointment of Attorney General Wegg as judge,[11] Arthur Gordon as advocate general,[12] Samuel Fontinello as register,[13] and James Johnstone as marshal.[14] All of these appointments were made on the governor's authority alone and in accordance with powers specifically delegated to him in his commission.[15] By virtue of a royal warrant Simon Amory

7. West Florida Commissions, pp. 12–15.
8. Ibid., Nov. 2, 1764, pp. 5–8.
9. Ibid., Jan. 21, 1765, pp. 9–11.
10. Minutes of Council, Jan. 22, 1765, C.O.5: 632.
11. West Florida Commissions, Feb. 8, 1765, p. 16.
12. Ibid., Feb. 1, 1765, p. 17.
13. Ibid., Feb. 9, 1765, p. 18.
14. Ibid., p. 19.
15. It is interesting to note in this connection that on July 9, 1766, Alexander Duncan was commissioned in England as judge of vice-admiralty under the great seal of High Court of Admiralty (ibid., pp.

was appointed register of grants, patents, and records.[16] Separately he was appointed clerk of the naval office, and was especially admonished not to infringe upon the rights of the Admiralty.[17] Amory was accorded the privilege of having a deputy, but was instructed not to absent himself from the province for more than three months without the king's permission. Civil government was thus inaugurated.

Several of the early ordinances of the council suggest the frontier character of the colony. It was resolved that not more than three retailers should be licensed to sell spirituous liquors in Pensacola;[18] in Mobile the number was limited to four. In the minutes of a meeting held at Mobile on December 11, 1764, is found this interesting item:

Resolved, That to prevent an abuse frequently complained of, that of killing the cattle of other persons and selling the carcasses at Mercates, that for the future all persons who shall expose any beef for sale, shall be obliged to hang out the green hide with the hair out, on his stockade fronting the street for four hours in the day.[19]

It was ordered that all cattle brands and ear marks be registered with the provincial secretary. When a horse was sold the bill of sale should be witnessed by a justice of the peace. Winchester measure was prescribed for measuring grain and wine measure for liquids.[20] The *Custos*

120–131); and on June 18, 1767 Alexander McPherson was commissioned in a similar way as register.

16. *Ibid.*, Nov. 2, 1764, pp. 21–24.

17. *Ibid.*, Nov. 1, 1764, pp. 25–26. Amory did not live to enjoy the fruits of his offices. A letter from Johnstone to Lord Halifax, Sept. 14, 1765 (*Miss. Prov. Arch.*, I, 288–290) mentions his death at the age of seventy-two and makes the following comment: "Mr. Amory had been educated in a very low situation of life, having lived as a retailer of pins, needles, and groceries in Taunton."

18. Minutes of Council, Nov. 25, 1764, C.O.5: 632.

19. *Ibid.*, Dec. 11, 1764.

20. The wine gallon of 231 cubic inches was established in England in 1707 but was superseded by the imperial gallon in 1824. It is still the standard in the United States. The Winchester bushel dates from the

Rotulorum was instructed to keep a set of English measures as a standard.[21] A resolution was adopted approving the building, by subscription, of a market at Mobile. Another resolution approved the erection of a church at Mobile through money to be raised in large measure by contributions. For this object the governor agreed to be responsible for £250,[22] of which £150 would come from his contingent fund and £100 from the Society for the Propagation of the Gospel.[23]

Pensacola had for many years been a settlement and a military port under Spanish rule. After the signing of the treaty and before the arrival of the British, several land speculators attempted to buy up the most desirable holdings in the town. The governor and council, however, subsequently declared the titles thus obtained to be faulty and refused to recognize any claims for land purchased from the Spanish, though consideration was given the holders of these claims in the distribution of town lots.

In accordance with instructions from the council, Elias Durnford, the surveyor, presented a plan for the erection of a town at Pensacola. After certain sections had been reserved for military, naval, and governmental purposes the remainder was divided into town building lots. All lots were eighty by one hundred and sixty feet, and with each was granted a garden lot bordering on the rivulet which flowed by the north side of the town. The council prescribed the conditions under which lots should be granted to petitioners. A quit-rent of sixpence sterling, payable March 25 of each year, was levied on each town lot. Each grantee must enclose his lot with a five-foot fence within eighteen months and must build within two years a good

time of Henry VII. Though it has been replaced in England by the imperial bushel, it is still the standard in the United States (*Encyclopaedia Britannica,* twelfth edition, and *The New International Encyclopaedia*).

21. Minutes of Council, Jan. 7, 1765, C.O.5: 632. This officer is the principal justice of the peace in an English county, and keeper of the rolls and records of the sessions of the peace.

22. *Ibid.*

23. *Ibid.,* Dec. 13, 1764. The proposed building was never erected.

tenantable house,[24] not smaller than thirty by fifteen feet and with at least one brick chimney. Failure to build or to enclose within the allotted time would result in an additional quit-rent of twenty shillings, and failure to do so within ten years would result in forfeiture. Failure to enclose the garden lot within two years and to drain and cultivate it in three would make it liable to forfeiture. A lot might not be alienated before it was enclosed. The right of fishing and "hawling the sean" on every part of the bay was free to all.[25]

For the purpose of receiving grants the petitioners were divided into five groups. The first was composed of those who were entitled to preference because of claims of purchases from the Spanish. There were fourteen persons in this group and to them twenty-six lots were granted. In the second class were the holders of official positions, mainly members of the council and the attorney general. To the five in this classification, six lots were granted. In the third class were those whom the council thought most able to improve the grants. Fifteen members of this group received a total of nineteen lots. Membership in the fourth and fifth classes was also determined on the basis of ability to improve the land, the most impecunious being placed in the latter class. Within these groups precedence in choice was decided by lots drawn under the supervision of a committee of the council. There were sixty-two grantees and an equal number of lots in the fourth class, and fifty-six grantees with fifty-five lots in the fifth.[26]

This very artificial procedure for land distribution in Pensacola, influenced by class distinction and wealth, furnishes an interesting contrast to the system in the early

24. The following council minute gives an interesting suggestion as to the kind of houses erected: "Read a petition from David Dewary praying for said lot No. 31. Granted the said petition, he engaging to His Excellency and the Honorable Council to raise a house upon it by tomorrow night." Aug. 8, 1765, C.O.5: 632.

25. *Ibid.*, Feb. 3 and 7, 1765. A poor copy of Durnford's plan, from the Public Record Office, is reproduced in P. J. Hamilton, *Colonial Mobile* (rev. ed.).

26. Minutes of Council, Feb. 7 and 8, C.O.5: 632.

New England towns where need was a major consideration.[27] This striking dissimilarity was due in part to the
fact that the founders of the New England towns had a
religious, moral, and social unity that was entirely lacking
among the first English settlers in Pensacola.

By the terms of the treaty of Paris the French in the
territory were given eighteen months to dispose of their
lands and to emigrate. In a memorial to Halifax, signed
by a number of French inhabitants, it was stated that although they desired to sell their lands and leave the
province they had no title except that of possession, cultivation, and use. Furthermore, it was stated, due to the
delay of the English in occupying the country, the eighteen months provided in the treaty was not sufficient. Consequently, these inhabitants asked for an extension of time
and for the right to sell their property without formal
title. Halifax instructed Johnstone to investigate the situation and to make an equitable adjustment. Shortly thereafter the council in Mobile directed all claimants to file
their original titles with the provincial secretary for examination by the attorney general and the surveyor. In
all cases where possession and cultivation, or buildings
erected at private expense, should appear, the titles would
be confirmed provided the parties were willing to abide by
the terms under which lands were usually granted.[28] However, all of the French claims were not settled for a number of years. Mobile, probably because it was better established and more substantially built, did not undergo a re-
organization similar to that in Pensacola, though a number of town lots were laid off and granted.

A question which greatly interested Governor Johnstone
and his successor, Lieutenant Governor Browne, was that
of the emigration of settlers from Louisiana to West
Florida. The announcement of the cession of Louisiana to
Spain, which was not made public until the spring of 1764,

27. R. H. Akagi, *The Town Proprietors of the New England Colonies.*
28. All this is explained in Minutes of Council, Dec. 13, 1764, C.O.5:
632.

put a new aspect on the anticipated movement of French inhabitants from Mobile and the surrounding country to New Orleans. Furthermore, it was felt that the inhabitants of that province, especially Germans and Swiss, had no desire for Spanish rule.[29] This impression was strengthened by the hostile reception which the people of New Orleans gave the first Spanish governor and the tumultuous times which followed his arrival. The authorities in West Florida were anxious to take advantage of this situation to encourage the immigration of prosperous settlers. On September 8, 1764, Halifax wrote Johnstone that he had lately been informed by his Majesty's Electoral Minister at Geneva, that there were several Swiss and German inhabitants of New Orleans who would probably choose to migrate to West Florida when the cession to Spain actually took place. Johnstone was instructed to investigate and if he found that a number of Swiss or Germans, who were likely to become good subjects and useful settlers, were anxious to remove to West Florida, he was to offer them every proper encouragement. Especially were Gaspard Pictet and Francois Caminade commended to his favor.[30]

Immediately after his arrival in West Florida Johnstone, who had no doubt discussed the possibilities of the situation with Halifax, sent Lieutenant Alexander Maclellan to New Orleans to induce inhabitants to emigrate to West Florida. This officer reported that he found most of the people of New Orleans, all of the Germans who were settled on the west side of the river, and some of the inhabitants of Point Coupée, willing to move. However, they hesitated because of the sterility of the soil

29. The Germans were probably descendants of those who had been brought over by John Law. They had a settlement just north of New Orleans called Carlstein. This section is called the "German Coast" today. H. E. Chambers, *History of Louisiana*, I, 115; Bernard Romans, Map of Florida, 1774, in *Publications* of Florida State Historical Society, No. 2.

30. *Miss. Prov. Arch.*, I, 151. Caminade came into West Florida and served for a time as a councillor, but he eventually returned to New Orleans.

around Mobile and Pensacola, the uncertain attitude of the West Florida government toward the Roman Catholic religion, and their inability to sell their property for negotiable money. Maclellan thought that the opening of the part of the province that bordered on the Mississippi where the land was very fertile, the adoption of a liberal policy toward the Catholics already at Mobile, and the providing of free transportation for household goods for a short voyage, that is, from eastern Louisiana to the western part of the province—across and in some cases up the river —would have a very stimulating effect on this movement.[31]

Inasmuch as the opening for settlement of the lands bordering on the Mississippi seemed a prime consideration not only in the encouraging of immigration, but also in the proper development of the province and the strengthening of communication with the Illinois country, Johnstone, with the coöperation of the military authorities, set about making this possible. To this end, two important engineering works were thought advisable. The first of these was the clearing of the Iberville River for navigation and the second was the establishment of a military post at Manchac, or Point Iberville, at the forks of the Iberville and the Mississippi.

The English were much hindered in their endeavors to take possession of the Mississippi region and to maintain communication with the Illinois country by the lack of a convenient route from Mobile to the western part of the province. The only water route was by way of the Gulf of Mexico and the Mississippi. This route was quite indirect and progress up the Mississippi was slow and laborious. The French, and later the Spanish, controlled the land on both sides of the river at the mouth and, though the free navigation of the Mississippi had been guaranteed to the English by the Treaty of Paris, the use of this arduous route was likely to result in delays and international complications; in case of war with Spain this line of communi-

31. Extract, [Alexander] Maclellan to Johnstone, Dec. 10, 1764, *ibid.*, I, 268–269.

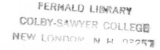

cation could easily be cut. Numerous creeks, rivers, and swamps made a direct land route impracticable. However, the Iberville River ran into the Amite and this stream emptied into Lake Maurepas, which had a connection with Lake Pontchartrain. The latter body of water had an outlet to the Gulf about one hundred miles west of Mobile. If this route could be made navigable, the distance to the western part of the province and to the Illinois country would be shortened, the toilsome journey against the current of the Mississippi would be curtailed, and difficulties with the authorities at New Orleans avoided.

The weak link in this chain of water communication was the Iberville, which, as a result of the annual spring overflows of the Mississippi, was filled with uprooted trees and other debris. It was thought that this stream could be cleared and that vessels drawing not more than eight or nine feet of water could navigate it without difficulty. The fatal difficulty in the scheme, the height of the bed of the Iberville above the low-water level of the Mississippi, was not appreciated at this time.[32] In the fall of 1764 Major Farmar authorized Captain James Campbell to attempt the operation. This officer set to work with a squad of fifty Negroes and in December wrote Governor Johnstone that the task would be completed within a month. He also mentioned the willingness of the inhabitants of Louisiana to migrate to West Florida and suggested the advisability of a military post at Manchac.[33] Johnstone immediately wrote Campbell, instructing him to reserve a place at Manchac for a fort, and authorizing him, with Charles Stuart, deputy Indian agent, to administer the oath of allegiance, to make temporary grants of land (which

32. There are interesting contemporary maps of the Iberville by Thomas Hutchins, William Brasier, and George Gauld in the Gage Papers. One by Brasier shows that the bed of the Iberville, in one place at least, was twelve feet higher than the surface of the Mississippi when that stream was low.

33. Campbell to Johnstone, Dec. 12, 1764, *Miss. Prov. Arch.*, I, 266–268.

would be made permanent later), and to encourage emigration from Louisiana.[34]

In the early part of 1765, Governor Johnstone conferred with Major Farmar, Major Arthur Loftus, Captain Campbell, and Engineer Archibald Robinson on the question of establishing a small post at Manchac. It was agreed, in view of the prospective opening of the Iberville, that this venture should be undertaken; and that Sir John Lindsay, commander of the Gulf Squadron, who had previously expressed his willingness to coöperate, should be requested to transport the necessary men and provisions by way of the Gulf and the Mississippi.[35] The funds necessary for the establishing of this post were procured through bills drawn by the governor on the Commissioners of the Treasury. Johnstone, apprehensive lest these expenditures should not be approved, wrote at length to John Pownall, secretary of the Board of Trade, setting forward the advantages of the proposed fort. Such a post was necessary in order to keep open the Iberville River, which had been recently cleared at great expense; it would encourage the emigration of Germans and Swiss from Louisiana, more than four hundred families of whom had agreed to come over with their slaves and stock if protection was offered; the passage of troops to the Illinois would be facilitated; such a post would aid in the capture of the fur trade of the Mississippi, which amounted annually to seven hundred thousand skins, all of which had been previously shipped from New Orleans; finally, settlements in a fertile and productive region were necessary to the life of the province. As proof of his belief in the value of the post Johnstone offered to allow the funds to be deducted from his salary until its utility had been demon-

34. Johnstone to Campbell, Dec. 21, 1764, in Minutes of Council, Jan. 7, 1765, C.O.5: 632. Charles Stuart is not to be confused with John Stuart, Indian superintendent for the southern district of North America.

35. Minutes of this conference, Jan. 7, 1765, in *Miss. Prov. Arch.*, I, 261–263.

strated beyond doubt.[36] The Board of Trade was so impressed by his case for the fort that it recommended not only the payment of whatever expense had been incurred, but also that provision be made in some future parliamentary estimate for enlarging the work.[37] The post was called Fort Bute. The expectations of large emigrations from Louisiana, however, were not realized. The failure of the Iberville project and the uncertainty of military protection, as well as the mildness of the Spanish rule, after it was finally established, contributed to keep the Louisiana settlers from coming to the province.

Equally pressing in its necessity for the governor's attention, along with the setting up of civil government and the encouraging of immigration, was the Indian problem. Three important tribes lived in or near West Florida and Johnstone was faced with the need of establishing friendly relations with these and of obtaining cessions of desirable land. The Creeks, Upper and Lower divisions, with an estimated strength of 3,600 fighting men, lived around Pensacola. The Choctaws with possibly 6,000 warriors inhabited the northern and western parts of the province.[38] The Chickasaws, less numerous and consistently friendly to the English, lived north of the Choctaws and south of the Tennessee River. These tribes were not confined to the rather narrow boundaries of West Florida, but all three had reached a fairly advanced stage of civilization and lived in towns which were more or less permanent in character. They raised Indian corn which they supplemented as a food supply with meat and fish. They were skillful hunters and sold many pelts to traders. The Choctaws and the Creeks were engaged in a chronic warfare and the English did little to bring about peace, believing themselves safe from attacks while the Indians were thus diverted.

36. Extract, Johnstone to Pownall, Feb. 19, 1765, *ibid.*, pp. 271–273.

37. Pownall to Charles Lowndes, secretary to the commissioners of the Treasury, Oct. 3, 1765, *ibid.*, pp. 269–270.

38. Johnstone and Stuart [to Lord Halifax], June 12, 1765, *ibid.*, pp. 184–188.

The impending war with France in 1756 and the inability of the colonies to coördinate their efforts had impressed upon the British government the necessity for a more direct agency for dealing with the Indians, especially in view of their potent possibilities as enemies or allies. For the purpose of Indian administration the English dominions in North America were divided into two districts, each in charge of an agent or superintendent. The now famous Sir William Johnson was appointed to the northern district and Edmund Atkin, sometime member of the South Carolina council, who was in England at that time giving a report on Indian conditions, was appointed to the southern district. Atkin's performance of his duties was not very vigorous and he died sometime before 1762. John Stuart, a native of Scotland, then living in South Carolina, succeeded him and held the office until his death in 1778.[39]

The Indians were upset in 1763 by the prospect of losing their hunting grounds to the land-hungry white settlers—in fact, Pontiac's outbreak is an evidence of this unrest. The proclamation of October 7 of that year was calculated both to quiet the Indian fears by prohibiting private purchase of their land and settlement beyond the line of the Alleghenies, and to divert the westward stream of immigration by opening for occupation desirable lands in the new provinces of East and West Florida.[40] By 1764 the Board of Trade had devised a plan which, if carried out, would put into operation the principles of the Proclamation of 1763 and provide a complete organization for dealing with all phases of the Indian problem.[41] It is of especial significance in the study of West Florida because of the efforts made to institute it there.

The plan provided for retention of the northern and southern districts under the direction of superintendents,

39. H. L. Shaw, *British Administration of the Southern Indians, 1756–1783*, pp. 1–20.
40. C. W. Alvord, "The Genesis of the Proclamation of 1763," *Michigan Pioneer and Historical Collections*, XXXVI, 20–52.
41. Plan is given in *New York Colonial Documents*, VII, 637–641.

but the division of jurisdiction was to be determined by the location of certain tribes which were assigned to each agent, and not by the Ohio River as was formerly the case. The superintendent for the northern Indians was to have three deputies and his southern colleague two. A commissary, to regulate relations between Indians and traders, and a smith or armorer for the repair of Indian guns, were to be located with each tribe. The commissary was expected to communicate fully with the superintendent, who would correspond with the Board of Trade. The agent was to be in complete control of relations with the Indians and no governor or military authority was to stop the trade with any tribe without his consent; nor was any public meeting or conference to be held with the Indians without his concurrence, though it was expected that civil and military officials would give their utmost coöperation to the superintendent. He had the right to confer rewards, honors, and commissions on influential chiefs. In the southern district the Indians of each town were to elect with the approval of the agent a "beloved" man who should represent them in their dealings with the traders, and the beloved men should elect a chief for the tribe who would deal with the commissary and the agent.

Trade with the Indians in North America was to be free and open to all of his Majesty's subjects who took out licenses from a colonial governor and obeyed certain regulations, except that no military officer or commissary should engage in trade, either directly or indirectly, and the charter of the Hudson's Bay Company should not be infringed upon. Prices were to be set from time to time by the commissaries in coöperation with the Indians and traders. Trade was to be conducted in the towns and posts and within certain limits specified by the commissaries; and within these limits the traders were authorized to erect huts and warehouses. Traders were forbidden to sell rum or other spirituous liquors, swan shot, or rifle-barrelled guns to the Indians, nor were they to give credit above fifty shillings. Standards of measure were to be kept in each post and town. No land was to be purchased from the Indians except by the crown (or proprietor) and then only at a general meeting. After a purchase had been consummated, representatives of the Indians should be present at the surveying. The annual expense of the plan was estimated to be £20,000 and it was thought that this amount could be raised by a duty on the Indian trade (except beaver 'skins), though this matter had not yet been submitted to Parliament.

In the spring of 1765 congresses were held in West Florida, at Mobile with the Choctaws and Chickasaws, and at Pensacola with the Upper and Lower Creeks, for the purpose of establishing friendly relations with the Indians, putting their trade on a regular basis, determining the Indian boundary lines, and securing, if possible, additional cessions of land. At this time Superintendent John Stuart attempted to put the new plan into operation.

The congress with the Choctaws and Chickasaws at Mobile continued from March 26 to April 4.[42] At this meeting were Stuart and his deputy, Monsieur Montbereaut (who had been active in Indian affairs under the French régime), Governor Johnstone with several members of his council, Colonel David Wedderburn of the military establishment, Arthur Gordon, who recorded the proceedings, and, of course, the principal chiefs of the Choctaw and Chickasaw nations, with numerous followers. Johnstone asserted that two thousand Indians came to Mobile. The congress was opened with the "usual ceremony of smoking the calumet . . . and prayers were read by the Reverend Mr. Hart; on which occasion the Indians behaved with great decency and listened with the utmost attention." The governor and superintendent then explained with great care the change from French to British rule and emphasized the friendly attitude of the English

42. Proceedings of this congress with the treaty are found in *Miss. Prov. Arch.*, I, 215–255. The letters of Stuart to General Thomas Gage, in the Gage Papers, deal in great detail with Indian relations in this period.

toward the Indians. At the same time it was subtly suggested that a cession of land was highly desirable in order that foodstuffs might be produced for the entertainment of the Indians on their next visit.

The Indians were equally emphatic in their protestations of friendship and as a token gave the English leaders Indian names. They appeared favorable to the proposed cession, but suggested, not quite so subtly, that, of course, presents were expected. A treaty of seven articles which had been prepared by Johnstone and Stuart was eventually approved and signed. The first article was a promise of peace and friendship between the English and the Indians and declared a "general oblivion" of all crimes and injuries that the Indians had heretofore committed. By the second article the governor agreed to encourage traders to supply the Indians with the goods that they needed. The third article was a promise on the part of the Indians to use their best endeavors to prevent damages to settlements, horse-stealing, and other disturbances, and to make restitution in case such outrages were committed; they also promised to put to death in the presence of two white people any Indian who murdered a white person. In the next article the English were bound to a similar procedure in case an Indian was murdered by a white man. The fifth article granted what Johnstone and Stuart termed "a tract of rich, convenient, and extensive territory." [43] By the sixth article the Indians bound themselves to support the authority of the commissaries and to aid in the return of white fugitives. The final article established a schedule of prices for items of the Indian trade in terms of pounds of half-dressed deerskins.

During the meeting the chiefs had surrendered their French medals, symbols of authority and respect from the French government. After the signing of the treaty, great medals were presented to six of the most important chiefs. The ceremony, according to the official chronicler, was

43. Johnstone and Stuart [to Halifax], June 12, 1765, *Miss. Prov. Arch.*, I, 184–188.

accompanied by the discharge of seven cannon from the fort and the playing of the drums and fifes of the 22nd and 34th regiments, proceedings well calculated to impress the Indians with the solemnity of the occasion. Similar though less elaborate ceremony attended the presentation of five small medals to less important chiefs.

Following the signing of the treaty with the Indians, a set of regulations governing the conduct of Indian traders was drawn up by Johnstone and Stuart. No spirituous liquor was to be sold or given to any Indian, though each trader was allowed a limited amount of rum. A trader was required to have written contracts with his employees and was responsible for their conduct. Furthermore, traders were prohibited from hiring Indians, half-breeds, or Negroes. White people were to be harbored in the Indian lands by the traders for only a brief period. All goods were to be sold at the prescribed rate and all measures were to conform to those of the commissary. No trade was to take place in the woods and no trader was to convene a meeting or deliver any message to the Indians without the concurrence of the commissary. Proper respect was to be shown commissaries and medal chiefs and under no pretense was anything to be taken forcibly from an Indian. Failure of any trader to observe these rules would result in the forfeiture of his license and bond.[44]

At the congress with the Upper and Lower Creeks held at Pensacola, from May 27 to June 24, the white delegation was made more impressive by the presence of Admiral Sir William Barnaby.[45] The most influential chief present was The Mortar, of the Upper Creek nation, on whom the English were especially anxious to make a favorable impression. Indeed, General Gage had designated him as one whose friendship should be won at all costs. The Mortar requested the governor and superintendent to meet him

44. Regulations are given in Shaw, *British Administration of the Southern Indians, 1756–1783*, pp. 195–196.
45. Proceedings of this congress with treaty are found in *Miss. Prov. Arch.*, I, 188–215.

and his warriors at the gate of the town, but they, perhaps not completely convinced of the pacific nature of his intentions, sent word that it was their "constant custom to receive Indians in the council chamber under the great king's picture." The Indians, therefore, came into the town and were saluted by a discharge of great guns. They gave Johnstone and Stuart each a white wing as an emblem of peace and friendship from the whole nation. "Sir William Barnaby, the Governor and Superintendent, were saluted with and fanned by eagles tails."

Notwithstanding these friendly gestures the conference was not as successful as the one held at Mobile. The Indians were almost insolent in their demands for presents. The Mortar doubted the good faith of the English. He complained that the red-crossed banners of the British signified hostility, and was opposed to any appreciable cession of land on the ground that not enough of his people were present to warrant such an action. He objected to the stationing of commissaries and armorers among his people and requested that a price unduly favorable to the Indians be established. The treaty as finally signed was similar to the one previously negotiated with the Choctaws and Chickasaws except that the clause in regard to commissaries was omitted. The Indians confirmed the eastern boundary that had been established at a conference held in 1764, at Augusta, Georgia, and granted a strip of land about fifteen miles wide—not broad enough to reach the fertile lands to the north—around Pensacola. The Mortar and three other chiefs of the Upper Creeks were made great medal chiefs with appropriate ceremonies and three chiefs of the Lower Creeks were given small medals.[46] A careful observance of the terms of the two Indian treaties and the regulations for traders would have been conducive

46. Superintendent Stuart and Governor Francis Grant of East Florida held a meeting with the Lower Creeks at Fort Picolata about twenty miles from St. Augustine, in the following November. After considerable diplomacy and intrigue the Indians agreed to a liberal cession. Grant and Stuart [to an unidentified correspondent, probably Secretary Conway], Dec. 9, 1765, ibid., pp. 174–176.

to agreeable relations with the Indians. Neither whites nor Indians, however, lived up to their obligations and the Indian question in West Florida was never satisfactorily solved.

One of the principal endeavors of Governor Johnstone was to tap the lucrative Spanish trade. Pensacola, with its fine harbor and proximity to Spanish settlements in Mexico, Central America, and the West Indies, was very favorably located for the purpose of distributing to the Spanish, articles of British manufacture and receiving in return silver, gold, and valuable tropical raw materials which would not compete with the products of British colonies. Such a trade in English bottoms was legal from the standpoint of the English navigation laws but was illegal under the Spanish laws, and was consequently extremely hazardous. When this trade was carried on in Spanish ships, though such a practice was contrary to both Spanish and English trade laws, it was less risky for the English; and inasmuch as it was in perfect accord with two cardinal tenets of mercantilism, namely, that of disposing of goods of British manufacture to an advantage, and that of obtaining desirable raw materials, it was thought that the enforcement of the English trade laws might be relaxed. The officers of the navy, however, were not inclined to allow this trade.[47]

Governor Johnstone, shortly after his arrival at Pensacola, put the situation pointedly before the Board of Trade in a letter to John Pownall. One of the conditions, he said, necessary to the complete prosperity of the colony was that his Majesty's ships should be clearly instructed to permit the commerce of Spanish vessels which brought in bullion or such products as would not compete with the commodities of the English colonies. As West Florida was conveniently located with reference to Mexico, Vera Cruz, Campeche, Havana, Merida, and New Orleans, nothing but downright folly could prevent riches from flowing into the colony. This trade, he estimated, would amount to

47. See pp. 13–14 above.

£200,000 a year. Nothing, he reiterated, would enable such a commerce to flourish but a "free egress and regress," where the ships brought bullion or such things as did not interfere with English manufactures, and took commodities in return; such a trade had long been allowed in the West Indies. He then recalled the regrettable incident which had occurred before his arrival at Pensacola when Captain Lucas, of the *Prince Edward*, had seized a Spanish vessel which had come in with 40,000 Spanish dollars in cash, and then after infinite perplexity, had towed it out of the harbor and dismissed it. "Three other vessels to the amount of £30,000 have been treated in the same way from a rigorous execution of the law under the late deputations, without any regard to the spirit of the act."[48] The great scarcity of hard money in the province at this time rendered such actions on the part of naval officers especially grievous.

The Board of Trade submitted the matter to Lord Halifax who laid it before the king. The decision was concise and disappointing. It was his Majesty's intention, Halifax wrote Johnstone, that Spanish ships and vessels, coming into the ports and harbors of West Florida, through distress or for refreshment, should not meet with any molestation, but should receive assistance in like manner as had always been allowed in Jamaica, provided they did not attempt to bring in any foreign goods or merchandise; the king's pleasure in that particular had been signified to the Commissioners of the Treasury and to the Lords of the Admiralty.[49]

This decision did not completely destroy Johnstone's hopes in regard to the Spanish commerce. In 1766 Parliament extended to two ports of Dominica and to four of Jamaica, privileges similar to those desired for West

48. Extract, Johnstone to Pownall, Oct. 31, 1764, *Miss. Prov. Arch.,* I, 167–170. "The captains and lieutenants are all swore [*sic*] and have deputations from the Commissioners of the Customs as customs house officers. . . ." Major William Forbes to Gage, May 20, 1764, Gage Papers.

49. Halifax to Johnstone, Feb. 9, 1765, *Miss. Prov. Arch.,* I, 172–174.

Florida.[50] On October 23, 1766, Johnstone sent the Board of Trade a number of recommendations for improving the commerce of the colony. He regretted that the privileges lately granted to Jamaica had not been extended to West Florida and suggested the advantages of admitting to the province the products of Europe in English-built ships, duty free, under a bond of re-exportation. This would increase British trade and make West Florida a center of commerce. If the liberty of exporting naval stores were allowed, the Spaniards would be dependent on West Florida in time of war. He also asserted that a remission of the British import duty on skins and a bounty of sixpence on half-dressed skins would draw a fur trade of £150,000 annually.[51] At the first meeting of the provincial legislature, which was held in November, 1766, a memorial from both houses made recommendations similar to those of the governor.[52] In the last council meeting which he attended before leaving the province, Johnstone again expressed his views on the Spanish trade and supported them with a variety of arguments. It was a particular maxim of English commercial law, he said, to encourage the importation of raw materials. The privileges lately extended to the West Indies would have been extended to West Florida had the importance of the province been known. English shipping would benefit from the raw materials re-exported. He was even willing to construe an isolated treasury minute as giving the council authority to encourage the trade.[53] Lieutenant Governor Browne concurred with Johnstone in these views and after the governor's departure continued, as we shall see, the effort to open this commerce.

By his commission and instructions Governor Johnstone had been authorized to summon an assembly, with the advice and consent of the council, when such an action was

50. *Statutes at Large*, X, 263 ff.
51. Johnstone to Pownall, C.O.5: 584, pp. 279–288, Miss. Trans.
52. *Ibid.*, pp. 295–322, dated Nov. 22.
53. Minutes of Council, Jan. 10, 1765, C.O.5: 632.

deemed expedient. Until such a body had met, the rules and regulations necessary for the good of the province were to be made by the governor and council, though no laws were to be passed that in any way tended to affect the life and limb of any subject.[54] Governor Johnstone held that this limitation did not prevent penalties of imprisonment and corporal punishment from being prescribed for infractions of council regulations, while Chief Justice Clifton held that such penalties were illegal. This difference of opinion was one of the contributory causes of a break between the two, and led to doubt as to the ability of the council to enforce its regulations. In February, 1766, a grand jury had, without positive result, memorialized the governor to call an assembly.[55] In July some inhabitants from Mobile petitioned for an assembly. The council was of the opinion that, in view of the need of sundry regulations and of the doubt as to the legal authority of the governor and council to enforce penalties effectually, the governor should summon an assembly. The council resolved: that six members be elected from each of the districts of Pensacola and Mobile and two from the township of Campbell Town; that the district of Pensacola embrace all of the territory east of the Perdido River except Campbell Town, and the district of Mobile all the territory west of the Perdido; that all the freeholders and householders within the districts and township have the right to vote; and that there be eight days' difference, at least, between the times of election at Pensacola and Mobile, and two days between the elections at Pensacola and Campbell Town.[56] The provision that elections in the different districts should not occur on the same day followed the English custom and was probably for the purpose of allowing electors to vote wherever they were able to qualify.

54. Instruction 11.
55. Mentioned in memorial to Pownall, April 1766, *Miss. Prov. Arch.*, I, 303–306.
56. Minutes of Council, July 28, 1766, C.O.5: 632.

The governor issued the writs of election, the elections were held, and the first assembly in West Florida met at Pensacola on November 3, 1766. After the representatives had been sworn by a committee of the council they elected Francis Poussett of Mobile speaker, and presented him to the governor and council for approval.[57] They then, in true legislative style, began the examination of credentials, and failed to seat one member, who had been returned from Campbell Town, because of fraudulent election.

During this first session of the assembly a memorial to the Board of Trade was passed by both houses and fifteen laws were enacted, and approved by the governor. The memorial, in an extravagant and exaggerated manner, enumerated the advantages and needs of the province and suggested a program of expenditure calling for an initial appropriation of £68,600 with an annual appropriation of £17,600 for the ensuing four years. The potential advantages were set forth as follows: a commerce with the Spanish dominions estimated at £300,000 annually; the strategic location of West Florida harbors in case of war with Spain; the staple commodities such as tar, pitch, masts, ships, lumber, cotton, indigo, rice, corn, wine, sugar, tobacco, hides, hemp, and fish, which might be produced with the proper encouragement of settlers; and the fine rivers which would engender a race of seafaring men "so peculiarly adapted to a nation maintaining the empire by sea." The needs were security against the Indians and stricter supervision of the Indian trade, a government house, churches, jails at Mobile and Pensacola, the opening of the Spanish trade, the securing of property by the issuing of new titles at public expense, remission of quitrents, the encouragement of agriculture by the distribution of slaves as premiums, the granting of bounties on rice and indigo, and an authoritative statement as to the powers of the civil and the military branches of the government. It is not probable that this bombastic petition had a great deal of effect on the home government.

57. *Ibid.,* Nov. 3, 1766.

The laws were such as might have been expected from
a frontier colony and, to a certain extent, they reflect local
needs and conditions. Elaborate regulations were adopted
for the governing of indentured servants and slaves.
Mobile with the surrounding territory was erected into the
county of Charlotte and a court of common pleas was established there. The legal rate of interest was fixed at 8
per cent and penalties were set on protested bills of exchange. The conditions by which foreigners might obtain
citizenship were established, and full political and religious privileges were promised to naturalized Catholics.
Masters of vessels, coasters excepted, were required to give
bond not to carry from the province any person who did
not have legal permission to leave. This law was probably
for the purpose of keeping debtors from escaping. Certain
import and internal taxes were granted to the king for the
support of the government of the province. It is interesting to note that most of the income thus raised was to be
used to meet the expenses of the assembly. The duration
of this tax law was limited to one year and the receiver
general was made collector with a salary of 5 per cent of
his collections. One act, in direct contravention of the governor's instructions, set the number of assemblymen for
each district, prescribed qualifications for electors and
candidates, and established a daily pay of ten shillings a
member and fifteen for the speaker. Other laws provided
for the regulation of workmen, and licensing of taverns,
and the clearing of weeds from streets.[58]

The Privy Council, acting on recommendation of the
Board of Trade, disallowed two of these acts. The law fixing the number of assemblymen and regulating electors
was pronounced an infringement on his Majesty's rights
and contrary to the governor's instructions. The act to
encourage foreigners was disapproved because it lacked a
suspending clause and because the encouragement it extended to Catholics was too general. The tax law was

58. Transcripts of these laws are in the Alabama State Department of
Archives and History, and photostats are in the Library of Congress.

severely criticized because most of the income was directed toward salaries of assemblymen. However, inasmuch as this law had been enacted for only one year and had already expired, to disallow it would have been an empty gesture. The governor was instructed, therefore, for the future, not to give his consent to similar acts.[59]

Notwithstanding the energy which Johnstone had exhibited in establishing the civil government, opening the province for settlement and encouraging immigration, treating with the Indians, and fostering the profitable Spanish trade, his administration was seriously marred by heated, and to a large extent, unnecessary, quarrels with officers of the West Florida military establishment. The frontier character of the province with the proximity of Spanish and Indians made strong garrisons essential to its welfare and development. The sparsity of population and its concentration, during the time of Johnstone, in the two principal military posts, Pensacola and Mobile, made inevitable some conflict between the civil and military unless the governor were a man of tact and diplomacy. These, unfortunately, were two qualities in which Johnstone seemed to be entirely lacking. He was bellicose and litigious by nature and determined that not one of the governor's prerogatives, as set forth in the formal phrases of his commission or as construed from a broad interpretation of this document, should be infringed upon.[60]

The first skirmish with the military occurred within a fortnight after Johnstone's arrival in the province. From the wording of his commission, which proclaimed him "Captain General and Governor in Chief of the province of West Florida," he claimed the right to command the garrison, to give the parole or countersign, and to receive the report of the guard. "For," he maintained to the local military commander, "imperium in imperio cannot exist

59. *Acts of the Privy Council, Colonial Series*, V, 158–159. For a more complete treatment of the assembly, see Chap. IV below.

60. "Governor Johnstone in West Florida," by C. N. Howard, *Florida Historical Quarterly*, XVII, 280–303, is concerned largely with the strife between the civil and the military.

in a commonwealth, much less within the fortifications of a garrison; either you must have the command of the fort or I; this is indubitable." [61] The fact that he lived within the fort complicated the situation. Captain Robert Mackinen, however, though averring his willingness to coöperate with the governor and council, quoted orders which placed him under the direction of the British commander-in-chief for North America and refused to surrender control of the fort.[62] Johnstone sent an account of the difficulty, with copies of the letters passed, to the Board of Trade, which referred the case to Lord Halifax.[63]

A dispute with Major Robert Farmar next occupied the governor.[64] This officer was preparing an expedition to the Illinois country[65] and was experiencing difficulty in persuading the merchants in Mobile and New Orleans to accept his New York bills of exchange drawn on General Gage. He eventually came into possession of a large number of deerskins (which he probably acquired by persuading some Mobile merchant to accept a New York bill of exchange). He planned to dispose of these in New Orleans for the hard money necessary to finance his expedition. The governor and council, though refusing official permission for this transaction, agreed, in view of the great need, to instruct the customs officers not to hinder the exportation of the first shipment of twelve hundredweight.[66]

61. Johnstone to Mackinen, Nov. 3, 1764, *Miss. Prov. Arch.*, I, 158–161.
62. Mackinen to Johnstone, Nov. 6, 1764, *ibid.*, pp. 162–164.
63. Board of Trade to Halifax, Feb. 1, 1765, *ibid.*, pp. 155–156.
64. On January 2, 1765, Johnstone wrote General Gage charging Farmar with misuse of government funds and supplies, lack of consideration for civilians, and failure to coöperate with, and to pay proper respect to, the civil governor. Johnstone to Gage, Gage Papers. This collection contains literally hundreds of papers relating to the disputes between the civil and the military in West Florida.
65. The attempt of Major Arthur Loftus in the spring of 1764 to lead an expedition up the Mississippi River to the Illinois country had been terminated tragically by an attack from the Indians at a point about a hundred miles north of New Orleans. Fifteen men had been killed and six wounded. *Collections* of the Illinois State Historical Library, X, 205-239.
66. Minutes of Council, Feb. 20, 1765, C.O.5: 632.

Permission to export a second lot of twelve thousand pounds was granted with the proviso that Farmar pay the customs officers an amount equivalent to the import duty that would have been paid had the skins been shipped to England.[67] Farmar thereupon drew on General Gage to the extent of £178 19s. 6d. in favor of Jacob Blackwell, collector of the customs at Mobile. Farmar reported the transaction to Gage with bitterness and charged the governor with using every means within his power to hinder and delay the expedition.[68] Though Farmar soon left for the Illinois country, his feud with Johnstone eventually ended in a court-martial for him in 1768, which after many delays resulted in an acquittal.

In the early part of 1765 Lord Halifax wrote Johnstone at length in regard to the relation of the military to the civil. It was the king's intention, he said, that the orders of the commander-in-chief for North America, and after him those of the brigadier generals commanding the northern and southern districts, should be supreme in all military matters and should be obeyed by all of the troops in the civil governments of America. Where no orders had been given by these officers, the civil governor in council, for the benefit of his government, might give orders to the local commander for the marching and disposition of troops; the latter should execute these pro-

67. *Ibid.,* Feb. 28, 1765.
68. Extract, Farmar to Gage, March 11, 1765, *Collections* of the Illinois State Historical Library, X, 464–466. A fellow officer commented on this controversy: "Johnstone imagined that his commission and instructions gave him more power than I think it has. Major Farmar and the officers would not allow him the power that he undoubtedly has. He desired Farmar to mark his own line, and that he would be satisfied 'til the dispute was otherwise determined. Farmar, not knowing his own powers, gave one point up one day and took it back the next; said and unsaid, puzzled and quibbled, 'til every part of civil and military government was driven into a most terrible confusion. . . ." Lieutenant Colonel David Wedderburn to Alexander Wedderburn, April 16, 1765, Wedderburn Papers in William L. Clements Library. Farmar attributed Johnstone's animosity to an unfavorable report on the climate and soil of West Florida that he, Farmar, had sent to the secretary at war before Johnstone came to the colony. Farmar to Gage, April 25, 1765, Gage Papers.

vided they were not contrary to, or incompatible with, orders that he might have received from the commander-in-chief or the brigadier general; and the local commander was, from time to time, to report to the brigadier general and the commander-in-chief the orders which he had received from the civil governor. The governor was authorized to give the word or countersign except when the commander-in-chief or the brigadier general was present. Returns of the state and condition of the troops, magazines, and fortifications should be made to the governor, as well as to the commander-in-chief and brigadier general. The governor, however, was not to interfere with the details of military duty and discipline.[69]

It would appear that these explicit instructions should have enabled the civil and military authorities to avoid further clashes of jurisdiction, but such was not to be the case. The letter from Lord Halifax reached Pensacola on May 20, just before the opening of the Creek congress, at a time when many strange Indians were present and coöperation between the civil and military was highly desirable both for the success of the conference and for the safety of the town. Johnstone immediately became involved in a dispute with the post commander, at this time Captain Andrew Simpson, over the possession of a house (which the governor wished an officer to vacate in order that he might assign it to the Indian superintendent), and over the keys of the garrison which the governor demanded be forthwith deposited with him. Finding that his contentions were upheld by all the members of the council except Chief Justice Clifton, and by Lieutenant Colonel Wedderburn, commander of the fort at Mobile, and Admiral Sir William Barnaby, both of whom were in Pensacola for the Indian congress, the governor decided, in spite of the unpropitious occasion, to press for his rights as he conceived them. Failing in an endeavor to place Captain Simpson under actual arrest, he persuaded Admiral Barnaby to land twenty marines and ordered Lieutenant

69. Halifax to Johnstone, Feb. 9, 1765, *Miss. Prov. Arch.*, I, 172-174.

Colonel Wedderburn to bring a detachment of troops from Mobile. With these forces he proposed to take forcible possession of the fort. In the face of such odds Captain Simpson felt constrained to yield. He publicly apologized and surrendered the keys to the garrison.[70]

General Gage, to whom the affair was reported, maintained that Johnstone had greatly exceeded his authority. He thought that Simpson was right in the main though he regretted that this officer had allowed himself to be moved from his original interpretation of his orders by the influence of others. He resented the fact that Admiral Barnaby, an officer of the navy, had been consulted in the matter. He roundly rebuked Wedderburn for his part and ordered him to return to his post at Mobile and to remain there until ordered to leave by a superior officer. He censured both Simpson and Wedderburn for allowing the letter of Halifax concerning the relation of the civil to the military to be published, as a general order, without his consent. He hoped that the arrival of Brigadier General Bouquet, who had charge of the southern district, would restore order.[71]

General Bouquet, however, died within two weeks of his arrival in West Florida. Johnstone, in notifying Lord Halifax of this event, remarked that the command of the troops within the province again fell on him. He "humbly" represented that the power of assembling a court-martial was much needed. If such a power was necessary to General Bouquet it seemed likewise necessary to his successor.[72]

A misunderstanding with Lieutenant Colonel Ralph Walsh, who had by this time become commander of the post of Pensacola, was not long in developing. Governor Johnstone learned of the severe criticism that General Gage had made of his conduct and on October 5 he wrote this officer a lengthy, satirical letter, showing that he felt

70. Extracts from Minutes of Council, May 23, 24, 26, 1765, *ibid.*, pp. 349–357; Johnstone to Gage, June 20, 1765, *ibid.*, pp. 384–387.
71. Gage to Simpson, July 31, 1765, *ibid.*, pp. 387–392; Gage to Wedderburn, July 31, 1765, *ibid.*, pp. 392–395.
72. Johnstone to Halifax, Sept. 14, 1765, *ibid.*, pp. 288–290.

very keenly on the subject of military command.[73] The trouble came to a head over the old questions of the right of disposing of government property, the custody of the keys of the garrison, and the honors due the governor. On January 20, 1766, the council, with Chief Justice Clifton dissenting, advised Johnstone to order Lieutenant Colonel Edward Maxwell, who had succeeded to the command at Mobile, to come to Pensacola with part of his force in order to arrest Walsh for disobedience and mutiny.[74] On the same day Johnstone dispatched the order. The greatest of haste was urged in order that Maxwell might take the command from Walsh and settle the disputes which bade fair to destroy the infant colony.[75] While waiting for the arrival of Maxwell the governor wrote General Gage applying, on the advice of the council, for a court-martial for Colonel Walsh, and charging: that he had seized the garrison; that he had withdrawn the sentinels from the governor's house and had ordered the guards to pay the governor no respect; that he had usurped the governor's prerogative by entertaining an Indian chief; that he had altered the parole prescribed by the governor; that he had seized materials purchased by the governor for the use of the garrison; that he had failed to make returns of the state of the troops to the governor; and, finally, that contrary to the orders of the governor, he had ordered the guns of the garrison to be fired on January 18, in honor of her Majesty's birthday, though the just respect due her Majesty had been duly observed on the real anniversary

---

73. *Ibid.*, pp. 405–408. General Gage's reply, incidentally, shows that the governor of West Florida had no corner on caustic rhetoric: "As the answer that I may be tempted to give to your letter . . . can't certainly be of use to the King's service, or indeed promote any good purpose, you will excuse me if I do no more than acknowledge receipt of that letter, and to add only, that it is my humble request to you, that you write me no more in that style, or that you would not take it amiss, if for the future epistles of that sort should be returned immediately to you." Nov. 18, 1765, Gage Papers.

74. Minutes of Council, *Miss. Prov. Arch.*, I, 373–374.

75. Johnstone to Maxwell, Jan. 20, 1766, *ibid.*, pp. 419–420.

of her birth.[76] These charges are in themselves pertinent commentary on the jealous regard in which Johnstone held his rights.

Lieutenant Colonel Maxwell arrived by water on January 31, with a force of sixty-five men. He was ordered by Johnstone to disembark his men on the following day and to take immediate possession of the garrison. On this occasion, however, the bluff of the governor was called. When Maxwell attempted to execute the order, he found that Walsh had closed the gates of the fort and increased the guard. A battle seemed imminent. Fortunately, Walsh and Maxwell held a conference in order to discuss the situation. When Walsh explained the very severe rebuke that Colonel Wedderburn had brought upon himself by an action similar to that of Maxwell, not twelve months before, the Mobile commander, who had already exhibited misgivings, backed down completely.

Governor Johnstone, not to be balked by the defection of his ally, issued a warrant for the arrest of Walsh charging him with giving orders, in opposition to the king's authority, for stopping the march of Lieutenant Colonel Maxwell's troops. He ordered the provost marshal to take Walsh into custody. It was amid scenes of great confusion that the governor himself eventually executed the warrant and turned the prisoner over to the provost marshal. Edmund Rush Wegg, whom the governor had two weeks previously suspended from the office of attorney general on the charge of incompetency, acted as attorney for Walsh. He drew up a writ of *habeas corpus* which Clifton signed. This order directed the provost marshal to bring Walsh immediately before the chief justice for a hearing. Clifton then stated that the charges against Walsh had arisen from a dispute of long standing between the officer and the governor over their several powers derived from the same authority—namely, his Majesty—to whom only, or to his commander-in-chief in America, belonged the decision. He

76. Johnstone to Gage, Jan. 27, 1766, *ibid.*, pp. 413–414.

ruled further, that there was not the least reason for legal prosecution or detention of Walsh and ordered that he be freed at once. He was, therefore, released after an imprisonment of several hours. Maxwell, after privately persuading Walsh to restore the governor's sentinels and to yield the point in regard to honors due Johnstone, was permitted, by the governor and council, at his urgent request, to return to Mobile.[77] Johnstone, baffled, poured out the vials of his wrath in a letter to the Board of Trade which referred the matter with full correspondence to the king.[78]

The results of this dispute were unfortunate and far reaching. The civil population took sides and Pensacola was torn by the struggles of violent factions. After the release of Walsh, peace between the governor and the chief justice, who held a seat in the council, *ex officio* and by virtue of a commission under the sign manual, was impossible. On February 26, Clifton resigned his seat, but Johnstone, contending that this office was inseparable from that of chief justice, refused to accept his resignation.[79] Thereupon Clifton referred the matter to the Board of Trade and ceased to attend the meetings. Governor Johnstone on July 23, preferred eighteen articles of complaint against Clifton and suspended him from the office of chief justice.[80] The charges comprehended ignorance of law, neglect of duty, and dishonesty, but it is not hard to see that Clifton's part in the difficulty with Walsh was the underlying reason for the governor's action. In the meantime Lieutenant Governor Montfort Browne, who had arrived at Pensacola in the midst of the Walsh episode, had sided with the military. With this as a basis for mis-

77. Documents relative to this fiasco are printed in *ibid.*, pp. 401–495.
78. Board of Trade to the king, Aug. 1, 1766, *ibid.*, pp. 342–343. Walsh gives a full account in a letter of Feb. 25, 1766 to Gage. William Tayler, the Brigadier who succeeded Bouquet, also had his troubles with Johnstone. On May 17, 1766, he wrote Gage in reference to the governor: "When madmen are sent out, it would be a proper precaution to send keepers and chains with them." Gage Papers.
79. Minutes of Council, May 26, 1766, *Miss. Prov. Arch.*, I, 331–332.
80. *Ibid.*, pp. 322–330.

understanding, he and Johnstone were soon at odds over the disposal of French Protestant refugees whom Browne had brought to the colony, and over the amount of respect due the lieutenant governor. In a short time each was sending to the home government unflattering reports about the other.[81]

In April a number of the friends of Wegg and Clifton sent a memorial to the Board of Trade stating that the capricious tyranny of the governor was imperiling the welfare of the infant colony. "We are still desirous of remaining here," they wrote, "but we cannot determine long so to do; for here our characters are subject to the most infamous and cruel aspersions; here despotism presides; here all laws are trampled on or wrested to the most arbitrary purposes, to overwhelm the victims of one man's displeasure; here, our lives, liberties and properties are endangered by the removal of their supporters, the opponents of oppression."[82] At the same time Johnstone was accusing his enemies of plotting to depose him and place Lieutenant Governor Browne in his place.[83] He attributed his lack of popularity to his energetic efforts to enforce the Stamp Act.[84]

Notwithstanding the efforts made in the congresses of 1765 to conciliate the Indians and to put into operation the new plan for the management of Indian affairs, the

81. Browne [to the secretary of state], March 27, 1766, *ibid.*, pp. 297–303; Johnstone to secretary of Board of Trade, April 1, 1766, *ibid.*, pp. 460–464.

82. Memorial to secretary of the Board of Trade, dated April, 1766, *ibid.*, pp. 303–306.

83. Extract, Johnstone to Pownall, April 1, 1766, *ibid.*, pp. 455–457.

84. Johnstone to the Board of Trade, Feb. 26, 1766, *ibid.*, pp. 417–419. That the unfortunate disputes in West Florida were paralleled by similar occurrences in other provinces is suggested by an extract from a letter of March 1, 1765, from the Board of Trade to Johnstone: "The misunderstandings and disputes, which have arisen in almost every one of His Majesty's colonies in America between the Civil Governor and Military Commanders since the appointment of a Commander in Chief have long called for some clear and explicit definition and adjustment of their respective powers and authorities." Quoted in Johnstone to Gage, Oct. 5, 1765, *ibid.*, pp. 405–409.

last months of Johnstone's administration were marked by much friction with the Indians, especially with the Upper Creeks. The failure of the plan was clearly set forward in a letter from Shelburne to Gage in the latter part of 1766: "The only province in which the above mentioned plan has been tried is West Florida, and it has not been at all recommended thereby, for although the expenses have increased very considerably the disorders and discontents among the Indians have increased in equal proportions."[85] The Upper Creeks under the leadership of The Mortar had always regarded the English with suspicion. They now claimed that English traders were not abiding by the established prices, that Creek territory was being infringed upon in violation of the late treaty, and that the English were inciting their ancient enemies, the Choctaws—in alliance with the Chickasaws—to make war on them.[86] The Mortar threatened to surrender his great medal.[87]

In a spirited reply Governor Johnstone denied that the boundary was being disregarded or that the Choctaws were being incited. He said that the hostility of that nation was caused by the fact that Creeks had recently murdered a Choctaw warrior. He complained of robberies and cattle-stealing recently committed by the Creeks. He quoted the words of a Creek chief to the Choctaws: "If you are for peace, say so, we wish to continue, if for war, say so, and we are prepared." "But," he concluded, "to receive our presents, eat our provisions, use our powder and balls, and cut our throats, it is neither felt that you should do so, nor

85. Dec. 11, 1766, *Collections* of the Illinois State Historical Library, XI, 454–459. Shelburne probably did not know that Sir William Johnson was attempting to introduce the plan in the northern district. *Ibid.*, p. 456n.

86. In this connection Johnstone wrote Stuart: "It is undoubtedly to our interest to foment the dispute between those nations [Creeks and Choctaws]. But considering the strong propensity mankind possesses for divulging what it knows, it was difficult to bring matters to this point without appearing as an accessory." May 19, 1766, Gage Papers.

87. Messages of Chiefs of the Creek Nation to Johnstone, May 16, 1766, *Miss. Prov. Arch.*, I, 526–531.

that we should permit it." [88] In June, 1766, Johnstone
sent Henry Seymour Conway, secretary of state, a rather
alarming account of the Indian situation. In the past thirteen months, the Creeks had killed five people and had
refused every kind of satisfaction. In addition to this they
were constantly engaged in cattle-stealing and in harboring runaway slaves and deserters. This conduct of the
Creeks, which the English had not been able to punish,
was having a bad effect on the other Indians, who "consider and calculate debts of blood as exactly as any banker
does his guineas." The safety of the settlements and the
necessity of retaining the respect of the other Indians demanded that the Creeks be punished, and in view of impending hostilities between this nation and the Choctaws,
the time was very favorable for such action. Johnstone,
thereupon, outlined a plan of campaign, which called for
an offensive alliance with the Choctaws, Chickasaws, and
Cherokees, and the assembling of eighteen hundred troops
at Pensacola and fifteen hundred at Augusta; two expedi-
tions from Pensacola and one from Augusta should be sent
out against the recalcitrant Creeks with orders to destroy
men, women, and children.[89]

On October 3, news was received at Pensacola of the
murder of two additional whites by the Creeks. The governor was not able to assemble a full council at this time,
but the members present advised that Brigadier General
Tayler, in command of the southern district and at this
time in Pensacola, be requested to erect fortifications at
the expense of the colony; traders were warned to withdraw from the territory of the Creeks and hostilities were
urged.[90] In view of the weak condition of West Florida
from a military standpoint, and in view of the fact that
General Tayler would doubtless not be moved to begin war
without orders from General Gage, the action of this

88. Johnstone's message to the Chiefs of the Upper Creek Nation,
June 9, 1766, *ibid.,* pp. 523–526.
89. Johnstone to Conway, June 23, 1766, *ibid.,* pp. 511–516.
90. Minutes of Council, Oct. 30, 1766, C.O.5: 632.

group, though later approved at a regular council meeting,[91] was hardly more than a warlike gesture. On February 19, 1767, Shelburne wrote to Johnstone that the king disapproved extremely of his action in rekindling Indian warfare without awaiting directions from England. Such an action, continued Shelburne, was contrary to the spirit of his instructions. On account of this and because of the spirit of disunion which had weakened and distracted the colony under his government the king had ordered his recall.[92] Johnstone, however, had left the colony on January 9 [93] on the strength of a six months' leave of absence.

Johnstone's administration was characterized by aggressiveness and action. Civil government was inaugurated, the assembly was established, Pensacola was laid out, meetings were held with the Indians and treaties were negotiated, efforts were made to tap the Spanish trade. The good results which accrued from these constructive measures, however, were largely dissipated as a result of the dissensions which were caused by the governor's belligerent and overbearing manner.

91. *Ibid.*, Nov. 6, 1766.
92. Miss. Trans., vol. X.
93. Lieutenant Governor Browne to [Shelburne], Jan. 12, 1767, C.O.5: 584, pp. 359–362, *ibid.;* Shelburne to Johnstone, Sept. 22, 1766, *ibid,* vol. X.

III

PROVINCIAL POLITICS, 1767–1772

THE period immediately following the establishing of civil government in West Florida, witnessing as it did five changes of administration and bitter factional strife, the violent death of one governor and the recall of a lieutenant governor, the unexpected withdrawal of most of the troops, Indian troubles caused largely by lack of proper supervision of the Indian trade, and struggles between the executive and assembly, was a time of almost continuous turmoil and confusion. Though the issues which at this time agitated the colonies of the Atlantic seaboard were either absent or dormant in West Florida, unrest and dissatisfaction certainly were not lacking.

Lieutenant Governor Montfort Browne,[1] who assumed

1. Montfort Browne had an active and even stormy career. He served in the French and Indian War as a subaltern. With the coming of peace he and his father and brothers were given a royal mandamus for 20,000 acres of land in West Florida, part of which was laid out on Dauphin Island near Mobile and part in the western part of the province near the present site of Baton Rouge. After his recall he interested himself in a scheme for establishing a new colony out of that part of West Florida which bordered on the Mississippi. In 1774 he was appointed governor of the Bahamas. He paid a brief visit to West Florida in 1775 to attend to his private affairs and no doubt to further his land schemes. When the Bahamas were taken over by the Americans in 1776 he was carried away as a prisoner but was exchanged for Lord Stirling. He was soon engaged in raising a corps of loyalists for service with the British around New York. The Bahamas having come under English control again, he returned as governor in 1778. Within a short while bitter strife developed between him and other provincial officials and in 1779 he was recalled. He and his opponents appeared before the Board of Trade two or more times in 1780. He won partial vindication from the Privy Council in 1781, though he was not returned to office. He returned to America in 1782 seeking his fortune again and not without success in the British Army. This writer has not found even a short biography of him, but numerous, though fragmentary, references to

the government on the departure of Johnstone, had arrived in the colony in the spring of 1766 with a group of
foreign Protestants, mainly Frenchmen, who had been
recruited and transported to West Florida at the expense
of the home government for the purpose of encouraging
the production of wine and silk. Arriving, as he did, in
the midst of the clashes between the civil and military,
Browne, after a brief support of the governor, allied himself with the opposing faction and quarreled with Johnstone over the place of settlement of the French emigrants.
However, he subsequently weakened his position with the
enemies of the governor by a violent dispute with Major
Farmar over the possession of Dauphin Island, near Mobile. Although he was senior councillor, he had little part
in administering the affairs of the colony, because of his
disagreements with Johnstone. When he took charge of
the government, therefore, he was unfamiliar with the
routine of the administration and was in addition opposed
by the friends of Johnstone who were referred to as "a
Scotch Party." A leader in this group was Daniel Clark,
a member of the council and an appointee of Johnstone
as receiver general of quit-rents.[2] The inexperience of
Browne coupled with the strength of the opposition boded
ill for the new administration.

The early policies of Browne, however, were of a constructive nature calculated to promote the public welfare
and prosperity and, except for a dispute with the assembly
over the salaries which the members had voted themselves,
there was at first little dissension in the government. The
quieting of the Creek Indians, with whom Johnstone had
been on the verge of open hostilities, was a matter of
utmost importance. The diplomacy of Browne and Briga-

his activities may be found through the indexes of: *Journal of the Com-
missioners for Trade and Plantations; Acts of the Privy Council,
Colonial Series*, vol. V; Peter Force, *American Archives*, 4th Series; and
Manuscripts of the Earl of Dartmouth and *Report on American Manu-
scripts in the Royal Institution of Great Britain*, both in *Reports* of the
Historical Manuscripts Commission.
    2. Browne to Hillsborough, July 1, 1768, C.O.5: 585, pp. 109–110.

dier General Tayler, commanding the southern district
of North America, was assisted in the solution of this difficulty by internal discord among the Creeks.[3] To meet an
accompanying difficulty, in the summer of 1767 Browne
assembled the Indian traders at Pensacola and required
them to take an oath to obey regulations recently prescribed by the Board of Trade for the purpose of preventing the evils caused by the presence of unlicensed and
disreputable traders among the Indians.[4]

Browne continued the efforts of Governor Johnstone to
foster the Spanish trade and for a while, at least, appeared to make marked headway. On September 29, 1767,
he informed the home government that, acting on the advice of the council, with the consent of the commodore of
the station and with the approval of the local merchants
engaged in the Spanish trade, he had sent the provincial
sloop to Havana under pretext of making inquiries which
would facilitate the collection of the insurance on an English ship, the *Don Carlos*, which had been wrecked in that
vicinity some two years previously. The real purpose of
this trip, of course, was to interest the Spanish in coming
to Pensacola for British merchandise. The sloop was received in a friendly manner and while none of the crew was
allowed to land, civil answers were given to the inquiries
about the *Don Carlos*. A short while after the return of the
sloop, a brig came to Pensacola from Havana and purchased 30,000 Spanish dollars worth of goods and brought
the information that other Spanish ships would soon follow.[5] The secretary of state chose to wink at this palpable,
but profitable violation of the trade laws. His Majesty,
wrote Hillsborough, approved the sending of the provin-

3. Same to Shelburne, June 29, 1767, C.O.5: 584, pp. 415–417.
4. Same to Board of Trade, Aug. 6, 1767, C.O.5: 575, pp. 281–283. In
a letter of March 10, 1767, John Stuart sent General Gage a printed
copy of *Regulations for the Better Carrying on the Trade with the
Indian Tribes in the Southern District,* and also a printed *Extract from
the Plan for the Future Management of Indian Affairs* drawn up by the
Board of Trade. Gage Papers.
5. Browne to Board of Trade, C.O.5: 575, pp. 305–307.

cial sloop to Havana for the records of the *Don Carlos* and was glad that the dispatches were so amicably received, since this would enable the merchants to recover the insurance.[6] Browne wrote the Board of Trade on February 1, 1768, that as a result of the visit of the sloop to Havana, no less than five or six Spanish ships had come to Pensacola, and more were expected daily; these were laden principally with bullion and logwood which were exchanged for British merchandise.[7]

In the spring and summer of 1768, the lieutenant governor made an extended trip through the western part of the province as far as Natchez, and on his return sent Hillsborough an interesting account of the undertaking and a glowing description of the country.[8] The journey had been made on water, by way of the Gulf, Rigolets, Lakes Pontchartrain and Maurepas, and the Amite, Iberville,[9] and Mississippi rivers. At the mouth of the Tangipahoa on Lake Pontchartrain he had administered the oath of allegiance to a number of French families who, having become disgusted with Spanish rule, had brought their Negroes and cattle into West Florida. He had smoked the calumet with several tribes of Indians on or near the Mississippi. In order to capture and hold the valuable Indian trade which came down the Mississippi from the Great Lakes region, he especially mentioned the need for a town at Fort Bute. He was much pleased with the fertility of the soil along the Mississippi and was particularly impressed with the desirability of the land around Natchez, where he declared he would be glad to spend the remainder of his days. His description of the place is noteworthy: "From the fort may be discovered the most charming prospects in the world, extensive plains intermixed with

6. Hillsborough to Browne, Feb. 23, 1768, C.O.5: 585, pp. 17–18.
7. C.O.5: 575, pp. 311–320. General Haldimand mentions these vessels in a letter to General Gage, March 17, 1768, but said that they brought little specie. Gage Papers.
8. Browne to Hillsborough, July 6, 1768, C.O.5: 584, pp. 147–164.
9. The trip was made during the flood season so the Iberville was navigable for small boats. Rigolets is the Gulf outlet of Lake Pontchartrain.

beautiful hills, and small rivers; here are, my lord, fruit trees of most excellent kinds, the grape, peach, plum, apricot, apple, pear, figs, mulberry, cherry, persimmon, medlars, and strawberries as good in their kind as any in the world and in as great abundance. . . . The nuts common in this part of the province are walnuts, chestnuts, hickory, and filbert."

Soon after his return to Pensacola, the monotony of governmental routine was broken and the course of petty disputes, which by this time were beginning to appear, was interrupted by an unexpected blow which threatened the prosperity if not the very life of the province and threw the entire population into a state of apprehension and unrest. In the latter part of August, Browne received a letter from General Gage, commander of the British forces in North America, informing him that in consequence of orders lately received he was transmitting directions to Brigadier General Haldimand, by this time commander of the southern district, to abandon the posts at Fort Bute and Natchez and to embark the two regiments which had been quartered in West Florida for St. Augustine. Only three companies were to be left in the colony and these were to be quartered at Pensacola and Mobile; Haldimand had been directed to confer with Browne as to the disposal of the forts and military property at Manchac and Natchez.[10]

This action, of course, was not aimed particularly at West Florida, but was a part of the policy, adopted by the British cabinet in the spring of 1768, for curtailing the expenses of colonial administration by reducing the number of military establishments west of the Alleghenies.[11] On the day following the receipt of this intelligence Browne wrote Hillsborough a letter of protest that was almost hysterical in character. The anxiety of the prov-

10. Gage to Browne, June 27, 1768, C.O.5: 585, p. 181. The orders to Haldimand were transmitted in a letter of the same date. Gage Papers.
11. C. W. Alvord, *The Mississippi Valley in British Politics*, II, 27–31; also Gage to Haldimand, June 27, 1768, Gage Papers.

ince, he said, could more easily be conceived than expressed. If the order were enforced, the number of poor families who had expended their small means in establishing themselves in the western part of the province must abandon their plantations and starve; the town of Pensacola even, which had increased so amazingly in the past twelve months, must be abandoned, for the inhabitants would never think their persons and effects safe in the midst of such a large number of savages.[12]

The assembly was immediately convened and previous disagreements with the lieutenant governor were forgotten, temporarily at least, in the endeavor to follow his suggestion and draw up, with the council, suitable memorials to the king and Lord Hillsborough setting forth in emphatic fashion the evil consequences of the withdrawal of the troops from the colony. In the last four years, the appeal to Hillsborough stated, houses and wharves had been built in Pensacola at a cost of £60,000; the value of British merchandise brought into the colony annually had increased to £80,000, most of which was disposed of in foreign trade; import duties on goods (largely skins) that had been sent from the colony to England had come almost to equal the parliamentary support fund. Furthermore, it continued, the colony was on the verge of a great development with people from Virginia and Pennsylvania planning to come to the province; the withdrawal of the troops would have a very detrimental effect and would, of course, prevent this development. In addition, the abandoning of the posts on the Mississippi would mean the loss of the valuable Indian trade which came down that river; and the danger to the province was increased by the fact that the Choctaws and the Creeks were on the point of making peace with each other.[13] Other memorials to Hillsborough signed by twenty-three merchants and firms of London and forty of Liverpool, including the mayor, set

12. Aug. 16, 1768, C.O.5: 585, pp. 177–179.
13. Aug. 24, 1768, *ibid.*, pp. 261–272.

forth the same or similar arguments against leaving the province without sufficient military protection.[14]

The military authorities in West Florida were inclined to discount the value of the province. The pessimistic reports of General Haldimand to General Gage, who as commander-in-chief had direction of the policy of retrenchment, were no doubt in part responsible for the removal of the troops. The land along the coast, Haldimand had written, was not fertile; that which lay inland was possessed by the Indians; trade at Pensacola was inconsiderable save to merchants who supplied the troops; the commerce of Mobile was not large.[15] He could not see any way by which one could hope that the province would ever be in a position to reimburse the nation for expenditures which had already been made, and still less for those necessary if the troops were to remain.[16] Both Gage and Haldimand thought that the posts on the Mississippi would be indefensible in case of a war with Spain.[17] Pensacola and Mobile could best be defended, they maintained, from the sea rather than by military posts.[18]

The orders of General Gage had been for immediate execution. Thus, on the advice of the lieutenant governor and council, the fort at Natchez was converted into a trading post, Fort Bute was dismantled and the troops at Mobile and Pensacola, except for three companies, sailed for St. Augustine. But the appeals of the assembly and the protests of the merchants were not without effect. On December 10, 1768, Hillsborough wrote that the king had

14. *Ibid.*, pp. 203–204, 280–281.
15. Haldimand to Gage, Dec. 6, 1767, Gage Papers.
16. Same to same, Dec. 20, 1767, Gage Papers. In 1771 Gage wrote Haldimand that he thought the amount needed for buildings and repairs at Pensacola and Mobile "more than the whole province of West Florida is worth." Aug. 4, 1771, Gage Papers.
17. Gage to Haldimand, May 16, 1770; Nov. 28, 1770, Gage Papers. The soundness of their judgment was vindicated by the easy fall of these posts to Spain in 1779.
18. Haldimand to Browne, Aug. 20, 1768; Haldimand to Gage, Feb. 11, 1770; Gage to Haldimand, March 23, 1770, Gage Papers.

received these memorials graciously, and that they had
been forwarded to General Gage, "and I doubt not," he
concluded, "from the manner in which my sentiment to
him upon this occasion is expressed, that he will give full
consideration to every circumstance of danger and inconvenience stated to attend the leaving so inconsiderable a
number of troops in West Florida." [19] As a result of
Gage's reëxamination of the situation, a reinforcement of
one regiment was sent to West Florida and the headquarters for the southern district were moved back to
Pensacola.

There is little doubt that factors in addition to appeals
of settlers and merchants made it advisable to maintain a
strong military force in the province. The arrival of the
Spanish governor O'Reilly in New Orleans with 3,500
regular troops perhaps gave the military authorities
pause.[20] And the diplomatic crisis which was precipitated
about this time between the courts of St. James's and Ma-
drid through the seizure of the Falkland Islands by the
governor of Buenos Aires doubtless added to the strategic
and military importance of the colony.[21] On September
28, 1770, Hillsborough in a confidential dispatch to the
Lords of the Admiralty said that unless the dispossessing
of his Majesty's subjects in the Falkland Islands was dis-
avowed by Spain and proper restitution made, war with
that country was very probable.[22] The posts on the Mississippi were not reoccupied, however, until after the Willing raid in 1778,[23] in spite of the insistence of Lieutenant
Governors Browne and Durnford and Governor Chester
that the proper protection for the western part of the
province would result in a general migration to the country, both by the dissatisfied French, Acadians, and Ger-

19. Hillsborough to Governor John Eliot, C.O.5: 585, pp. 283–284.
20. Gage to Haldimand, Nov. 10, 1769 and May 14, 1770, Gage Papers.
21. Same to same (secret and confidential), Nov. 30, 1770, Gage
Papers.
22. C.O.5: 71, pp. 385–386.
23. See pp. 209, 212 below.

mans in Louisiana and by the land-hungry settlers from
the English colonies on the Atlantic seaboard.

Though John Eliot had been appointed governor of
West Florida early in 1767, soon after the recall of Johnstone, for some reason he did not reach the colony until
April, 1769.[24] This long delay gave the enemies of Browne
opportunity to work against him and the daily expectation that he would be relieved of his power did not
strengthen his position. As early as November 15, 1768,
Hillsborough wrote the governor of West Florida ordering an investigation of Browne's accounts, saying that
complaint had been received from the province that the
lieutenant governor had issued false vouchers for expenditures charged to the contingent fund. This letter reached
Pensacola while Browne was still in control and fell into
his hands.

Governor Eliot arrived on April 2, 1769.[25] He took the
appointed oaths before the council and his commission was
read with due solemnity from the gallery of the house used
for governmental purposes. Browne was at Mobile at the
time of Eliot's arrival but he soon went to Pensacola and
requested an investigation of his accounts before the governor and council. This request was granted and the investigation began on April 27. "This inquiry," wrote
Browne to Hillsborough, "continued through several days
during which time His Excellency frequently expressed
his surprise at the malice and iniquity with which it [the
charge against him] was attempted to be supported, but
the intervention of a most unforeseen and melancholy circumstance, which, when I call to mind chills me with horror,
deprived me of the happy opportunity I had so long and
ardently wished for, and [deprived] the world of His
Excellency, who on the second of May hanged himself in
his study. I had had the honor of dining and spending

24. Commission as vice-admiral is dated March 23, 1767; commission
as governor, May 15, 1767.
25. Eliot to Hillsborough, April 3, 1769, C.O.5: 586, pp. 207-208.

the preceding day with him when he seemed cheerful and composed and showed me the utmost politeness." [26]

The sudden and tragic demise of Governor Eliot, whose administration had been expected to remove Browne from the control of public affairs and to put an end to factional struggles, was the signal for the outbreak of great confusion.[27] A petition to the council signed by a number of inhabitants, including several members of the assembly, requested that the lieutenant governor not be allowed to reassume the government. When the council failed to take action, a number of the petitioners persuaded the chief justice to attempt to exact from Browne a promise to write home for permission to resign his commission; they threatened to send to England a memorial against him if he declined to do as they requested. This proposition, Browne says, he refused with the contempt it deserved. On the other hand, a number of inhabitants, among whom were officers of the Mobile garrison, sent the lieutenant governor a letter of confidence and appreciation. Browne asked Hillsborough for an immediate opportunity to defend himself, adding that if there were irregularities in his accounts, they were caused by his lack of familiarity with the methods of accounting and by the great inconvenience he had suffered through the death of two secretaries.

Browne reassumed the government (this was the only constitutional move that could have been made) and Elias Durnford, surveyor of the province and a member of the council, who was on the point of going to England under the authority of a leave of absence, carried an account of the condition of affairs to Hillsborough. The lieutenant governor, it appears from the correspondence, looked upon Durnford as his friend and advocate, and sent by him a

26. May 13, 1769, *ibid.*, pp. 123–134.
27. Browne's letter above gives a vivid account of the situation. Copies of the memorial and letter mentioned below are found in *ibid.*, pp. 335–341.

letter of defense. In the meantime the province was in a state of extreme unrest.

While Browne was at Pensacola defending himself before Governor Eliot and the council, Major Farmar had seized the opportunity to expel the tenants and take forcible possession of the lieutenant governor's plantation on Dauphin Island near Mobile. The unexpected turn of affairs, placing Browne again in control of the administration and in a position to defend himself effectively, and the ensuing lawsuit between a man of Farmar's popularity and one of Browne's official position, which was necessary to put the lieutenant governor in possession again, considerably aggravated the spirit of confusion which already existed.[28] Browne's letters are filled with bitter diatribes against his enemies.[29] He removed two men from the council. The report that the Spaniards from Havana were tampering with the Creeks and planning to hold a meeting with them at the mouth of the Apalachicola River proved an additional disturbing factor. In order to prevent this meeting Captain Phillips, commander of the local naval forces, was requested to cruise in that direction,[30] but he failed to meet any Spaniards.

What account Durnford gave in England of the situation in West Florida, we do not know, but we do know that on August 4, Hillsborough wrote Browne that the minutes of the council which had examined his accounts and a memorial of certain inhabitants of West Florida against his conduct had been received from Mr. Hannay, the legislative agent of the colony. These materials had been laid before the king, who had ordered Browne's recall and the appointment in his stead of Elias Durnford, from whom he would receive the letter.[31] The arrival of

28. A full account of trial is found in *ibid.*, pp. 285–303.
29. Browne to Hillsborough, Oct. 8, 1769, C.O.5: 577, pp. 397–404.
30. Same to same, Aug. 20, 1769, *ibid.*, pp. 377–386.
31. C.O.5: 586, pp. 203–204. Durnford's commission which contains a revocation of Browne's is dated July 31, 1769 (Florida State Historical Society photostats).

72   BRITISH WEST FLORIDA

Lieutenant Governor Durnford,[32] though he appears to have enjoyed the respect and regard of most of the people, did not bring immediate calm and peace. Browne was naturally humiliated over his recall and doubtless enraged at what he considered the duplicity of his friend. Durnford charged Browne with reluctance to surrender the papers and archives of the government, while Browne accused Durnford of trying to prevent him from obtaining copies of documents necessary for his defense in England.[33]

Among the first acts of the new administration were the reinstatement of councillors who had been removed by Browne and an examination of the late lieutenant governor's accounts. As a result of the latter, Durnford charged that Browne had furnished his family and Negroes with supplies from the Indian presents.[34] The situation was brought to a crisis by a duel between Browne and Evan Jones, one of the Durnford adherents. An eyewitness gave a graphic but laconic account of the affair: "Phillips Comyn maketh oath and sayeth that about seven o'clock this morning Montfort Browne and Evan Jones did go out with firearms as far as Gage Hill, where said Evan Jones cocked his pistol which missed fire, and said Montfort Browne did then fire at said Evan Jones and shot him through the body so that his life is despaired of." Browne surrendered himself to the authorities but, since the recovery of Jones appeared to be very doubtful, Chief Justice Clifton refused to allow bail or to issue a writ of *habeas corpus*. After several days, however, Browne was released on an order of Alexander Moore, a justice of the peace. Clifton was greatly incensed that his authority had been disregarded by this irregular action and brought

32. Elias Durnford was perhaps the most able of the provincial executives. He served the colony as surveyor general, councillor, and lieutenant governor, and was in command of Mobile at the time of its surrender in 1780. There is a biographical sketch of doubtful value in the appendix of Hamilton's *Colonial Mobile* (rev. ed.).
33. A copy of an acrimonious correspondence between the two is found in C.O.5: 577, pp. 253-333.
34. Durnford to Hillsborough, Jan. 27, 1770, *ibid.*, pp. 209-215.

the matter before the council. Since the boat on which Browne had planned to go to England was on the point of sailing and since Jones appeared by this time to be on the way to recovery, it was finally decided to allow Browne to depart without molestation; as Durnford sagely remarked, any attempt to detain him might be construed as an effort to prevent him from defending his administration.[35] It is probable, too, that Durnford saw in his departure an essential step toward the restoration of tranquillity.

The remainder of Durnford's brief period as chief executive was of a more peaceful character. There were the usual occasional Indian outrages caused largely by encroachments on the Indian lands, abuses of the traders, and lack of military protection in the western part of the province. The most noteworthy of these was an attack on the trading post at Natchez which was in the charge of one John Bradley, who had the reputation of being too free in his distribution of rum to the Indians.[36] Perhaps the most significant accomplishment of the administration was the passage of an act for the regulation of trade with the Indians. During the French and Indian War the English government had gradually assumed control of colonial relations with the Indians, and in 1764, as already indicated, the Board of Trade had drawn up an elaborate

35. A full account of this episode is given in Minutes of Council, Feb. 14, 17, 18, 1770.

36. Bradley to Durnford, Feb. 1, 1770, C.O.5: 577, pp. 233–240. The pattern of relations between traders and Indians was colorfully described by Alexander Cameron, a commissary, in a letter of September 23, 1766, to John Stuart: "Many of them [the traders] alter their steelyards, some augment the price of their goods, others lower their prices and shorten their measures. . . . the white men cheat the red and steal their horses, the Indians, in return, rob and steal the rum from the traders, and are very nigh up with them in horse stealing." Abstract enclosed in Stuart to Gage, Dec. 19, 1766. Gage Papers. The traders as a group had a bad reputation. One observant writer said of them: "It is true that those monsters in human form, the very scum and outcast of the earth, are always more prone to savage barbarity than the savages themselves." Bernard Romans, *A Concise History of East and West Florida*, p. 60.

plan for the regulating of Indian affairs. However, because of the large expenditures for which the plan called,
it had never been put into full operation. In West Florida,
where it had been applied to a fuller extent than in the
other southern colonies, the plan had not proved a success. In 1768, it was decided to return the control of Indian trade to the colonies, though the offices of superintendents for the northern and southern departments
were retained and some allowances were made for deputies;
in West Florida, at least, commissaries and armorers were
withdrawn. It was desirable, therefore, that each province
make some provision for the management of Indian trade,
and West Florida was the first colony to pass a law for
this purpose. The act, dated May 19, 1770, is significant
as a commentary on the way the trade should have been
regulated rather than on the way it was regulated, for the
law was weak in structure, containing no adequate provision for enforcement. A glance at its important features
is desirable at this time.

A heavy penalty was provided for persons who traded
with the Indians without licenses or who disposed of skins
at New Orleans or to any person other than subjects of
the British king. Licenses might be secured from the governor of West Florida or from the governor of any colony
in the southern district; the names of all employees of a
trader were to be inscribed in the license, as well as the
particular villages in which the employer and his helpers
were to operate; each trader was required to post bond
for £200 sterling, in order to guarantee for himself and
his employees due observation of the regulations prescribed in the act; he was to have a written contract with
every person in his employ and was not to hire Negroes,
Indians, or half-breeds; he was forbidden to harbor in his
house in the Indian lands for more than four days any
white person not in his employ, unless the person was ill
or had permission from the governor to stay longer. He
was required to aid in the apprehending of fugitives from
justice and was to appear, when summoned, at meetings or

congresses held by officials with the Indians; but he was not, under pain of a severe penalty, to bring Indians to Pensacola without authorization, nor to convene any meeting or deliver any "talk" without written permission from the governor. Any information that came into his hands which was of consequence to any of the colonies was to be delivered immediately to the governor or to other proper officers. No trader was to abuse or maltreat any Indians, and especial respect was to be paid to medal chiefs. No trader was to have in his possession at any time more than eighteen gallons of rum or other strong drink, and under no circumstances was any of this to be bartered to the Indians for skins; credit above thirty pounds weight of half-dressed skins was not to be allowed, and the sale of swan shot and rifle-barrelled guns was forbidden. No trading was to take place in the woods. It was stipulated that the weights used by the traders should contain eighteen ounces to the pound and that other standards be the English yard and the Winchester pint. A price list in terms of pounds of leather was established for some forty-six articles of the Indian trade. These regulations, of course, were not to apply to trade with Indians who lived outside the limits of the province. It was further stated that, if any commissaries were appointed by the governor or the superintendent to reside among the Indians, the traders should register with them and they should have general supervision of the trade. The law with such slight provisions for enforcement was little more than a gesture.[37] Another law passed at the same time provided a heavy penalty for infringement on Indian lands and for private purchase of land from the Indians.[38] Experience was to show that it was to be difficult if not impossible to enforce.[39]

37. C.O.5: 623, pp. 220–226.
38. *Ibid.*, pp. 227–229.
39. In 1771 Superintendent Stuart complained to Chester of the futility of attempts to secure convictions for infractions of this law. Minutes of Council, Oct. 12, 1771.

The arrival on August 10, 1770,[40] of Governor Peter Chester,[41] who had been appointed in the place of Eliot, brought an end to the administration of Durnford and marked the beginning of a government which was to continue until the province was lost to Spain in 1781. Though he reached the province in safety, Chester was unfortunate in the loss of some of his goods. Shortly after his arrival he wrote Hillsborough of the wreck of the Florida packet and the loss of his chariot, which was not insured. "But the loss I most regret," he continued, "is that of the pictures of my royal masters which have shared the same unfortunate fate." [42] It is not known whether the pictures of the sovereigns were replaced, but in 1776 Bartram, the noted botanist, recorded that as he approached Pensacola he met Governor Chester, who was riding in his chariot.[43]

One of the main problems which faced Chester was that of Indian relations. The mild bromide which was very poorly administered by the recent acts had not relieved the difficulties arising from a policy inherently unsound; for the plan of allowing the colonies to control the Indian relations and to regulate Indian trade had several fundamental weaknesses. Six colonies in the southern district

40. Chester to Hillsborough, Sept. 24, 1770, C.O.5: 588, p. 1.

41. Little is known of the life of Chester before or after his service in West Florida. In a memorial of April 12, 1782, to the Commissioners of the Treasury, he stated that he had been appointed to a lieutenancy in the army in 1740, and that he had served in the last two wars, having been present at the siege of Belle Isle and at Martinique; he had held the rank of lieutenant colonel since 1761, but had been retired on half pay because of poor health. C.O.5: 581, pp. 15–16. His administration was lethargic. Apparently he never visited the western part of the province during his stay of eleven years in West Florida. He quarrelled with the military and his attitude toward the assembly was overbearing and high-handed. With his secretary, Philip Livingston, Junior, he was charged with grave irregularities in office and the home government was investigating his conduct at the time of the fall of the province. See Mrs. Dunbar Rowland, "Peter Chester," in *Publications* of Mississippi Historical Society, Centenary Series, V, 1–183. This is a short sketch of Chester and a number of his letters and enclosures to the home government.

42. Chester to Hillsborough, Sept. 27, 1770, C.O.5: 578, p. 79.

43. William Bartram, *Travels through North and South Carolina, Georgia, East and West Florida*, p. 414.

were involved in the Indian trade. In the regulation of this commerce some uniformity was highly desirable, yet there was no way by which pressure could be brought to bear on the different assemblies to force them to pass uniform laws, or any laws at all, for that matter, on the subject. Therefore, the effort of any one colony to make for the trade reasonably strict regulations would tend, if it were possible to enforce such regulations, to drive the trade from that colony to other colonies where trade was unregulated. Thus the Indians could still be cheated out of their deerskins with impunity by means of rum and short measures. Only coördinated and unified efforts could bring about a satisfactory handling of the Indian trade, and coördination and unity could not be expected from six different provinces.

This was the situation when Chester assumed the reins of government. The West Florida law was not enforced and the other colonies concerned had made no laws on the subject; the trade was almost unregulated. The Indians were clamoring for a congress and claiming that they were being robbed by the traders, and that their lands were being trespassed upon. The traders and frontiersmen on the other hand claimed that they were being plundered by the Indians.

Charles Stuart, deputy Indian agent at Mobile, who was thoroughly familiar with the situation, wrote Chester a letter in the spring of 1771 which shows keen insight and understanding. The Chickasaws, he said, had always been the most steadfast friends of the English; at this time they very justly complained that the Indian traders were encroaching on their lands and establishing plantations with overseers; they also complained that the traders were competing with them in the hunting; finally, they deplored the amount of rum which was being brought among them, by which they were cheated of their skins, and to which they attributed all of their disorders. A commissary placed among them would settle disputes and an armorer would keep them from coming to town so often.

The Creeks and Choctaws, continued Stuart, were treacherous and less loyal and required careful attention; the encouraging of war between these two tribes was a nice question, for when peace was eventually made the fomenter would then be in a difficult situation.[44]

Chester, for his part, attributed the Indian unrest to the failure to call congresses, which the Indians had expected, and to the activities of licentious traders who were not restrained by the law. He pointed out the necessity of uniform laws in all of the colonies concerned, the enforcement of these laws by commissaries, and the strict licensing of traders. As an alternative he suggested control through an act of Parliament.[45] Hillsborough, in reply to Chester's report, stated that the views of the governor coincided rather closely with the views of the Board of Trade, but the alternative of control through act of Parliament, however desirable and sound in principle, was at that time inexpedient in view of the hostile opinion in the colonies toward parliaméntary enactments.[46]

At the congresses which had been held during Johnstone's administration the Indians were promised that similar meetings would be held frequently. Such conferences,

44. Enclosed in Chester to Hillsborough, April 13, 1771, C.O.5: 578, pp. 185–191. In this connection it may be noticed that Lord Shelburne had not approved of the practice of encouraging one tribe to make war against another. Convincing Indians, he said, that their lands would not be encroached upon and that they would not be cheated by traders was a much superior policy of conciliating them than that of setting one tribe against another. Shelburne to Stuart, Dec. 11, 1766, enclosed in Stuart to Gage, April 18, 1767. The devious policy of the British government in this matter is naïvely set forth in a letter from Gage to Stuart, Feb. 5, 1771: "The war continuing between the Creeks and the Choctaws may be the means of rendering West Florida secure by finding employment for those Indians. But it appears to me that the greatest caution should be used on our part that they may not discover our intrigues to obstruct the peace, which several of the tribes of Creeks as well as all the Choctaws seem so desirous to conclude, and in which work we have engaged to assist." Feb. 5, 1771. See also Stuart to Gage, Feb. 8, 1771. These letters are in the Gage Papers.

45. Chester to Hillsborough, March 9, 1771, C.O.5: 578, pp. 129–134.

46. Hillsborough to Chester, July 3, 1771, C.O.5: 588, pp. 201–206.

conducted with great ceremony and with a nice regard
for rank, and accompanied by great feasts and the liberal
distribution of presents, were occasions of gratification to
the Indians. On the other hand, by the English, who were
not fond of intimate association with the Indians, they
were likely to be regarded as expensive and unpleasant
necessities. In 1771, however, several considerations
pointed to the advisability of calling together the Indians.
Their plundering activities demanded some remedy, and
their complaints in regard to encroachments on their land
and abuses of the traders called for investigation; an additional cession of land on the Escambia near Pensacola by
the Creeks was highly desirable; and, finally, the Indians
themselves were demanding meetings. In view of these
facts the English government ordered Superintendent
John Stuart, who had his home and made his headquarters
in Charles Town, to repair to West Florida for this purpose. It is interesting to note that on his arrival there he
presented a mandamus from the king and was admitted
to the council as councillor extraordinary, with full privileges, except that of assuming the government in case of
the death or absence of the governor, lieutenant governor,
and councillors senior to him.[47]

Since the Creeks and the Choctaws were not on friendly
terms, two congresses were necessary. The Creeks were
summoned to meet at Pensacola in the latter part of October, while the Choctaws and Chickasaws were directed to
assemble at Mobile some two months later. While waiting
for the Indians to arrive, the governor and council with
the aid of the superintendent took several steps to correct
abuses. Stuart appointed John McIntosh and John
Thomas commissaries, the former to the Choctaws and
Chickasaws, and the latter, with headquarters at Manchac,
to the Indians on the Mississippi. In order to strengthen

47. Minutes of Council, Aug. 2, 1771 and Stuart to Gage, May 24,
1772, Gage Papers. The superintendent was eligible in a similar way for
membership in every provincial council in his district.

the authority of these officers they were commissioned justices of the peace.[48] The governor and council also directed that the traders who dealt with towns within the limits of the colony should take out licenses according to provincial law and that those who traded with towns outside the province should take out licenses in accordance with the Proclamation of 1763. As the northern boundary of the province had never been run, the surveyor was ordered to make a map and locate the towns and boundary as best he might.[49]

The congresses in form and procedure were much like those of 1765. There were the usual smoking of the calumet, the eloquent speeches couched in figurative language, the attendance of the military and provincial dignitaries, the exchange of compliments, the round of feasting, and, finally, the inevitable and, in the eyes of the Indians, all-important distribution of presents. The Choctaw and Chickasaw chiefs were with pomp and ceremony invested with great and small medals, but this rite was omitted with the Creeks, who apparently did not hold the medals in high regard. The negotiations with the Choctaws and Chickasaws were more friendly than those with the Creeks. Philip Livingston, Junior, a member of the council, was official recorder of proceedings.

The congress with the Creeks met from October 29 to November 2.[50] Emistisiguo was the principal chief present. The Indians complained mostly of encroachments on their lands and of white people driving cattle through their territories. The governor explained that the encroachments had been made through error and that they would not be repeated. Then Chester tactfully suggested a cession of land on the Escambia in order that the fertile fields might be utilized for the production of food for the entertainment of the Indians on their next visit. Emisti-

48. Minutes of Council, Aug. 17, 1771.
49. *Ibid.*
50. Chester to Hillsborough, Dec. 20, 1771, C.O.5: 589, pp. 13–16; minutes of the congress, *ibid.*, pp. 85–115.

siguo evaded this request with the same sophistry that had been used effectively by the Creeks in 1765. The title to the land, he said in reply, was vested in all the members of the tribe, including women and children, and those present had no authority to alienate lands without the consent of all concerned. He offered a counter proposal, however, of ceding to the English a small barren strip near Pensacola and a tract between the Tombigbee and the Coosa, which the English already claimed by virtue of the cession from the Choctaws in 1765. The first of these offers was diplomatically rejected as worthless, but the second was accepted as a necessary confirmation of title to land already occupied. The English were rather chagrined at their failure, but pharisaically congratulated the Indians on their adherence to high principles.[51]

The congress with the Choctaws and Chickasaws convened in Mobile from December 31, 1771, to January 6, 1772.[52] Paya Mattaha of the Chickasaws was the most important chief present and because of the consistently friendly attitude which his tribe had maintained toward the English he occupied a place of honor. The Indians complained of the sale of too much rum. "It flows in upon our nation," said one chief, "like a great sea from Mobile and from all the plantations and settlements roundabouts." They also complained of short measures and weights and deviation from the established price lists on the part of the traders, and of the withdrawal of the commissaries and "gun doctors," meaning the armorers. The traders, a number of whom were present, complained of robberies by the Indians. The governor and the super-

51. General Gage understood perfectly the reluctance of the Indians to give up their land. He wrote Stuart that "long experience has shown them that as the white people advance the natives are annihilated, and their policy is good to prevent us from extending ourselves into their country as long as they can." June 21, 1772. At a later date Stuart himself wrote, "I am certain that the Indians can have no such powerful motive for quarrelling with us as our insatiable avidity for their land." Stuart to Gage, Jan. 18, 1775, Gage Papers.

52. Chester to Hillsborough, Feb. 20, 1772, C.O.5: 589, pp. 23–26; minutes of the congress, ibid., pp. 125–162.

intendent heard the Indians with patience. They promised redress but chided the chiefs for countenancing the activities of traders who sold rum; they rebuked the Indians for their past misdemeanors and announced the reëstablishing of the commissaries. They also urged that Indians be deputed to accompany a party for the survey of the boundary of the cession of 1765, which had never been definitely marked. The meeting adjourned with the Indians in good spirits, and Chester wrote Hillsborough that the support of these Indians could be counted upon in case of a rupture with Spain. After the congress was ended a party accompanied by Indians set out to survey the boundary. This task, however, was not completed, for the Indians, complaining that swamps through which the surveys must be made were flooded at that season of the year, soon quit the expedition.

It is not to be thought that these meetings solved the problems of Indian relations. Difficulties continued chronic until the outbreak of the Revolution. This event made the question of Indian adherence one of great importance and both the English and the Americans made energetic efforts to win and keep Indian support.[53]

53. H. L. Shaw, *British Administration of the Southern Indians, 1756–1783*, pp. 84–162.

IV

THE LEGISLATURE

THOUGH the assembly in West Florida met only from 1766 to 1771, with a short but turbulent session in 1778, its various activities, its *esprit de corps*, its methods of procedure, and its quarrels with the governors, which militated so effectively against the welfare of the young province, warrant a fuller discussion than its brief existence would indicate. It may be said that the history of the West Florida assembly is an epitome of the more lengthy history of the assembly of the usual royal province. Inasmuch as the period of activity of the assembly coincides closely with the interval considered in the preceding chapter, it is now in order to examine this institution, tracing its origin and election, observing the procedure which it effected, noting the laws which it enacted, and evaluating its significance to the province and in the whole colonial scene.

A bicameral legislature was characteristic of all of the older colonies with the exception of Pennsylvania and Delaware, where the lawmaking bodies consisted of only one house. Because of its unpeopled state it was thought at first that West Florida was not ready for a legislature, and the early representations of the Board of Trade on the subject suggested for the proposed colony an administration by governor and council. In the final draft of the Proclamation of 1763, however, the governor was authorized to call an assembly, with the consent of the council, "so soon as the state and circumstances" of the colony permitted. In an accompanying representation, the board explained that the change had been made in order to encourage settlement.[1] The commission and instructions to

1. See pp. 4, 5 above.

Governor Johnstone amplified this authority and prescribed with a great degree of exactitude the way in which
the legislative body should be summoned, the means by
which it should exercise its power, and the limits within
which this power should be employed. Following the usual
custom the lower house was to be elected by the freeholders, and the members of the governor's council, when
sitting in a legislative capacity, were to compose the upper
house.[2]

Johnstone arrived in West Florida in the latter part
of 1764 and the first assembly met in November, 1766,
two years after his arrival and more than three years after
the creation of the province. When one considers the sparsity and heterogeneity of population, the frontier character of the colony, and the difficulties of communication
and transportation, this delay does not seem unreasonable.
On August 18, 1766, the governor issued a proclamation
directing that elections be held and that the assembly meet
in Pensacola on November 3, following. In view of the
small number of freeholders and the time necessary for
the making of grants to acquire land, the franchise was
extended, for the time being, to all persons occupying
houses (except that only one person from a house could
vote). For the district of Pensacola, which included all
of the province east of the river Perdido except the township of Campbell Town, six persons were to be chosen;
Campbell Town was to have two representatives; the district of Mobile, which comprised all of the province west
of the Perdido, was to have six.[3] The writ of election,
issued on the same day, directed the provost marshal to
see that "a sufficient number of inhabitants from each
district of the best most able and discreet men for busi-

2. See Chap. I for analysis of instructions.
3. Proclamation opposite first page of manuscript volume of Assembly Minutes in Library of Congress. Campbell Town was soon deserted and degenerated into a "rotten borough," whence came charges
of corruption at almost every election. Assembly Minutes, Jan. 25, 26,
30, 1769.

ness" be chosen as representatives.[4] The execution of the writ was signed by James Johnstone, deputy provost marshal, who was the governor's nephew. There is evidence that this officer sometimes exercised an unseemly influence in the choice of representatives.

As the actions accompanying the organization of the first assembly are typical and indicative of its future attitude, they may well be observed with care. The members of the commons house, as the elective branch was frequently called, met on November 3, according to the governor's proclamation, and two members waited on the governor to inform him of their coming together. Three members of the council then attended "the house and administered the usual oaths to the members who took the same and made and subscribed the Declaration."

And then the said gentlemen of the council informed the members, His Excellency, in His Majesty's name, had ordered them to command the house to proceed to the choice of a speaker immediately.

Then the house unanimously chose Francis Poussett, Esqr. their speaker and thereupon he was conducted to the chair.

Ordered that Mr. Ward and Mr. Williams attend His Excellency and acquaint him that the house had made choice of a speaker and desire to know when they shall attend His Excellency to present him; who, returning, reported delivery thereof and that His Excellency was pleased to say when the house pleased.

Whereupon the house attended and presented their speaker, who being approved of, demanded in the name of the house the usual privileges, viz.,

4. *Ibid.,* Nov. 3, 1766. Part of the assembly minutes has been printed by James A. Padgett in the *Louisiana Historical Quarterly:* minutes for Nov. 3, 1766–Jan. 3, 1767 in XXII, 311–384; for Feb. 23–June 6, 1767 and Dec. 15, 1767–Jan. 11, 1768 in XXII, 943–1011; for Aug. 23–Oct. 21, 1768, Jan. 25–Feb. 2, 1769, and May 22–June 29, 1769 in XXIII, 5–77. The citations in this study are to originals or to transcripts or photostats in the Library of Congress.

1st. That they have liberty of speech and freedom of debate.

2nd. That on all urgent occasions, the house may have liberty of access to His Excellency.

3rd. That they may be exempted from arrests during the sitting and continuance of the assembly.

Which His Excellency was pleased to grant.

Mr. speaker further made his humble request to His Excellency on his own behalf, that His Excellency had, from too favorable an opinion of him, been pleased to agree with the house in the choice of him to be their speaker, that he would give the most favorable interpretation to his conduct, and to impute any error or mistake he [the speaker] might have committed now before him [the governor], not to the house, but to himself.[5]

The members then returned to their own chamber where Thomas Robert Hardy and William Cox were elected clerk and messenger, respectively. These two men, it is interesting to note, were reëlected by succeeding assemblies until Governor Chester ceased in 1772 to summon the legislature; their yearly salaries were set at £70 and £50, respectively.[6] The speech of the governor and the writ of election, with the return, were read and entered in the minutes. A committee was appointed to draw up an address of thanks to the governor for his speech.[7]

The first standing committee appointed was on privileges and elections. Immediately after this action Dr. John Lorimer, of Pensacola, presented a petition alleging

5. Assembly Minutes, Nov. 3, 1766. It may be noted that on one occasion Mr. Richard Carpenter, member from Mobile, took the affirmation prescribed by law for Quakers, rather than the oath. *Ibid.,* May 24, 1769.

6. *Ibid.,* Nov. 20, 1766.

7. Compare this procedure with that described in an essay by Mary P. Clarke, "Parliamentary Privilege in America," *Essays in Colonial History,* pp. 124–144, especially pp. 125–127. It will be found to be very similar to the proceedings in all of the royal provinces and to show an indebtedness to the English House of Commons. See also *The Cambridge History of the British Empire,* I, 422–426.

that at the close of the poll at Campbell Town sixteen votes had been cast in his favor and twelve for David Williams, but that the marshal or sheriff had taken upon himself, on the sole advice of David Williams or his friends, to alter the poll in such a manner that David Williams was returned as a member from the said township, to the great prejudice of the petitioner and his constituents. The petitioner had no purpose to serve, save the good of the province, and was sorry to see his name connected with any contested point. He was conscious that every cause of dispute should be avoided especially at the commencement of an assembly for an infant province, but the affair was so well known and of such a tendency that it could not be silently passed over. The petitioner, therefore, presented a copy of the poll and hoped that the house would come to some resolution "as may be at once equitable for the present and safe for the future." The petition was referred to the committee on privileges and elections, and the deputy provost marshal and Robert Collins, who had acted as his clerk at the Campbell Town election, were ordered to attend the committee at four o'clock in the afternoon.[8]

On the same day, and with a promptness that leads one to suspect it had been prepared in advance, the committee on privileges and elections presented a set of twenty-nine standing rules which was immediately adopted. These rules, though changed from time to time, formed a basis for procedure. The assembly was not to be considered met unless the speaker were present. A later rule provided for a speaker *pro tempore* in case of the speaker's sickness or necessary absence. Each member was to place himself as he came in so that there might be no disparity. The quorum for the transaction of business was eight, but five might adjourn from day to day and send for absent members. The speaker was authorized to sign warrants for those members absent without leave; these were to be taken into custody and were to pay the messenger two dollars

8. Assembly Minutes, Nov. 3, 1766.

and the clerk one dollar for every day of detention. No one was to leave the house while it was in session without the speaker's consent. The seat of any member who left the province without proper leave was to be declared vacant. In order "that all might be governed by right and decency," the speaker and house might imprison any member who misbehaved. No member was to presume to speak without standing up and addressing the speaker, nor was any member to speak twice on the same subject without leave of the house. No member was to be held liable by another member for any words spoken or motion made except at the same sitting and before an adjournment; nor was the house to receive any charge against a member, brought by an outsider because of words spoken openly within the house.

The minutes were to be read each morning and if approved were to be entered in the journal, which was to remain in the hands of the speaker. A motion, made and seconded, should be put to a vote whether there was any debate or not. When a resolution had once been taken by the house it was not to be altered during the session. A bill, before passage, should be read three times with amendments. Committees were to be appointed by the speaker and approved by the house. The standing committees were usually authorized to send for persons, records, and papers and to question all persons in the most solemn manner. Anyone summoned to appear before a committee or before the house was under the protection of the house.[9] Persons giving false evidence before a committee or the house, or tampering with those who had been summoned to appear before a committee or the house, would be proceeded against with the utmost severity. No committee should meet while the house was in session. Any question in regard to an election return should be made within twenty days after the return was brought in (this period

9. A comparison of these rules with those outlined in Dr. Clarke's essay (p. 134) will reveal that they were quite similar to those in vogue in the older colonies.

was later reduced to five days). When a question regarding the election or privilege of a member came up, he should withdraw until the question was decided; by a later rule he was allowed to be present during the debate but was to withdraw before the vote was taken. When the house judged any petition concerning an election to be "frivolous or vexatious" it should order satisfaction to be made to the person petitioned against. No member of the council, it was declared, had the right to interfere in, or to vote in any assembly elections. This rule was doubtless derived from the custom in England that members of the House of Lords did not participate in elections for the House of Commons.[10] The house promised to proceed with utmost severity against any one who appeared to have procured his election by bribery or other corrupt practice.[11]

The assembly which met in the fall of 1778, if one may look ahead, adopted a few new rules that added color to the procedure.[12] On the demand of any member for that purpose a roll call must be made; this was later expanded into a specific regulation that a record of the votes of the members be incorporated into the minutes.[13] Any member of the house was permitted to introduce a private gentleman as a spectator, but should any business arise that ought not immediately to be made public, the speaker was to order the house and lobby cleared. The speaker was directed to seat himself in the chair with his hat on. But should he take off his hat, on putting a question or on similar occasion, every member was to be uncovered out of respect to him as speaker. It was ordered "that when the house do rise, every member keep his seat until the speaker go, and then every one in course orderly as they do sit. That the doorkeeper or messenger or both do attend

10. W. R. Anson, *The Law and Custom of the Constitution* (Fifth Ed.), I, 130.

11. Assembly Minutes, Nov. 3, 1766. Most of the colonial assemblies adopted standing rules. See Dr. Clarke's essay, pp. 137–138.

12. Assembly Minutes, Oct. 19, 1778.

13. *Ibid.*, Oct. 22, 1778.

the speaker to and from the house, bearing the mace or carrying a wand before him."

On the second day of the first session the committee on privileges and elections reported a resolution which the house adopted: "That this house are the sole judges, and alone have right to take cognizance, hear, and determine the right of voters at any poll of election, and of the qualification of members returned." [14] Dr. Lorimer, at his request, was by vote of the house given leave to be heard at the bar. The speaker produced a letter from David Williams, member from Campbell Town, in which he asked to be excused from attending on account of indisposition. After debate it was ordered that Williams should either send a certificate from his doctor or attend the house immediately. "Mr. Williams accordingly attended." After Dr. Lorimer had spoken in support of his petition, Williams was called to the bar in order to be heard. He made the error of accusing the committee of partiality in their proceedings. On order of the house Williams' behavior was taken into immediate consideration and after debate it was "Resolved, That Mr. Williams be called to the bar of this house and be severely reprimanded, and make a concession to the house for the reflections made on the proceedings of the committee of privileges and elections." The house then resolved that the deputy provost marshal had made a false return for David Williams, and that he be expelled from the house; that Dr. John Lorimer had been duly elected and that he take his seat accordingly. Then, according to the resolution, Williams was severely reprimanded and made an apology. [15] Dr. Lorimer received the oath from the speaker and another member, one Ross, to whom a *dedimus* had been issued by the governor. Immediately afterwards, James Johnstone, the deputy provost marshal, was called to the bar to answer for his conduct. [16]

14. *Ibid.*, Nov. 4, 1766. All colonial assemblies claimed the right to decide disputed elections. See Dr. Clarke's essay, pp. 135–136.

15. Such a procedure was common in the other colonies. See Dr. Clarke's essay, pp. 131–133.

16. The sheriffs of English counties were frequently summoned to the

He said that he was sorry for his part in the affair and that it had proceeded from his inexperience. This statement was accepted and he was discharged. Thus did the assembly, in the second day of its existence, vindicate its honor and exhibit an *esprit de corps* which would have done credit to a much older institution.

This jealousy of honor and privilege, though not usually exhibited in such a dramatic way, characterized the whole history of the assembly. In 1767, William Duncan, a constable, was ordered confined to the common jail during the pleasure of the house, for admitting disorderly company into the assembly chamber.[17] On January 27, 1769, for an offense against the committee on privileges, William Collins, deputy provost marshal, was summoned to the bar of the house and made the following apology: "I had no intention to offer any insult or to give any offence to this committee, and if any words by me spoken have given offence, I am heartily sorry for it and ask pardon of the committee."[18] The house was frequently called upon to decide contested elections. On one or two occasions it was agreed that there had been a tie vote, and the seat was declared vacant and writs were issued for another election.[19]

The assembly, though small in size (the average attendance was not over ten, and there were frequent adjournments because of the lack of a quorum) used committees to a large extent in routine business. The committees were of three kinds: select, standing, and of the whole house. The terms "select" and "standing" were not used contemporaneously, however. A select committee, usually composed of from two to four members, was, of course, one appointed for some specific purpose, such as to carry a message to the governor or the upper house, or to prepare

bar of the House of Commons and made to apologize for irregularities in connection with elections. E. P. Cheyney, *The European Background of American History*, p. 268.

17. Assembly Minutes, May 25, 1767.
18. *Ibid.*, Jan. 27, 1769.
19. *Ibid.*, Dec. 15, 1767.

an address, and it went out of existence without formality when the function for which it had been appointed had been performed.

The standing committees were named when the assembly convened, and served during the session. They were composed of from six to nine members, and other members of the house who desired to do so were sometimes allowed to attend meetings. It was not unusual for a prominent member to belong to several or even all of the standing committees. Talent was probably so scarce that it was necessary to use it when available. The functions of the committee on privileges and elections have already been suggested. The committee on laws inquired as to what acts were expiring and prepared and introduced bills; it was perhaps the most important of the committees. Petitions of complaint were referred to the committee on grievances, and before a great while this group was styled the grand committee on grievances. It also corresponded with the colonial agent until a separate committee of correspondence took over this function. The committee of accounts, whose function it was to examine the treasurer's books, had made its appearance by 1771. The committee of the whole house considered and discussed bills and addresses much in the manner of modern legislative bodies. An early standing rule provided that when the house went into the committee of the whole, the door should be locked and the key laid on the table before the chairman; and any member presuming to depart without leave should incur the censure of the house. The chairman of this committee was changed from time to time.

Most of the bills originated in the committee on laws, and none came from private members. Sometimes, however, a motion was made and carried that a bill be introduced for a certain purpose. In such a case, a select committee was appointed to prepare the bill, and a member of this committee presented the bill to the house. A bill once introduced was read twice, sometimes on the same day, and then referred to the committee of the whole. After consideration by this body during one, two, or three sittings, it was reported back to the house, with or without amendments, as the case might be. Then it was read a third time and ordered "that the bill do pass." The speaker was directed to sign the bill and a select committee was appointed to carry it to the council and to request its concurrence. This committee usually reported back to the house that it had delivered the bill and that the council had promised to consider it. The council or upper house, as it was frequently called, might agree to the bill without change, agree to it with amendments, or reject it entirely. In the last case, of course, the bill was lost. In the second case the assembly might accept or reject all or some of the amendments. Disagreements between the houses were sometimes removed by a conference of select committees. After a bill had been passed by both houses it was sent to the governor for his approval. It was the usual procedure for the governor to go to the council chamber near the end of each session and to send for the assembly to meet him there. Then in the presence of both houses he gave his assent to the bills which had been presented to him and prorogued or dissolved the commons house. As the governor usually had almost complete control of the council, it was rarely necessary for him to withhold his approval.

There remain to be noticed several items of procedure. The house usually began its daily meetings in the mornings; frequently there were afternoon sessions; evening sessions occasionally were held. If a member were elevated to the council, his seat automatically became vacant and writs were issued for an election. On one occasion the seat of one Weir, who was not expected to return to the province during the session, was declared vacant. On another occasion, Valens Stephen Comyn, having been forced to apologize to the house, asked permission to resign his seat. This was, by a vote of the house, refused.[20] But in 1771 writs were issued to fill the places of Richard Car-

20. *Ibid.*, May 31, 1769.

penter and James Amoss, who were returned from Pensacola, when they signified that it would be impossible for them to attend.[21] Occasionally the same man was returned as a representative from two constituencies. This occurred in 1769 when James Ross was returned from both Pensacola and Mobile. He declared that he took his seat for Pensacola.[22] The opinion of the chief justice was requested in 1767 on the legality of a principle that was involved in a proposed law.[23] At irregular intervals the journal of the assembly was inspected by a committee from the council, and the commons house invariably responded by appointing a similar committee for the inspection of the journal of the upper house. These inspections took place with all good humor. The assembly, however, was inclined to be sensitive in regard to suggestions from the council, and on one occasion when that body sent a message remonstrating gently with the lower house because of the extravagant salaries they had voted themselves, the assembly replied: "This species of condescension and good nature which your Honors have been pleased to manifest toward the house, they are determined shall never become a precedent for their own conduct, which shall always be ruled by their own and not the reason and judgment of others."[24] Nevertheless, the members agreed that their salaries for the session be used for the relief of the poor at Pensacola and Mobile.[25]

The procedure in the upper house was similar to that in the assembly and equally formal. There were no standing committees. Communication with the governor was by means of a select committee; with the commons house, by the clerk or the master in chancery. Bills frequently originated in the upper house, where they were introduced by individual members rather than by a committee. Money or tax bills, however, always originated in the lower house, and though carefully considered in the upper house, were

21. *Ibid.*, June 29, 1771.
22. *Ibid.*, Jan. 25, 1769.
23. *Ibid.*, May 27, 1767.

24. *Ibid.*, Dec. 22, 1766.
25. *Ibid.*, Dec. 24, 1766.

passed there without amendment. The rules of order were similar to those of the commons house but with certain variations. Each member took his seat according to seniority; a quorum was five; the senior member present presided. No member was to speak more than twice on a bill except to explain himself, or unless the house was in committee of the whole. A member, when speaking, rose and addressed, not the chair, but the house, viz., "Honorable Gentlemen." When a question was put, the junior member voted first by saying "content" or "not content," and thus every member in his turn; the clerk took note of the votes.[26] The upper house, composed as it was of men favorably inclined toward the government, selected by the governor and appointed by the crown, was, of course, a much more conservative body than the lower house. Its journal is a rather dull record of legislative procedure and is almost entirely without those flashes of feeling and drama which raise the journal of the other chamber above the commonplace.

The governor, and in his absence the lieutenant governor, communicated with the houses through letters conveyed by the deputy provost marshal. Although he sometimes went to the room occupied by the upper house in order to address both bodies, it does not appear that he ever participated in the deliberations of either house. The West Florida legislature always convened in Pensacola, despite the fact that Governor Johnstone in summoning the first assembly to Pensacola promised that the next should meet in Mobile. On leaving the province he recalled his promise to the council, but stated rather cynically that he did not believe that his successor could be held to it. Apparently no effort was ever actually made to have the assembly meet in Mobile. Probably the fact that Pensacola was designated in the governor's instructions as the seat of government prevented the question of sessions at Mobile from being agitated.

26. Minutes of Upper House, March 1–May 19, 1770, C.O.5: 626; also Oct. 6, 1778, C.O.5: 628.

The records do not indicate the building in which the
first assembly met. A council resolution of March 7, 1767,
was to the effect that the house of Sir John Lindsay should
be temporarily rented for a courthouse and a meeting
place of the assembly. The rent of seventy pounds a year
was to be paid from the contingent fund. On July 6 of
the same year, the council was of the opinion that the
house of William Aird should be rented for £100 annually.
This building because of its "commodiousness" would answer for the courts of judicature, the council chamber, the
house of assembly, and the public offices. Apparently this
arrangement continued until February 7, 1769, when the
council voted to rent the house of General Haldimand as
a home for Governor Eliot (whose arrival was daily expected) and to convert the building within the fort, which
had been used as a residence by Johnstone and Browne,
into a government house. Governor Eliot, however, stated
to the council on April 5, that he intended to occupy the
house within the fort and he designated the Haldimand
structure for business of state. Chester on his arrival in
1770 chose to reverse the arrangement. It appears that
the house within the fort, though frequently reported to
be desperately in need of repairs, was used for official
purposes until the end of the period.[27]

27. The home government in 1771 made a provision of £2,500 for the
erection of a suitable governor's home, and construction was immediately begun under the direction of Lieutenant Governor Durnford, who
was also engineer and surveyor general of the province. It was thought
that on the completion of this structure General Haldimand's house
would be purchased for the use of official agencies or that the old government house would be restored or rebuilt. However, these optimistic
expectations were not fulfilled. The funds were exhausted before the
building was completed, in spite of the explicit warning of the home
government against this contingency. This unhappy situation, according to Chester, was to be attributed entirely to the mismanagement of
Durnford, who, in spite of repeated admonitions, had planned on too
large a scale; Durnford, however, placed the blame on Chester's desire
for a fine home. No additional appropriations were forthcoming. The un-
finished building was eventually taken over by the military and used as
barracks. Hillsborough to Chester, Feb. 11, 1771, C.O.5: 588, pp. 65–68;
Chester to Dartmouth, April 22, 1775, C.O.5: 592 (original pagination
not preserved in transcript); Durnford to Germain, Oct. 7, 1778,

The appointment of a colonial agent was a function that was assumed by the West Florida legislature. On January 2, 1767, near the close of the first session of the first assembly, the council suggested to the commons house that in view of the various memorials and other provincial business to be laid before the different public boards in England, it was expedient to appoint an agent, "who by being at the fountain head may give that attention which is due to the business of the province, and who from his situation may be enabled to seize these opportunities for the public good." The council further suggested that Samuel Hannay of London, who had on former occasions exerted his warmest endeavors to promote the interest of the colony, be requested to accept this office, and that it be recommended in strongest terms to the good faith of succeeding sessions of the general assembly that an allowance be given him. The lower house agreed to this proposal and a letter signed by James Bruce, as senior councillor, and Francis Poussett, speaker of the assembly, was accordingly dispatched to Hannay, requesting him to assume the duties of agent.[28] Hannay, a London merchant, was at this time, by virtue of a royal patent, provincial provost marshal, but he exercised the office by deputy. He acted as agent for the colony at least until 1778, when he was active in presenting charges against Governor Chester. He usually corresponded with the speaker of the assembly and the committee of grievances; later the committee of correspondence was directed to take over this duty.[29]

C.O.5: 595, pp. 17–22; Chester to Germain, Sept. 21, 1778, C.O.5: 595, pp. 389–392. All of these letters are in Miss. Trans.

The difficulties relating to the construction of a government house in West Florida were quite different from those which developed in North Carolina at the same time over Governor Tryon's "Palace" at New Berne. This beautiful edifice, erected from money appropriated by the North Carolina assembly, was the cause of much popular discontent.

28. Assembly Minutes, Jan. 3, 1767. A council minute of June 16, 1770, condemned the practice of the assembly in appointing a committee to communicate with the colonial agent without the coöperation of the council. Governor Chester expressed a similar sentiment to Hillsborough a short time later. March 10, 1771, C.O.5: 578, pp. 137–138.

29. Hannay's agency is not to be confused with that of John Ellis.

Not much can be said definitely in regard to the personnel of the assembly. The position of representative seems not to have been greatly desired. Though there were several examples of contested elections, there were also instances where men refused to serve or requested permission to resign, and members appear frequently to have been elected from outside the district which they represented. A seat in the governor's council, precarious though it was in the hectic times of Browne and Eliot, seemed more desirable. The membership of the assembly did not vary a great deal from session to session. The influence of the merchant class can be seen through the numerous laws which were passed to regulate the mechanics of business and trade. James Ross, Valens Stephen Comyn, and John McGillivray, of Mobile, whose firm was heavily involved in the Indian trade, were representative of the commercial interests of the province. Major Robert Farmar, who was prominent in the military occupation of the province, had led troops to the Illinois country after the failure of the expedition under Major Loftus. On his return to West Florida he had been acquitted by the court martial which Johnstone had prevailed on General Gage to order, and he settled at Mobile and was elected to the assembly. Since he had quarrelled violently with Lieutenant Governor Browne over the possession of Dauphin Island, he was doubtless a thorn in the side of this luckless executive. Dr.

West Florida, unlike most royal provinces, had two agents. The functions of these two officials were entirely different and their appointments came from widely separated sources. John Ellis was appointed by the crown under the sign manual and his duty was to disburse, on proper warrants, the parliamentary support fund. Commission dated April 2, 1764, is found in C.O.324, folio 21, Florida State Historical Society photostats. His salary of £200, annually, was paid from this fund. Ellis served until his death about 1778, when he was succeeded by Christopher Newsham, whose lax and inefficient administration of the office provoked much complaint. (Memorial of certain merchants trading to West Florida, June 16, 1781, C.O.5: 580, p. 347.) See statement in Andrews' *Guide*, I, 238n. There are two articles in the *Political Science Quarterly* on the general subject of colonial agents: E. P. Tanner, "Colonial Agencies in England during the Eighteenth Century," XVI, 24–49, and B. W. Bond, "The Colonial Agent as a Popular Representative," XXXV, 372–392.

John Lorimer, a military surgeon, who was held in high esteem, served during one session as speaker *pro tempore* and was very active in the business of the house. A counterpart of Dr. Lorimer was "Doctor" George Brown, a representative from Pensacola, of whom little is known except that his name appears with great frequency in the assembly journal for several sessions. Arthur Neil, the ordnance storekeeper, played a relatively unimportant part in the proceedings. Francis Poussett, the first speaker, was a merchant and also belonged to the local bureaucracy. He was at one time deputy provincial secretary and was recommended by a subsequent assembly to Browne as provincial treasurer, but he was never appointed. Edmund Rush Wegg, who also served as speaker, was the attorney general who had been suspended by Johnstone. Following a trip to England he was restored to office. Wegg was also, for a while, judge of the provincial vice-admiralty court. Elihu Hall Bay, prominent in official circles of the province, was judge of vice-admiralty, by deputation, and also deputy provincial secretary. Adam Chrystie served as speaker of the assembly which met in 1778. He was the hero of a skirmish which had taken place at Manchac with members of the Willing expedition, and it was probably because of this that he was elected from both Mobile and Manchac and elevated to the speakership.[30] He was soon at odds with Governor Chester, however, apparently over the representation of Mobile, and, with John McGillivray, was the leader in the movement against him. Anthony Hutchins, member from Natchez, received the thanks of the assembly for his leadership in the recovery of Natchez from the Willing forces.[31] He had several years before led a number of families from Virginia and the Carolinas to the Natchez district. Another interesting member of the assembly of 1778 was Thaddeus Lyman, a son of General Phineas Lyman of Connecticut, who was one of the leaders in the Company of Military Adventurers.

30. Assembly Minutes, Oct. 1, 2, 1778.   31. *Ibid.*

The attitude of the assembly toward the executive was alternately friendly and hostile. It is a curious anomaly that Governor Johnstone, whose fierce quarrels with the military and judicial officers caused repercussions which threatened to wreck the colony, should have had very cordial relations with the only popular branch of the government. It is possible that the establishing of a legislature in a new country appealed to his imagination and that in his mind he compared himself with the Solons of Greece and the Catos and Ciceros of Rome, characters with whom he was well acquainted and to whom he frequently referred. The platitudes of his opening address to the assembly would seem to give credence to this theory. After congratulating the members upon the establishment of a complete legislative authority and emphasizing the responsibility which rested on them, he said, "I shall not presume to recapitulate the particular laws which have appeared to me as necessary to be enacted, respecting our peculiar situation. Where the society has felt the inconvenience, these will naturally occur to the different members, when I make no doubt that proper remedies will be provided, in which as well as in everything else that can promote the public good, you may depend on my hearty concurrence. In general, it is my opinion that the basis of our legislation should be as mild as human vices will admit; that we should ever remember the most virtuous people have had the fewest coercive laws, and that such laws have always been penned in the plainest language; that those colonies who have shown the greatest moderation in the speculative points, toward the prejudice of others, have flourished most; that all punishments where nature revolts even when inflicted on the worst of malefactors, serve only to vitiate a society, and in short, that the great principle of good living lies in the fear of shame, which must always depend more on the example we are to give in our private capacities, by the encouragement of virtue and the discouragement of vice, than on the multiplicity of regulations we may enact." [32] The assembly thanked the governor for his "generous sentiments of humanity and moderation," asked his indulgence over their lack of "more perfect abilities" and looked forward to a period of prosperity under a "governor of your Excellency's abilities." [33]

At the conclusion of the session, just before his departure from the province, the governor offered additional aphorisms on the sacredness of private property, the superiority of the civil authority over the military, the evils of paper money, and the dangers of too much governmental interference with commerce. He gave his assent to fourteen laws, one of which was in direct violation of his instructions, and was subsequently disallowed in England. He did not comment on the salaries which the assemblymen had allowed themselves.[34] Since the tax bill provided that provincial funds should be placed in the hands of the receiver general, the question of the appointment of a treasurer was not raised. After his departure, and even after his recall, Johnstone appears to have continued his interest in the province, and a later assembly passed a vote of thanks to him for his efforts in behalf of the colony.[35]

The relations of Lieutenant Governor Browne with the assembly were far from friendly. From the beginning of his administration the assembly was antagonistic, and the executive and the lower house were usually in a state of disagreement. In the first session after the government had devolved upon Browne, a set of resolutions was adopted which pledged the support of the assembly to the lieutenant governor as long as he abided by his instructions, but complained further that he had, on the advice of some weak and ill-disposed persons, assumed to himself

32. *Ibid.*, Nov. 3, 1766.
33. *Ibid.*, Nov. 5, 1766.
34. *Ibid.*, Jan. 3, 1767.
35. *Ibid.*, March 1, 1770.

certain functions of government which should not have been exercised without the consent of the council.[36] Browne's reply to these resolutions was a forty-day prorogation.

When the house reassembled, it had, figuratively speaking, a chip on its shoulder, and the situation was not eased by the fact that Browne was not in Pensacola to greet the members. In a few days an address to Browne was prepared, which summarized the work of the session thus far and presented a program for the future. For the most part this document was couched in very respectful terms, but it contained one paragraph which might have been objectionable: "We shall always look upon it as an essential part of our duty to detect and redress such grievances as far as in our power, or to present them to your honor in the most glaring terms." Browne was still offended because of the recent resolutions and when a committee informed him that the house wished to present an address, he replied with a brief letter: "I am extremely happy to find that you proceed with the public business. I will not, therefore, take up any of your time in receiving addresses or in answering them." [37] The house, nonplussed and disturbed by this unexpected spiking of its guns, "Resolved, nem. con., That His Honor's letter and refusal to receive the address of the house are unprecedented."

On the final day of the session, a committee appointed to inquire into the state of the courts of justice, reported that the chancellor of the province had lately reversed the verdict of a jury. This, of course, was a reflection on Browne, who, as chief executive of the province, was chancellor. The house, therefore, resolved that in all cases where the plaintiff had a remedy at common law, he ought not to be relieved in chancery, and that the court could not relieve when the substance of the suit tended to overthrow an act of Parliament or any fundamental part of the common law. The house then attended the lieutenant

36. *Ibid.*, April 3, 1767.
37. *Ibid.*, May 23, 1767.

governor, who gave his assent to seven bills. At the conclusion of this ceremony, his Honor delivered to the assemblymen a scathing address. He reproached them for their "shameful resolutions" and reviled them for their cupidity. "What must the other colonies think of you," he demanded, "when they know that you tax the subjects merely for your own benefit and advantage. . . . Such grievances cry aloud for redress and I will redress them and make them publicly known so that the people may have an opportunity of contributing to their own happiness hereafter by a more proper choice of their representatives." He then dissolved the assembly without allowing time for a reply.[38]

Browne's relations with the next assembly were somewhat more happy. The assemblymen set their salary at five shillings *per diem*, with seven shillings, sixpence for the speaker.[39] Instead, however, of designating the receiver general as custodian of funds raised by the revenue law, a provincial treasurer was named in the body of the act. Browne, in giving his assent to the law, declared that he considered the appointment of a treasurer by the assembly as an infringement upon the prerogative of the crown, but inasmuch as funds were needed he consented to the act with the statement that he would not yield the point to any future assembly or allow his yielding this time to be pleaded as a precedent.[40]

Since the establishment of the assembly in West Florida, warrants for writs of election to fill vacancies in the house had been issued by the speaker. In 1769, just previous to the arrival of Governor Eliot, Browne complained to the speaker, Edmund Rush Wegg, that the method pursued in the other colonies, more particularly Georgia, was for

38. *Ibid.*, June 6, 1767. *The South Carolina Gazette* devoted three-fourths of the front page of the issue of July 13-20, 1767, to this dispute. Both the messages of Browne and the resolutions of the assembly were given with an explanation very favorable to the assembly. A file of the *Gazette* is in the collections of the Charleston Library Society.

39. Assembly Minutes, Dec. 23, 1767.

40. *Ibid.*, Jan. 7, 1768.

the governor to issue the warrant on application from the house.[41] The matter was referred to the committee on privileges and elections. This committee reported, and on order of the house drew up an address to the lieutenant governor setting forth that it had been the constant practice in West Florida for the speaker to sign the warrants; that the best precedents in their possession from the time of Queen Elizabeth to the present had been consulted, especially the second statute of the thirtieth year of Charles II, and that the method in use was the nearest and most agreeable to the laws of England.[42] Browne replied by letter, quite civilly, that the precedents offered were not drawn from practice in America, and that he did not think them sufficient authority for deviating from the custom established in the neighboring provinces; but as the arrival of Governor Eliot was expected daily he would leave the determination of the matter to him; the assembly was then prorogued for forty days.[43] Whereupon the house, although it had been legally prorogued, resolved: That in its address to his Honor, it had not particularized upon the forms of any colony because the colonies differed among themselves; that the order of adjournment had frustrated those plans and schemes which the members were concerting for the welfare of the colony; that those persons who had advised his Honor to issue this order were the enemies of his Majesty, to the intentions of the mother country, and the settlement and welfare of the colony; that the clerk be ordered to furnish members with copies of the proceedings of this meeting in order that they might show their constituents the great desire of the house to proceed with moderation and dispatch in those matters essential and expedient to the welfare and prosperity of the province.[44]

41. *Ibid.*, Jan. 30, 1769.
42. *Ibid.*, Feb. 1, 1769.
43. *Ibid.*, Feb. 2, 1769. This question was never settled. In 1771 the house requested Governor Chester to issue the warrants, but in 1778 the speaker was ordered to issue them.
44. *Ibid.*, Feb. 2, 1769.

Thus did the assembly meet in extra-legal session in order to bring forth a political document.

Governor Eliot, during his brief interlude, had no disagreements with the assembly. He brought with him to the colony an order of the Privy Council that disallowed the law under which the existing assembly had been elected. The assembly, therefore, was dissolved and an election ordered under regulations prescribed by the governor and council.[45] But Eliot killed himself before the new assembly came together.

When this assembly did convene, the issue over the appointment of the treasurer was joined in earnest. David Ross and Francis Poussett were nominated in the house for this office and Poussett was elected.[46] A committee which had been appointed to notify Browne of the choice reported that his Honor refused to agree.[47] In a formal communication the lieutenant governor informed the assembly that the sole right of appointment lay in him. The house then weakened to the extent of making an effort to get Browne to divulge the name of the person whom he intended to appoint. When Browne refused this gesture of conciliation the members resolved, without dissenting vote, that they would proceed no further with the tax bill until the person appointed treasurer, and the security which he gave for execution of his office, received the approbation of the house.[48] And there the matter rested until the recall of Browne.

Lieutenant Governor Elias Durnford had no difficulties with the assembly. He had been appointed to succeed Browne largely because of irregularities in Browne's administration, and also because of disorders in the province which had developed on the death of Governor Eliot. The harmony of his régime was in marked contrast to the confusion which had preceded it. He was a man of ability,

45. Eliot to Hillsborough, April 17, 1769, C.O.5: 586, pp. 115–117.
46. Assembly Minutes, June 10, 1769.
47. *Ibid.*, June 12, 1769.   48. *Ibid.*, June 14, 1769.

well-acquainted with the province and the people, and his intercourse with the assembly was friendly. When, on May 10, 1770, Benjamin Ward was recommended by that body to him for appointment as treasurer,[49] the appointment was made without comment [50] and the money bill was promptly passed.

Governor Chester clashed with the assembly over appropriation and privilege. Probably taking his cue from Hillsborough, he was rather high-handed in his attitude toward the popular body. The king had every reason to expect, Hillsborough wrote Chester, that so distinguished a mark of his royal favor as that of allowing an assembly to be summoned, would be productive of real benefit and advantage to the colony; but there was too much ground to apprehend that the personal interest of the members, and not the general welfare, had been the object generally held in view. The money bills devoted almost entirely to the upkeep of the assembly, and the claim of that body to the right of nominating a treasurer were especially reprehensible. It was to be hoped that Chester would explain the spirit and the privileges of the constitution more perfectly.[51]

In his first speech Chester urged that appropriations be made to defray the expenses of criminal justice in the colony.[52] The assembly replied that it would cheerfully do this but that the inhabitants could not bear the additional taxes that such an appropriation would necessitate.[53] In assenting to the tax bill of the year, the governor regretted that his request had not been granted. Though Chester had complained to Hillsborough of the arrogance of a previous assembly in presuming to nominate a treasurer,[54] this question did not cause an open rift between the executive and the legislature after 1770.

49. *Ibid.,* May 10 and 16, 1770.
50. West Florida Commissions, p. 84.
51. Hillsborough to Chester, Oct. 3, 1770, C.O.5: 587, pp. 419–422.
52. Assembly Minutes, July 10, 1771.
53. *Ibid.,* July 30, 1771.
54. Chester to Hillsborough, March 10, 1771, C.O.5: 578, pp. 137–138.

The real difficulty that Chester experienced with the assembly was not over finance but over privilege, and the roots of the trouble went back to the time of Johnstone. The form of the indenture executed between the provost marshal and the electors at the election of the members for the first assembly is not entered in the minutes, but the form used at the time of the second election stated specifically that the representatives were to be chosen for one year.[55] This infringement on the right of the king to determine the frequency of elections provoked little notice at the time and the fixing of the term at one year became customary. The lieutenant governors, however, usually were careful to dissolve the assemblies before the expiration of a year in order that the king's prerogative in this particular might be preserved.[56] The irregularity of fixing the tenure of assemblymen was observed by Durnford, however, and on his visit to England at the time of his appointment as lieutenant governor in 1770 he asked for guidance in regard to the matter. In the election of members for the fourth assembly in 1771 (the first elected under Chester) the limitation was still retained.[57] In issuing the writs for the following election, however, the governor ordered the provost marshal not to allow this restriction to be inserted in the indenture. The Mobile electors refused to make a choice of representatives unless the term of service was limited. Pensacola representatives were elected, but they were evidently in sympathy with the Mobile electors. The time for convening the assembly arrived, but since a quorum could not be secured, Chester ordered a prorogation. He laid the situation before the secretary of state in England and informed that officer that if the Mobile electors continued in their determination he would issue no more writs of election for this town.[58] His stand was ap-

55. Assembly Minutes, Dec. 15, 1767.
56. *Ibid.*, May 19, 1770. Apparently Browne overlooked this formality on one occasion (*ibid.*, Oct. 21, 1768).
57. *Ibid.*, June 25, 1771.
58. Chester went into the situation at length in a letter to Hillsborough, July 8, 1772, C.O.5: 589, pp. 261–262.

proved by Dartmouth who had by this time succeeded Hillsborough.[59] The governor also suggested that the failure of the Mobile electors to select representatives was caused largely by the fact that the principal people there were engaged in the Indian trade and did not wish to see the law governing this trade renewed or strengthened.

For reasons that are not entirely clear another assembly was not summoned until 1778. It is probable that benefits derived from provincial legislation were so few, and dangers of the contagion from the revolutionary spirit which was rampant in the colonies of the Atlantic seaboard so great, that the game was not thought worth the candle. But the disastrous Willing raid of 1778, which was keenly felt on the Mississippi and regions adjacent, made a militia law highly desirable. An assembly, therefore, was summoned to meet in Pensacola on June 6, 1778, but owing to sundry prorogations, it did not actually convene until October 1. A copy of the form of the indenture is not included in the assembly minutes but it seems probable that the term of the assemblymen was not limited. The apportionment of representatives for this assembly presented a radical departure. The town of Pensacola was alloted four, the district of Pensacola four, and the districts of Mobile, Manchac, and Natchez four each.[60] It is important to note in this connection that apparently the town of Mobile was deprived of representation and the western part of the province which had hitherto been included in the district of Mobile was divided into two districts and given eight representatives.

When the members came together Adam Chrystie, of the district of Mobile, was elected speaker and Chester made a lengthy speech reviewing the unhappy relations of the mother country with the seaboard colonies and urging the passage of laws for establishing a militia, regulating the Indian trade, raising funds for administering criminal justice, and providing for a place of custody for prisoners

59. Dartmouth to Chester, Nov. 4, 1772, *ibid.*, pp. 303–305.
60. Assembly Minutes, Oct. 1, 1778.

taken on American privateers.[61] This speech in character and form more nearly resembles a modern executive address to a legislature than any other made by a West Florida governor to an assembly. In spite of desperate need for provincial protection, the question of the representation of the town of Mobile soon became the dominant issue. The committee on privileges and elections was instructed to investigate the situation and it reported that in previous assemblies six or eight representatives had been allowed for the town and district of Mobile or for Charlotte County, which embraced the same territory; and that in the present assembly the town of Mobile was without representation.[62] The assembly then addressed an inquiry to the governor concerning the failure to issue writs of election for the town of Mobile.[63]

On the following day a bill was introduced for establishing the number of representatives for the different towns and districts, for ascertaining the rights of the electors, and for limiting the duration of the assemblies. The reply of Chester, though sound enough from the legal standpoint, was not in a form calculated to allay discord and restore harmony. He rebuked the assembly for neglecting matters of importance in order to spend time on questions of privilege; his Majesty alone was the judge of these matters and had imparted his power in this respect to the governor of the colony who was clearly within the authority of his commission and instructions when he failed to issue the writs for the town of Mobile. Besides, this municipality was included in the district of Mobile.[64] He failed to point out that under the existing apportionment the part of the province west of the Perdido was entitled to twelve repre-

61. *Ibid.*
62. *Ibid.*, Oct. 8, 1778.
63. *Ibid.*, Oct. 20, 1778.
64. *Ibid.*, Oct. 21, 1778. Chester's defense to the authorities in England is found in an undated manuscript from the Library of Congress, "The Reply of Peter Chester, Governor of West Florida, to Complaints Made against His Administration," printed by James A. Padgett in *Louisiana Historical Quarterly*, XXII, 31–46.

sentatives, which was more than a majority of the whole
and four more than it had ever had before.

The reply as given did not satisfy the assembly and two
days later the bill regulating privileges was passed and
sent to the upper house for concurrence.[65] This body was
more conservative and more tractable. When the bill was
shown to be at variance with the seventeenth article of the
governor's instructions, it was rejected on the motion of
Philip Livingston, Junior.[66] The governor informed the
upper house that he had withheld the writs of election
from Mobile because of the unwarranted action of the electors of that place in refusing, when the assembly had been
last summoned, to execute indentures of election except for
one year.[67] The lower house then attempted to persuade
the council to join in a memorial to the governor to issue
writs of election for Mobile, but these efforts were unsuc-
cessful.[68] On November 5, the governor brought the abortive session to an end by prorogation,[69] and the legislature
of West Florida never met again. One is inclined to think
that Chester, by diplomatic concession in the emergency
which confronted the province, might have induced this
assembly to pass several salutary laws. He might also, in
this way, have forestalled the action of Adam Chrystie
and others in presenting to the home government charges
against him which were to prove embarrassing.

Of the six assemblies which were elected for West
Florida, only four passed acts which were concurred in by
the council and approved by the governor. The fifth assembly, because of the refusal of the Mobile electors to execute an indenture which did not limit the term of the representatives to one year, never formally convened. The sixth,
as we have seen, became involved with Governor Chester in
a dispute over the question of privileges and passed only

65. Assembly Minutes, Oct. 23, 1778.
66. Minutes of Upper House, Oct. 27, 1778.
67. *Ibid.*, Oct. 28, 1778.
68. Assembly Minutes, Oct. 31, 1778.
69. *Ibid.*, Nov. 5, 1778.

the bill apportioning the representatives for each district, and even this was promptly rejected by the council. The acts passed were doubtless inspired both by local conditions and needs and by the example of the neighboring province of Georgia, whose circumstances were similar to those of West Florida and whose legislature had been in existence since 1754. One is struck by the fact that for almost every law of West Florida there was a similar law in Georgia.[70] Chief Justice William Clifton, who was a very influential member of the council, had been, before his arrival in West Florida, attorney general of Georgia, and it is possible that he was responsible for some of the similarity in legislation. But it is probable that this likeness was due more to the geographical proximity of Georgia and conditions common to both provinces than to the influence of any one man or group of men.

There are several aspects of West Florida legislation which are worthy of note.[71] The revenue laws were always enacted for a period of one year. In this respect the assembly followed a tendency which was prevalent in the other colonies rather than the wishes of the mother country.[72] A provision of the law for governing slaves provided that a master be reimbursed by the province for a slave legally executed, and the money bills carried appropriations to meet this provision. The provincial treasurer was allowed a percentage of his collections rather than a salary. Import duties were always less on Negroes imported directly from Africa—"new Negroes" as they were called—than on Negroes brought from other colonies. The revenue act of 1770 provided for an appropriation of £50 for the pur-

70. See A. D. Candler (ed.), *The Colonial Records of the State of Georgia*, vols. XVIII and XIX, for colonial laws of Georgia.

71. The laws are found in C.O.5: 623; there are photostats in the Library of Congress and transcripts in the Alabama State Department of Archives and History at Montgomery. See also Peter J. Hamilton, "Acts of the Assembly of British West Florida," *Gulf States Historical Magazine*, II, 273–279, which gives a brief statement about the laws enacted and lists them by title.

72. See L. W. Labaree, *Royal Government in America*, pp. 268–311, for an interesting discussion of finances in royal colonies.

chase of a piece of silver plate for Samuel Hannay in appreciation of his services as agent of the colony. The building of a road from Pensacola to Mobile, the maintenance of a ferry at the Perdido, and the erection of forts at Natchez and Manchac were among the few constructive works for which the assembly voted appropriations.

Several laws were enacted to regulate business relations. In order to make easier the recovery of small debts, an act was passed establishing a court of requests. Another act passed for the relief of debtors established means whereby a person confined on account of debt might be released on certain conditions provided he consented that his wages be assigned to the person whom he owed, and provided this person agreed to the arrangement; if the creditor did not concur, then he was forced to pay a certain amount weekly for the support of the person confined. A related act provided punishment for ship captains who carried debtors from the province. From various petitions presented to the council and assembly it is apparent that such laws were needed. The prevention of fraudulent mortgages was the purpose of another law. The law establishing a legal rate of interest and providing penalties for protested bills of exchange has already been mentioned.

Another set of laws governed local conditions of buying and selling. Provision was made for the erection of a market in Pensacola and regulations were established for its conduct. Forestalling was forbidden. A scale of bread prices dependent on the price of wheat was set up and every baker was required to put his mark on his loaves; a penalty was provided for those guilty of adulterating bread or selling loaves that were under weight.

The laws designed to regulate Indian relations have already been discussed.[73] Those relating to slaves and indentured servants and the Anglican Church will be treated in a later chapter.[74]

Of the forty-six laws enacted, ten were disallowed by

73. See Chap. III above.
74. See Chap. VII below.

the Privy Council. It is surprising that the number disallowed is so small, for the assembly had scant respect for the wishes or policies of the home government. The passing of revenue bills for one year and the levying of duties on imported Negroes are examples of the way in which it flouted English standards for colonial government. The reasons for disallowing West Florida laws were various. The act regulating the assembly was an infringement on the prerogative and not consistent with the governor's instructions.[75] The act to encourage foreigners contained no suspending clause and the favors it extended to Roman Catholics were too general.[76] The act to encourage the settlement of the part of the province west of Charlotte County created a power within a power and exceeded the authority that the provincial legislature could exercise with propriety.[77] Two acts to facilitate the collection of debts were not sufficiently limited in their scope and were open to abuse.[78] The act to allow magistrates and freeholders of Charlotte County occasionally to prohibit the sale of rum to the Indians gave the magistrates a legislative and inquisitorial power that was not conformable to British principles.[79] The act erecting Mobile and the county adjacent into a county and allowing the three senior justices to hold a court of common pleas was disallowed on the representation that this law enlarged the powers of a court of common pleas established by the governor, and gave to the county court final jurisdiction in causes up to thirty pounds.[80] An act for the governing of slaves did not set forward with sufficient clarity the right of appeal to the crown in capital cases.[81] The act to indemnify officers and others commanding on Rose Island was too general in scope and liable to abuse.[82] The act to

75. *Acts of the Privy Council, Colonial Series*, V, 158.
76. *Ibid.*, p. 159.
77. *Ibid.*, p. 286.
78. *Ibid.*, pp. 312–313.
79. *Ibid.*, p. 313.
80. *Ibid.*, pp. 317–318.
81. *Ibid.*, p. 318.　　　　　82. *Ibid.*, pp. 344–345.

improve the coasting trade was disallowed because the collector of customs at Pensacola claimed that its enforcement would interfere with the royal customs service.[83]

As a branch of the government, the assembly did not play a very significant rôle in the history of the province. The parliamentary support fund deprived it of its most effective weapon and made the governor secure from legislative control—a matter of great constitutional importance. It is worth noting that this independence of the executive did not prevent a struggle between governor and assembly over finance—a struggle which occurred in other royal colonies. Because of this independence, however, when in 1772 a dispute arose over privilege, Chester was able to carry away the honors by not summoning the assembly for a period of six years; nor did the province seem to suffer appreciably because of this interruption in the process of legislation. The revenue produced by the tax laws was little more than enough to pay the expenses of the assembly. The laws which it passed appear to have been loosely drawn and carelessly observed.

The attitude of the assembly, in spite of its weakness in colonial administration, illustrates clearly the legislative consciousness which was characteristic of all the British seaboard colonies of the period. It was, in its own eyes at least, the commons house of a parliament modeled after that of Great Britain, and as such, held itself entitled to all respect and consideration. This infant institution assumed all the rights and privileges which had been claimed by the older assemblies and jealously guarded them against infringement. The West Florida assembly, coming into existence as it did near the end of the colonial period, represented the summation of the colonial attitude toward legislative privilege which had developed during the preceding century and a half.

83. *Ibid.,* p. 346.

V

THE DISTRIBUTION OF LAND

IN the American colonies as a whole two general methods for the distribution of land were employed. In New England grants were customarily issued by the general court to a group of individuals or proprietors. In the seventeenth century, the members of such a group were bound together by ties of blood, friendship, and religion, forming a congregation, and any attempt to understand the distribution of land in New England without considering the social, moral, and ethical ideals of these congregations will necessarily fail. The different groups distributed the land to individuals in small parcels under regulations which were remarkably uniform in spirit and purpose. Thus were formed the settlements or towns so characteristic of New England.[1] The general court occasionally granted land to an individual; this was frequently as a reward for some service to the colony and the tract thus granted was often an island. The quit-rent, save to a very limited extent in New Hampshire and Maine and rarely in Massachusetts, was not collected in New England.

In the colonies south of New England the land was distributed to individuals by the crown or by proprietors or groups of proprietors to whom the king had given large tracts. The grant to the individual and to the proprietors, and by the proprietors to the individual, was always subject to an annual quit-rent, which might be a fat buck, a few arrow heads, a white rose, or some other token. More often it was a small money payment. The quit-rent should

1. See R. H. Akagi, *The Town Proprietors of New England.* However, he fails to stress sufficiently the religious element. The settlement by towns continued in the eighteenth century, but in this period the religious and social solidarity was not so pronounced.

not be confused with rent in the modern sense of the word; it was not paid for the use of the land and the amount was not necessarily in proportion to its value. It was a commutation of service to which all holders of free land were subject in medieval times, an acknowledgment of the higher ownership of the king or the proprietor.[2] The quit-rent, though small in individual cases, was a sizable amount in the aggregate and was an important source of revenue. In few cases was it conscientiously paid, the settlers were chronically in arrears, and attempts to collect it caused discontent in both royal and proprietary colonies.

By the time of the French and Indian War desirable land in the English colonies of the Atlantic seaboard was becoming scarce; most of that thought to be profitable had been granted to settlers or was in the hands of speculators who demanded for it a higher price than the crown or the proprietors had asked. The increase in population, from natural causes and from immigration, tended to crowd the colonies and to cause the pioneers and backwoodsmen to press against and to infringe upon the Indian frontier. The invasion of Indian lands gave offense to the natives, whose friendship at this time was very important to the English. With the British in possession of all the territory east of the Mississippi as a result of the Treaty of Paris, the colonists looked forward to the occupation of the desirable lands which had been gained, to a certain extent, at least, by their own efforts. It is not likely that the necessity of maintaining the good will of the Indians, however important it might be to the home government, would weigh heavily with the frontiersmen; nor would they view with equanimity their exclusion from such a broad and fertile area because of questions of Indian policy. Indeed, the main purpose of the Proclamation of 1763 was to quiet the fears of the Indians, by assuring them of the continued possession of their lands, and to divert the tide of westward expansion from the west to

2. See B. W. Bond, *The Quit-rent System in the American Colonies*, and especially the Introduction by C. M. Andrews.

the south and southwest, by establishing the new provinces of East and West Florida, where good lands might be secured on reasonable terms.[3] The very circumstances of the creation of the province, as well as the exigencies of settling new territories, made the distribution of land in West Florida a matter of fundamental importance. On the whole the method used was that in vogue in the colonies south of New England, more particularly the royal colonies, but there were certain variations which were peculiar to East and West Florida.[4]

All land distributed in West Florida was granted by the governor (or in his absence by the lieutenant governor) under the authority of royal mandamuses or orders of the king in council, the royal instructions, or the Proclamation of 1763.

On recommendation of the Board of Trade the Privy Council, on November 14, 1763, authorized the insertion of advertisements in the *London Gazette* inviting persons to offer proposals for settling, at their own expense, townships in the new governments of Florida with Protestant inhabitants, either from the other English colonies or from foreign parts, under such conditions of quit-rent, cultivation, and improvement as might be thought necessary and expedient.[5] Interested parties were invited to communicate with John Pownall, the secretary of the board. In due time a notice to this effect appeared in the *Gazette* and was copied in *Scots Magazine*.[6]

The issuing of royal mandamuses for grants of land was characteristic of the period which followed the French and Indian War. Between 1764 and 1777 such orders were

3. C. W. Alvord, "The Genesis of the Proclamation of 1763," *Michigan Pioneer and Historical Collections*, XXXVI, 20–52.

4. This chapter has appeared in almost its present form in *Louisiana Historical Quarterly*, XVI, 540–553. A similar though briefer article on East Florida is Charles L. Mowat, "The Land Policy in British East Florida," *Agricultural History*, XIV, 75–77.

5. *Acts of the Privy Council, Colonial Series*, IV, 610; *Journal of the Commissioners for Trade and Plantations*, Nov. 21, 1763, XI, 407–408, gives the advertisement.

6. *Scots Magazine*, XXV, 627.

issued for lands in Georgia, South Carolina, New Hampshire, Canada, Quebec, Nova Scotia, and New York, as well as East and West Florida. It was only in the last four of these provinces, however, that the number of grants was significant; there were thirty-nine in Nova Scotia, sixty-seven in New York, forty-five in West Florida, and more than two hundred in East Florida.[7] Most of these were issued in the four years that followed the close of the French and Indian War, and doubtless found their inspiration in the great wave of land speculation which accompanied England's undisputed claim to such vast and desirable territory. They varied in size from two thousand to one hundred thousand acres.

The terms for all of the mandamus grants in the Floridas were practically the same. The grantee was required to settle the land with white Protestant inhabitants in the proportion of one person for every hundred acres and within ten years of the date of the grant. If one third of the grant were not thus settled within three years, the whole was to revert to the king; likewise, any part not thus settled in ten years would similarly revert. Beginning in May, 1767, this condition was reworded in such a way as to prevent the settlers from being recruited in England and Ireland. The annual quit-rent was set at one-half penny sterling per acre and was due on half of the grant after the expiration of five years, and on the whole after ten years. Lands suitable for military and naval purposes were reserved to the king as were all mines of gold, silver, copper, lead, and coal. If any of the land appeared, from the surveyor's report, well adapted to the growth of hemp or flax, the grantee was required to sow annually and to cultivate these valuable commodities in the proportion of one acre to every thousand of the grant.[8]

7. *Acts of the Privy Council, Colonial Series,* vol. IV, appendix V; *ibid.,* vol. V, appendix V. The fact that East Florida was better known and more easily accessible than her sister province perhaps accounts for the greater demand for land there.

8. *Ibid.;* C.O.5: 607, pp. 216–225. This is an order in council for land for Phineas Lyman.

The forty-five orders in council which were issued for land in West Florida called for a total of approximately three hundred and fifty thousand acres, with individual allotments varying in size from two thousand to twenty-five thousand acres. If all the lands which the royal orders provided for had been granted and the conditions met, the province would have gone through a period of very rapid development, but such was not the case. Perhaps not more than half of these orders were ever presented in West Florida, and there was practically no effort on the part of those to whom grants were made to meet the conditions. Some of the finest and most favorably situated land in the colony was thus placed beyond the reach of actual settlers. Chester, soon after his arrival at Pensacola, made note of the large tracts embraced in some of those unimproved grants, and asked the secretary of state if they could not be forfeited to the crown. This officer, however, though admitting that the situation was undesirable, was unwilling or unable to give the necessary permission.

Among the large grants actually surveyed for patentees who did not reside in the province were tracts of twenty thousand and five thousand acres on the Mississippi for the Earl of Eglinton and Samuel Hannay, and tracts of twenty thousand and ten thousand acres for Lord Ellibank and Count Bentinck near Pensacola.[9] The Eglinton grant, located as it was in the fertile district around Natchez, was an especial grievance to Chester. Apparently Thaddeus Lyman, to whom was granted the land authorized by an order in council June 6, 1770, for his father Phineas

9. Map of West Florida by Samuel Lewis, 1772, from the surveys of Elias Durnford, photostat in Library of Congress; original in the Crown Collection in British Museum. This is a most interesting map showing all of the grants that had been surveyed before August 1771. There is a printed map, from an unidentified source, in the Mississippi Department of Archives and History which shows grants on the Mississippi in 1770; a manuscript map by William Wilton, assistant provincial surveyor, in the archives of the Mississippi River Commission at Vicksburg, showing the grants in 1774, offers an interesting basis for comparison. Photostats of these two maps are in the Library of the University of North Carolina. See p. 141 below.

Lyman, was one of the few grantees to make a real effort to settle his holding. Amos Ogden was in the province for a while and imported some settlers, but it appears that he took out land for these on the basis of family right, rather than settle them on his tract of twenty-five thousand acres, which was laid out near Natchez.

The governor's instructions contained full and specific directions in regard to the local distribution of land.[10] As soon as possible after his arrival he was to appoint some competent person to make a survey of the physical characteristics of the province and to make recommendations as to the best method of settlement. But as such a task would take some time, he was to begin settlement at once under such means as appeared expedient from the general information he was able to collect.[11] Inasmuch as experience had shown that from the standpoint of civil coöperation and protection from Indians it was more profitable to settle planters in townships, he was instructed to cause such areas to be laid out in units of about twenty thousand acres each. In every township he was to reserve sufficient space for military purposes and suitable land for the production of naval timber; in or near each township a particular spot was to be reserved for a church with four hundred acres of adjacent land for the maintenance of a minister and two hundred for a schoolmaster.[12] Unfortunately the conditions accompanying the occupation of West Florida were not to make for such an orderly settlement, and with the exception of Campbell Town, which was a complete failure, the township system was not used.

Since great inconveniences had arisen in other colonies, the instructions continued, because huge tracts had been granted to persons who had never cultivated or settled them, the governor was told to take care that all grants which he made should be in proportion to the ability of

10. Instructions to Johnstone, Nos. 44–56. Johnstone's instructions are found in C.O.5: 201, pp. 131–177.

11. Instruction 44.

12. Instructions 46, 47.

the grantee to cultivate. Every master (or mistress) of a family who came to the colony was entitled to one hundred acres for himself and to fifty acres for every black or white man, woman, or child in his establishment actually present in the province at the time of making the grant.[13] This was known in West Florida as the "family right." Persons who desired to take up more land than they were entitled to by the family right might do so in amounts up to one thousand acres if the governor thought they were able to cultivate and improve it, provided they paid, on the day of the grant, to the receiver general of quit-rents or other officer designated for that purpose, five shillings for every fifty acres. Land acquired in this way was by "purchase right." Two years after the grant had been made the land became subject to an annual quit-rent. The original instructions to Johnstone provide that this should be two shillings a hundred acres, which was the amount frequently required in other royal provinces, but an additional instruction of May 25, 1764, issued doubtless before Johnstone left England, raised this to one half penny per acre, or four shillings twopence a hundred.[14]

For every fifty acres of land accounted plantable, the patentee was required to clear and work at least three acres within three years; for every fifty acres considered barren he was required to pasture within three years three neat cattle. If no part of the grant was fit for cultivation without manuring or improving, the grantee was obliged to erect a good dwelling house, at least twenty feet in length and sixteen in width, in addition to meeting the requirement in regard to neat cattle. If any land was stony and fit neither for cultivation nor for pasture, the employing of one good hand in a quarry or a mine within three years and for a period of three years would be considered sufficient improvement for every one hundred acres. The ful-

13. Instruction 51.
14. C.O.5: 599, pp. 168–169; *Acts of the Privy Council, Colonial Series,* IV, 668–669. At the same time the quit-rent was similarly increased in East Florida and Nova Scotia.

fillment of these conditions would insure the patentee against forfeiture; after they had been met he was directed to offer proof of this improvement at the court of the county wherein he resided and to have such proof certified in the register's office in order that his title might be secure.[15] All of the terms and conditions were to be recorded in the grant.[16]

The governor was directed to see that each grant contained a proportionable number of profitable and unprofitable acres; that the breadth of each grant be one-third of the length; and that the length of any tract did not extend along the banks of any river, "but into the mainland, that thereby the said grantees may have each a convenient share of what accommodation the said river may afford for navigation or otherwise." [17] In order that people elsewhere might be informed about West Florida the governor was instructed to issue a proclamation soon after his arrival setting forth the terms of settlement and the natural advantages of the province, and he was to take the proper means for having this published in all of the colonies of North America.[18] The governor was to consider ways and means for the most effectual collection of quit-rents and prevention of frauds. If he deemed a law on this subject necessary, he was to prepare the heads of such a bill and present it to the Board of Trade for consideration.[19] Each year he was to require the surveyor general or some other competent person to inspect all the grants that had been made and to make a report on the progress of the grantees in meeting the conditions; this report was to be forwarded to the Board of Trade.[20]

15. Instruction 51.
16. Instruction 16.
17. Instruction 52.
18. Instruction 53. *The South Carolina Gazette* of December 10–17, 1764, carried excerpts from such a proclamation by Governor Johnstone, dated November 1, 1764, which gave a glowing account of West Florida from the standpoint of natural resources and trade with the Spanish and Indians.
19. Instruction 55.
20. Instruction 56. These instructions were substantially the same as

Under the authority of the governor's instructions towns were laid out and lots were granted in four places in the province: Pensacola, Mobile, Campbell Town, and Manchac or Harwich. The surveying and planning of Pensacola by Surveyor General Durnford and the granting of lots with the conditions of improvement and quit-rent have already been described.[21] Mobile, inasmuch as it was a more considerable settlement at the time of British occupation, was not as completely organized, but lots were laid out and granted under similar conditions. Campbell Town, at the mouth of the Escambia River, near Pensacola, was a more rural community than either Mobile or Pensacola. Lands there were granted to the French Protestants who had come over with Montfort Browne to introduce the production of wine and silk. Due partly to the unhealthfulness of the place, partly to the erratic leadership of the French pastor, Peter Levrier, and partly to the instability of the settlers, the project was a failure, in spite of the fact that the Protestants were provisioned for a while from the provincial contingent fund; the town, as such, was soon abandoned.

Manchac had from the first occupation of the province been regarded as a place of importance. It was the key to the only possible intra-colonial waterway communication between the eastern and western parts of the province; it was strategically located for the interception of the valuable Indian trade which came down the Mississippi; from it trade could be carried on with the Indians, with the English who were fast settling the eastern banks of the Mississippi, and with the French who resided in and near the prosperous village of Point Coupée, which was across and not far up the river.[22] Fort Bute had been established

those issued contemporaneously to the governors of East Florida, Georgia, Nova Scotia, and Quebec. See *Royal Instructions to British Colonial Governors, 1670–1776,* collated and edited by L. W. Labaree, II, 527–533.

21. See Chap. II above.

22. The letterbook of John Fitzpatrick gives ample evidence of the commercial significance of Manchac. See pp. 194–195 below.

there in 1765 but had been abandoned in 1768. There was a good deal of talk of moving the capital of the province to this place, especially when it was seen that the Spanish trade, for which Pensacola was favorably placed, would not materialize. A town was planned for this location soon after the arrival of Governor Chester, who wrote enthusiastically of the western part of the province. Secretary of State Hillsborough also appeared very favorable to the reëstablishing of the military post, but Dartmouth, who succeeded him in 1772, was not an advocate of westward expansion. Despite this lack of coöperation from the mother country, after 1777 a number of town lots were granted, largely to officers of the provincial government, the conditions of the grants being similar to those for lots in Pensacola and Mobile.[23] But the war with Spain which broke out in 1779 prevented the development of the new town.

Since we have examined the effect of the orders in council and the governor's instructions on the distribution of land, it is now in order to note the influence of the Proclamation of 1763. This document, it has already been pointed out, was issued in part for the purpose of diverting the immigration from the Indian lands. Inasmuch as the king was desirous on all occasions, the proclamation stated, of testifying his royal approbation regarding the conduct and bravery of the officers and soldiers of the armies, the governors of Quebec and East and West Florida were empowered to grant, without fee or reward, to such reduced officers and soldiers who had served in North America during the late war, quantities of land with exemption from quit-rent for a period of ten years. The applicants for grants, however, must be actually residing in the colonies in which the grants were made and must apply personally. The terms of improvement were iden-

23. Petitions, Warrants, and Grants of Land, May 1774–April 1777, manuscript volume in Library of Congress. Eight of these grants were made to Elihu Hall Bay, ten to Alexander Ma'Cullagh, and thirteen to Philip Livingston, Junior (C.O.5: 610).

tically the same as on the lands granted on family and purchase rights. A field officer was entitled to five thousand acres, a captain to three thousand, a subaltern or staff officer to two thousand, a non-commissioned officer to two hundred, and a private to fifty. Like quantities were offered to reduced officers of the navy who had served at the capture of Louisbourg or Quebec.[24] Such a blanket offer was, of course, open to great abuse, unless it were very carefully and conscientiously administered. The speculative spirit, which gripped the times and was apparent in all places where desirable land was available, was not conducive to careful administration. In fact, after 1770 the provincial officers most concerned in the distribution of land, namely, the governor, provincial secretary, and surveyor, were very much interested in speculation.

The process of securing a grant in West Florida was complicated, expensive, and slow. There was no general land office, but the office of the provincial secretary at Pensacola was the headquarters for land business. A person desiring a grant drew up a petition (or had it drawn up), setting forth his eligibility for a grant under the terms of the governor's instructions or the Proclamation of 1763, and requesting a certain number of acres, to which he claimed a right. This petition was read in council and accepted, rejected, or postponed by the governor on the advice of the council. In the event the petition was accepted (and a vast majority were), a warrant was issued by the governor to the surveyor general directing him to mark out the desired land and to return the survey with a general description of the natural characteristics of the land, together with a plat, within six months. The survey was accordingly made by the surveyor general or his deputy and a description and plat brought in. The governor then issued a fiat directed to the provincial secretary and the attorney general instructing them to draw up a grant for the survey in accordance with the usual terms. The final grant, usually on a printed form after 1769 (ex-

24. *Michigan Pioneer and Historical Collections,* XXXVI, 14–19.

cept those made as a result of royal warrants), contained a description of the land and a statement of the terms under which the grant was made. It was issued under the great seal of the province and was signed by the governor in council. To the grant proper were usually attached a number of certificates: a statement that the grant had passed the secretary's office, signed by the secretary or his deputy; an abstract of the return of the survey, signed by the surveyor general; a certificate that pursuant to a fiat issued by the governor the grant had been examined and found without error, signed by the attorney general; and finally, the certificate that the grant and the above papers had been examined and recorded. In the summer of 1774 Governor Chester assumed to himself the right of issuing, without consulting the council, warrants of survey and of signing grants to reduced officers and to those holding royal warrants.[25]

This cumbersome process, patterned after the practice of other royal colonies, was the subject of much complaint, especially because of the fees that were encountered at every step.[26] There was a fee for the preparation of the petition and another to the messenger for reading it in council; a payment must be made for making out the warrant of survey, and the governor must be remunerated for signing it; the fee of the surveyor was determined by the size of the grant and its distance from Pensacola; and, naturally, there was an additional charge for the plat which accompanied the return. The provincial secretary must be paid for preparing the grant and passing it through his office; the governor was again rewarded for signing the grant and for attaching the great seal; the attorney general received a fee for his examination of the

25. Preface to Petitions, Warrants, and Grants of Land to Officers of the Army and Navy 1774–1777, manuscript volume in Library of Congress.

26. The Board of Trade in 1779, after receiving memorials and hearing individuals on the subject, wrote the governor ordering him to adhere to the table of fees that had been adopted by the governor and council in 1765. *Journal*, Feb. 23, March 2, 12, 1779, XIV, 229, 232, 233.

grant. When Thaddeus Lyman received in 1775 a grant
of twenty thousand acres, on the authority of a mandamus
that had been issued to his father, Phineas Lyman, he
was forced to allocate three thousand acres to men who
advanced the funds necessary for issuing the grant.[27]
There is small wonder that provincial officials encouraged
the granting of land when one considers the lucrative returns which they enjoyed therefrom.

In 1774 for a grant of five hundred acres or less there
were seventeen fees due the governor, secretary, and messenger of the council, and these amounted to approximately twenty Spanish dollars. Of this sum, more than six
dollars went to the governor, more than twelve dollars to
the secretary, and only five reals to the messenger; the fees
on grants between five hundred and one thousand acres
amounted to about twenty-four dollars. It is interesting
to note that these fees were calculated in Spanish rather
than in English money, and that they did not include
either the fees of the surveyor, which at this time were
levied in shillings and pence, or the fee of the attorney
general.[28] The surveyor's fees on a grant of five hundred
acres were about four pounds sterling.

In connection with official procedure in distributing
land it is worthwhile to observe that lands often changed
hands. It would appear from casual observation that in
a frontier province such as West Florida, where population was sparse and land plentiful, there would be little

27. Petition of Thaddeus Lyman to Governor Chester, C.O.5: 607, pp.
216–225.
28. Fly leaf Secretary's Office Account Book 1774–1778, manuscript
in Library of Congress. The fees that were actually collected in this apparently unimportant province are almost unbelievable. In the year
1777 the fees of the secretary and governor amounted to about 11,000
Spanish dollars, of which approximately 8,000 went to the secretary. Of
the total amount over 1,700 dollars came from the contingent fund; some
of the remainder came from clearing ships, marriage licenses, and Indian traders' licenses, but the greater part of it came from land fees.
West Florida Secretary's Office Account Book 1775–1780 in Library of
Congress. In this period a Spanish dollar was worth four shillings sixpence sterling. A real was one-eighth of a Spanish dollar and the contemporary equivalent of the modern bit.

occasion for private sale of land. But the speculative fever of the times, which is the key to the explanation of a great part of the land history of the province, caused great activity of this kind. Desirable town lots in Pensacola and improved and unimproved plantations were frequently sold; and, if one is to believe the records, the consideration was usually silver—Spanish milled dollars. The term occurs repeatedly and the number of dollars mentioned is occasionally more than a thousand. Yet it is difficult to believe that there was much specie in the province, for both governor and military commanders frequently referred, especially in the period before 1770, to the scarcity of hard money.

The means of transferring land from one person to another was usually by "lease and release." The first step taken by a person wishing to buy a certain tract, was to pay a few shillings, "lawful money of Great Britain," and to agree to pay the owner one pepper corn "if the same shall be lawfully demanded." This gave him a lease on the land for one year. Such a lease, the indenture stated, was for the purpose of putting the lessee in actual possession of the land, in order that he might be qualified under the statute made "for transferring uses into possession" to receive a grant and a release of the reversion and inheritance of the tract, from the owner for himself and his heirs. The next step in transferring land was an indenture between the owner and the lessee reciting the terms and purposes of the lease and stating that in consideration of a certain sum, this time not nominal (usually given in Spanish milled dollars, but sometimes in pounds sterling, and occasionally in both), the owner had transferred the carefully described tract to the lessee. To this was usually attached a certificate that the money consideration had actually been paid.[29] The price of land varied, of course, according to the location and quality and to the improve-

29. See C.O.5: 601–606 for a large number of these leases and releases; also manuscript volumes of conveyances in Library of Congress.

ments that had been made upon it. In 1774 Edwin Thomas, a surgeon, sold Attorney General Wegg a tract of five hundred acres on the Mississippi for two hundred and fifty Spanish milled dollars.[30] In 1775 Thomas Wescott sold a tract of three hundred acres on the Amite, which had been granted to him in 1772, for three hundred and fifty Spanish milled dollars, and in each case the money was paid in cash.[31]

From a perusal of the records one comes to the inevitable conclusion that the distribution of land in West Florida was administered in a very inefficient and loose manner. There is much to indicate that terms of the grants were in many instances totally disregarded. Around Mobile, where travelers frequently commented on the herds of black cattle, and in the western part of the province, where the land was more suitable for agriculture, the conditions of the grants were doubtless met in some cases; but it is probable that large numbers of the grants were never occupied. There is no indication that any appreciable amount of quit-rent was ever collected,[32] though the receiver general reported on one occasion that he had in his possession more than four hundred pounds sterling which had been received for grants made on purchase rights. Not only was the distribution inefficiently administered and were the terms of grants rarely met, but there were undoubtedly many "jobs" and questionable transactions. The conditions set forth in the Proclamation of 1763 invited abuse. Though this document provided that grants should be made only to reduced officers and soldiers actually resident in the province, apparently land was given to many who never came to the colony and to almost every military or naval officer whose duty brought him to West Florida.

30. West Florida Conveyances of Land, April 2, 1774–Oct. 1, 1775, pp. 329–334, manuscript in Library of Congress.

31. *Ibid.*, pp. 457–461.

32. Bond, *The Quit-rent System in the American Colonies*, p. 382, concurs in this conclusion.

The name of Philip Livingston, Junior,[33] is closely connected with many questionable deals. He was, by deputation from the patentee, who did not reside in the colony, provincial secretary. Chester soon made him a member of the council and receiver general. He acquired several other offices and in 1778 his enemies claimed that, either personally or by deputy, he held no less than nine. He was much interested in the acquisition of land both for himself and for the members of his family. His methods are illustrated by several transactions. In the summer of 1772 he purchased from five military and naval officers for 248 Spanish dollars, five tracts, aggregating 2,950 acres, which had been granted to them in the previous six weeks.[34] It is easy to conjecture, though difficult to prove, that Livingston suggested to these officers that they apply for the grants and that, in his official positions as provincial secretary and member of the council, as well as in his private capacity as friend and favorite of the governor, he did much to get the patents through the complicated granting process. In August of this year he purchased from Chester, for 326 Spanish dollars, five tracts, comprising 6,050 acres, which the governor had shortly before granted to himself.[35] On April 5, 1777, Chester granted Livingston eleven lots in Harwich.[36] It is not difficult to believe the charge made in 1778 that Livingston had by various means acquired the title to one hundred thousand acres.

Provincial officials, not surprisingly, were anxious to enrich themselves by the acquisition of land. A number re-

33. He was a member of the famous Livingston family of New York but had been in London at the time of the appointment of Governor Chester, with whom he had come to the colony as private secretary under the promise of preferment in the way of an appointment to a lucrative provincial office. Livingston, under the patronage of Chester, became a very important personage in the province, and the activity of his relatives in New York during the Revolution was a source of embarrassment to the governor.

34. C.O.5: 605, pp. 503–524.

35. *Ibid.*, pp. 490–493.

36. Petitions, Warrants, and Grants of Land, May 1774–April 22, 1777, manuscript volume in Library of Congress.

ceived grants by royal mandamus. Among these were Lieu-tenant Governors Montfort Browne and Elias Durnford; James Bruce and Jacob Blackwell, customs collectors and councillors; Arthur Neil, ordnance storekeeper; and David Tait, sometime deputy surveyor and Indian com-missioner. Each official, of course, was entitled to land on family right. In addition, as suggested above, there is ample evidence of collusion for the obtaining of further grants. In a council meeting in 1772, petitions from Jane Chester, Rebecca Durnford, Ann Raincock, Rebecca Blackwell, Isabelle Bruce, and Elizabeth Hodge, praying grants of one thousand acres, each, were received and favorably acted upon.[37] These ladies were the wives of the governor, lieutenant governor, and four of the councillors.

To summarize, the system of land distribution in West Florida followed roughly the systems in operation in other royal colonies. The land was granted by the governor, usu-ally with the consent of the council, under authority of royal mandamus, instructions to the governor, or the Proc-lamation of 1763. The process of taking out a grant was complicated and the payment of numerous fees was neces-sary. Each grant was made under stated conditions, which were rarely met by the grantee, and subject to a quit-rent that was seldom paid. The spirit of speculation which else-where was so characteristic of the period was much in evi-dence in West Florida, and, seizing as it did a number of provincial officials, did much to promote inefficiency and laxity in administration and to make possible frauds and other irregularities. Lands were granted with a prodigal hand and only the large amount of good land available on the Mississippi and the early fall of the province to Spain prevented the scarcity of land from becoming a real problem.

37. Minutes of Council, Feb. 4, 1772.

VI

WESTWARD EXPANSION, 1770–1779

T HE selection of Pensacola, almost in the southeastern corner of the province, as the seat of government was doubtless made with the view of utilizing
to the best advantage its fine harbor and favorable location in the Spanish trade.[1] But there were several conditions and circumstances which were unfavorable to the development of the section around Pensacola and which
made probable a more rapid development of the regions
to the west, especially those adjoining the Mississippi. In
the first place, Pensacola itself was isolated. By sea it was
a long distance from Charles Town and Jamaica; mail and
supplies were usually relayed from these places and were
nearly always late and uncertain. While communication
overland to Charles Town was possible, it was very dangerous and highly unsatisfactory because of the sullen
attitude of the Creeks. In the next place, the soil immediately surrounding Pensacola was sandy and barren. Romans, who gave a rather optimistic account of the province, said that it would not even support a garden during
the summer months. There was valuable land on the Escambia to the north which the English tried several times
to persuade the Creeks to cede, but these Indians with
characteristic shrewdness always pleaded some excuse, and
the English were afraid or powerless to attempt to coerce
them.

On the other hand the western part of the province was
not much more distant by sea from the south Atlantic and
West Indian colonies than was Pensacola, and the mouth

1. This chapter has been revised and amplified since it appeared in
the *Mississippi Valley Historical Review*, XX, 481–496, under the title
"Expansion in West Florida."

of the Mississippi was a magnet for commerce. The river, extending as it did with its tributaries into the heart of the continent, was a natural means of communication with the back country of the English colonies, whence many backwoodsmen, ever restless and in search of adventure and better lands, might be drawn. The land in the west, up the Tombigbee from Mobile, on the Pearl and the Pascagoula, on the Comite and the Amite, around Lakes Maurepas and Pontchartrain, and especially on the Mississippi between Manchac and Natchez, was very fertile and desirable, and capable of rendering great returns for efforts expended. The Indian menace, though always present in a greater or lesser degree, was not so imminent as in the eastern part of the province. In 1765 the Choctaws had made a liberal cession around Mobile and to the west. Along the Mississippi the Indians were less numerous and were inclined to be friendly; the Natchez had not been a power since a punitive expedition, sent by the French after the massacre of Fort Rosalie in 1729, had almost exterminated them, and the Chickasaws always prided themselves on their friendship with the English. Though these Indians were constantly goaded into minor plunderings and robberies by infringement on their lands, the dishonesty of traders, and the too profuse introduction of rum, they did not present a real barrier to westward expansion.

Another factor which entered into the development of the west was the trade of the Mississippi River. This commerce was of two kinds: the valuable skin trade which came down the river and for which New Orleans was the natural mart, save for the part the English were able to intercept at Manchac and other posts; and the trade in European manufactured goods and slaves, supplied to those who lived on both the English and Spanish sides of the river. The sale of these commodities by the English to the settlers in the Spanish territories was forbidden by the navigation laws of Spain, but the provision of the Treaty of Paris which guaranteed to the English the free naviga-

tion of the river made it difficult if not impossible to enforce these laws. As a matter of fact the Spanish governors
were so busy establishing themselves in Louisiana, and
slaves and articles of foreign manufacture were so needed,
that they usually made little effort to break up this clan-
destine trade, though there were occasionally annoying exceptions to this policy of official connivance.

There were several conditions, however, which militated
against and hindered the settlement of the Mississippi
region. Pensacola, the seat of civil government, where justice was administered and from which all land titles must
come, was several hundred miles distant. Communication
between the capital and the western part of the province
by means of the Gulf, Rigolets, Lakes Maurepas and
Pontchartrain, and the Rivers Amite and Iberville was
slow and unsatisfactory. Nor was the journey by way of
the Gulf and the Mississippi much less difficult. Trips
down the river were made with ease and dispatch but
progress up the river by sail, by warping, or by oarsmen,
was uncertain, laborious, and expensive. Not only were
the physical aspects of navigation of the river formidable,
but, though free use of the stream had been promised by
the Treaty of Paris, there was always the possibility that
a boat might be held up under some pretext by the Spanish
authorities at New Orleans. Finally, there was lack of protection. The exposed position of the region, the presence
there of the lawless element characteristic of the frontier,
the proximity of the Spaniards with whom the English
had often been at war, and the danger from prowling Indians, made military protection highly desirable. Small
posts had been established at Manchac and Natchez in
the time of Johnstone, but these were abandoned in 1768
and were not reëstablished until after the Willing raid of
1778. While these conditions doubtless hindered and delayed western development, they by no means prevented it.

The early administrators of the colony, with the exception of Eliot, whose brief period hardly deserves to be
called an administration, recognized the value of the land

on the Mississippi and bent their energies toward settling
it. Johnstone was responsible for having the northern
boundary moved from the thirty-first parallel of latitude
to a line drawn east from the confluence of the Yazoo and
Mississippi rivers, in order that the region around Natchez
might be included in the province. He had encouraged the
ill-fated project of making the Iberville navigable, and
had been largely responsible for the establishing of Fort
Bute. He realized the disadvantages of Pensacola and suggested that, if the Spanish commerce was not to be encouraged, it would be advisable to move the seat of government to some place on the Mississippi. In 1768, Lieutenant Governor Browne made an extended tour of the western part of the province. Part of his rhapsodic description
has already been quoted.[2] On several occasions he urged
the advantages of erecting the district around Natchez
and Manchac into a separate government, and suggested
himself as a suitable governor for the new province. In
1769, during the period of great dissatisfaction in Louisiana with the administration of General O'Reilly, Browne
sent an agent to New Orleans to encourage the discon-
tented subjects of Spain to move across the river and settle
in the fertile English territory.[3] Elias Durnford, surveyor
and engineer that he was, worked out plans for fortifying
the Mississippi, for the erection of new towns, and for dig-
ging a cut from a point on the bank of the Mississippi
which the current struck with great force, to the Iberville,
in order that a part of the Mississippi might be diverted
into this sluggish stream and so make it a dependable
waterway. All three of these men obtained for themselves
large tracts of this valuable land.

Though lands were granted in the western part of the
province from the time of Johnstone, the great influx of
settlers does not appear to have begun until the time of
Durnford. In 1768, during the administration of Browne,
but while he was away from Pensacola, Surveyor Durnford

2. See pp. 64–65 above.
3. John Campbell to Browne, Oct. 9, 1769, C.O.5: 577, pp. 413–424.

wrote Hillsborough that many people from the back country of Virginia had found the markets for their produce inaccessible and during the preceding few months had visited the colony with a view to becoming settlers on the Mississippi and Mobile rivers. Inasmuch as they were impecunious, Durnford suggested that it might be advantageous to charter a sloop at the expense of the colony, for the purpose of transporting them, and to furnish them with supplies for two months after their arrival.[4] In May, 1770, Durnford, by this time lieutenant governor, informed the council that a Mr. Holt, who had been deputed by a number of people from Virginia to look over the lands on the Mississippi, had been in the province and had been very favorably impressed; Durnford was reserving for him and his associates a strip about ten miles long on the Mississippi. The council approved this action.[5] In June of the same year, a ship load of immigrants from Maryland missed the mouth of the Mississippi and put in at the Spanish port of Espiritu Santo where their effects were plundered. Durnford sent a vessel to Vera Cruz to demand redress (and to find out something about the fortifications of the place), but the commandant gave him little satisfaction, referring him to the Spanish court and refusing to allow his emissaries to land.[6]

By the time of the arrival of Chester in the summer of 1770, the movement of settlers from the colonies on the Atlantic seaboard to the fertile lands of West Florida had assumed substantial proportions. In August of this year, Daniel Huay arrived at Pensacola with the information that he had piloted a party of seventy-nine white people and eighteen Negroes, mostly from Pennsylvania, by way of Fort Pitt, to Natchez, and that they planned to settle on the fruitful lands of the Mississippi. Huay, himself, was from North Carolina and expected to bring to the prov-

4. Durnford to Hillsborough, June 5, 1768, C.O.5: 69, p. 443.
5. Minutes of Council, May 1, 1770.
6. Durnford to Hillsborough, June 12, 1770, C.O.5: 587, pp. 337-339; same to same, June 13, 1770, *ibid.*, pp. 357-358.

ince in the near future his family and a number of other families from that colony and from Virginia and Pennsylvania.[7] Huay brought with him to Pensacola a letter from John McIntyre, who was one of the leaders of the Pennsylvania emigrants. McIntyre said that there were a number of tradesmen in the party and that he had with him "all the furniture for erecting a saw mill and a grist mill." He requested the protection of the province and the bounties usually offered to new settlers. He also asked for a copy of the laws, in order, as he said, "to know our duty." A hundred families in the western parts of Pennsylvania and Virginia, he claimed, would come to the province if his party gave a favorable report of the situation.[8]

Chester, in notifying the home government of these new arrivals, took occasion to emphasize the value of settlements on the Mississippi. The soil was fertile and not held tenaciously by the Indians; products could with great ease be shipped down the Mississippi and then to England; the settlers would use articles of British manufacture. He had a project for making the Iberville navigable and strongly urged the reoccupation of the posts at Manchac and Natchez. "I flatter myself," he concluded, "that we have great tracts of very excellent land, that if protection and encouragement is given to us, and your Lordship would deign to adopt and patronize this infant child, that measures might be pursued to place us in a more respectable situation." [9] Chester intended to visit the western part of the province in order that he might report personally on its needs and possibilities, but because of illness and the requirements of provincial business, he was prevented from carrying out his purpose. In his stead, however, he sent Lieutenant Governor Durnford, who, on his return, gave a glowing account of the land between the Mississippi and the Pearl and made recommendations as to its settlement.

7. Deposition of Daniel Huay, Pensacola, Aug. 25, 1770, C.O.5: 578, pp. 71–72.
8. McIntyre to Chester, July 19, 1770, *ibid.*, p. 75.
9. Chester to Hillsborough, Sept. 26, 1770, *ibid.*, pp. 59–69.

He pointed out the need of military protection and urged that the immigrants be settled in townships and allowed some supplies at provincial expense. At that time, he said, there were few colonists on the Mississippi.[10]

Definite steps were taken and concessions made to encourage settlers to take up claims in this region. In August, 1771, the council authorized John Thomas, a justice of the peace and Indian commissary residing at Manchac, to take affidavits of family rights. This was for the purpose of relieving those who lived in the western part of the province from making a trip to Pensacola in order to obtain a warrant for a grant of land.[11] Soon after this body recommended that the surveyor appoint deputies to reside on or near the Mississippi so that the cost of taking out grants might be decreased.[12]

In the autumn of the same year occurred another pointed encouragement to new settlers. Colonel John Clark informed the council that he had been deputed by more than two hundred families who lived on the Holston River to represent their intention to come to West Florida and settle on or near the Amite, but that they would need arms, ammunition, and provisions for six months. The board was of the opinion that these families would be a great acquisition to the province, and agreed that they should be allowed, from the contingent fund of the colony, a barrel of corn a man, monthly, and salt in proportion, until they were able to support themselves.[13]

Interest in the western part of the province continued to increase. On April 20, 1772, ten petitions for town lots in Manchac were presented to the council.[14] Three months later, Chester wrote Hillsborough, suggesting that the seat of government be moved to the proposed town of Harwich or to some other place on the Mississippi.[15] In Oc-

10. Durnford to Chester, June 23, 1771, *ibid.*, pp. 233–235.
11. Minutes of Council, Aug. 17, 1771.
12. *Ibid.*, Oct. 14, 1771.
13. *Ibid.*
14. *Ibid.*, April 20, 1772.
15. Chester to Hillsborough, July 13, 1772, C.O.5: 579, pp. 135–137.

tober, under authority of a mandamus, twenty-five thousand acres near Natchez were granted to Captain Amos Ogden, and a strip of fifteen thousand acres was reserved for those who were expected to come with him from New Jersey.[16]

In March, 1773, an interesting group composed of Colonel Israel Putnam, later to become famous in the Revolution, Lieutenant Rufus Putnam, Captain Roger Enos, and Thaddeus Lyman, appeared before the council. They explained that they were representatives of the Company of Military Adventurers, a New England organization composed largely of officers who had fought in the late war. One of their number, General Phineas Lyman, was at that time in England soliciting a royal grant for the company, and they had come to look over the province and to reserve suitable lands. They were cordially received by the governor and council and invited to select choice tracts, which would be reserved for them. In the event that the royal grant did not materialize, the land would be granted under the terms prescribed by the instructions to the governor.[17] Nineteen townships of about twenty-three thousand acres each were eventually reserved for the company, to be granted half on family right and half on purchase right.[18]

There are numerous other instances of large tracts being reserved during this period. On April 19, twenty-five thousand acres near Natchez were reserved for Samuel Sweesy, a minister from New Jersey, who had already

16. Minutes of Council, Oct. 27, 1772, C.O.5: 630.

17. *Ibid.*, March 5, 1773. The journals kept by Israel and Rufus Putnam have been edited by Albert C. Bates and were published by the Connecticut Historical Society in 1932 as *The Two Putnams: Israel and Rufus in the Havana Expedition 1762 and in the Mississippi River Exploration 1772–73 with some account of the Company of Military Adventurers.* It is interesting to note, in this connection, that General Lyman had obtained an order in council for twenty-five thousand acres for himself in 1770. Minutes of Council, July 7, 1773, C.O.5: 630.

18. *Ibid.*, July 9, 1773; *ibid.*, Feb. 11, 1774, contain interesting minutes of meetings of the Company of Military Adventurers. The map described in note 26 below shows the townships reserved for the Military Adventurers.

brought in a number of people from "the northward" and planned to bring more. On the same day Jaques Rapalje informed the council that he was looking over the province in the interest of his father, Garrett Rapalje of New York, and his associates, and a reservation of twenty-five thousand acres was promised to them.[19] A month later, in a letter to Dartmouth, Chester mentioned that several gentlemen from the north had come down to prospect and had asked that land be reserved for them on the promise of influencing several thousand people to come to the province. A considerable number of families had come from the older colonies by means of the Ohio and Mississippi rivers, and, all in all, prospects for settling the western part of the colony were flattering.[20] In June, Thomas Hutchins and associates petitioned for the reservation of a tract of twenty-five thousand acres near Natchez, on the ground that they intended to bring in a number of families from Pennsylvania and New Jersey. The request was granted on the condition that this tract was not petitioned for by Colonel Putnam and his party on their return from the Mississippi.[21] On July 10, tracts of twenty-five thousand acres each were reserved for Peter Van Brugh Livingston and associates, and James and Evan Jones and associates, who planned to encourage settlers from New York.[22] Peter Van Brugh Livingston was doubtless interested in the province by his kinsman, Philip Livingston, Junior, while the Jones brothers were Pensacola merchants. Two weeks later, 152,000 acres near Natchez were reserved for Colonel Anthony Hutchins and associates, who were to settle this tract with families from Virginia and the Carolinas.[23] On September 27, Captain Amos Ogden and associ-

19. Minutes of Council, April 19, 1773, C.O.5: 630.
20. Chester to Dartmouth, May 16, 1773, C.O.5: 579, pp. 357–359.
21. Minutes of Council, June 2, 1773, C.O.5: 630. Hutchins was an English staff officer who later, as geographer to the United States, published a valuable topographical and historical description of Louisiana and West Florida.
22. *Ibid.*, July 10, 1773.
23. *Ibid.*, July 23, 1773.

ates reported that they had brought in enough persons to
entitle them to 3,550 acres on family right.[24] Ogden, a
short while before, had been made a justice of the peace
and a member of the quorum.[25]

The development of the Mississippi region in this period is graphically suggested by two contemporary maps.
The first is a printed map of 1770 from an unidentified
source in the Mississippi Department of Archives and History. Entitled "Plan of the River Mississippi from the
River Yasous to the River Ibberville in West Florida," it
indicates ninety-nine claims of which some had been surveyed and some had not. The second, which has only recently come to light, is an original manuscript map in the
archives of the Mississippi River Commission at Vicksburg. It is entitled "Part of the River Mississippi from
Manchac to the River Yazous for Governor Chester by
Wm. Wilton." It was apparently made about the year
1774 and shows more than two hundred claims that had
been laid out in the same region. In addition, it covers
more than one hundred claims along the Iberville, Amite,
and Comite rivers in a nearby area that is not shown on
the first map.[26]

The enthusiasm of the governor and council for granting lands was chilled a trifle by a letter which Chester received from Dartmouth in the late summer of 1773, warning him not to increase those improvident grants which his
predecessors had made on the Mississippi. In view of this
admonition the board decided to issue no more warrants

24. *Ibid.*, Sept. 27, 1773.
25. *Ibid.*, Aug. 25, 1773.
26. The second map turned up in the survey of Federal Archives in
Louisiana under the direction of Stanley C. Arthur. Attached to the
map is a statement made by the owner in 1881 that he purchased the
map about 1848 from the parish surveyor of East Baton Rouge, and
dating the map 1774. From internal evidence it seems that this date is
at least approximately correct. Mr. Arthur has made a study of the
map which has not been printed, but copies with photostats of the map
are in the Howard Memorial Library in New Orleans and the Louisiana
State University Archives at Baton Rouge. Photostats of both maps are
in the Library of the University of North Carolina.

for land on purchase right until his Excellency should receive further directions.[27] In October, the governor received a circular instruction dated April 7, which threatened to put an end to the prosperous expansion which the
colony had enjoyed for the past three years. Inasmuch as
it had been represented to his Majesty, the instruction
ran, that the state and condition of the colonies in America, both in justice and expediency, required that the conditions of granting land, as prescribed in the instructions
to the governors, be revised, the Board of Trade had been
directed to take the matter under consideration. Governors
were therefore ordered, under the pain of the king's highest displeasure, to issue no more warrants nor to pass any
additional grants, except under authority of a royal order
or of the Proclamation of 1763.[28]

The consternation that the publication of this instruction created in West Florida can well be imagined. After
it had been read in council, Chester mentioned the great
number of people who had arrived in the province with
their wives and families from the northern colonies, many
of whom were at that time in Pensacola, under the expectation of receiving grants on family and purchase rights,
which he was by this instruction forbidden to make. The
council was unanimously of the opinion that any families
that were already in the province without grants of land,
and any who might arrive in the future, should have the
liberty of settling on any unoccupied land in the colony,
and that this occupation should give them a prior claim
to the land when his Majesty's further pleasure in regard
to granting land was made known.[29] It is instructive to
note that a large number of land petitions in 1776 and

27. Extract, Dartmouth to Chester, Dec. 9, 1772, quoted in Minutes of
Council, Aug. 23, 1773, C.O.5: 630.
28. *Ibid.*, Oct. 16, 1773. This was a step in the plan of the British
ministry to make uniform the conditions under which land was granted
in the various colonies and to convert the ungranted land into a source
of revenue. C. W. Alvord, *The Mississippi Valley in British Politics*, II,
212–215.
29. Minutes of Council, Oct. 16, 1773, C.O.5: 630.

1777 mention this squatter occupation. In the meantime, the number of grants to reduced officers showed no decrease.

Philip Livingston, Junior, immediately notified the Company of Military Adventurers of the prohibition on the granting of land; but the members of this organization, who had received with enthusiasm the report of their committee and who had voted for the immediate occupation of four of the nineteen townships which had been set aside for them, decided that the land had already been reserved for them and that they would not be deterred. On March 5, 1774, Major Timothy Hierlichy, in behalf of the company, presented a petition to the council which recited the history and plans of the organization. This document indicated that as a result of the report of the committee and the reservation of the land, a large number from the company had already sold their possessions in New England and were on their way to the province. Indeed, one hundred and four heads of families had already arrived in West Florida. The council was at a loss to know what action they should take and advised the governor to refer the memorial to the British secretary of state.[30]

Meanwhile the frontier of the Mississippi was developing apace and the need of civil government was keenly felt. The settlers in that region petitioned for a court of pleas and general jail delivery, and a court of requests for the collection of small debts. As a consequence, a new commission of the peace was ordered, with justices from Manchac and Natchez as well as from Pensacola and Mobile, and another commission was issued establishing a court of requests which was to meet alternately at Manchac and Natchez.[31] In response to another petition Chester appointed John Selkeld English pilot at the mouth of the Mississippi.

The injunction on the granting of land did not entirely destroy the hopes of those who were interested in coloniz-

30. *Ibid.,* March 5, 1774.
31. *Ibid.,* April 20, 1774.

ing the district adjacent to the Mississippi. In June, 1774, Adam Chrystie petitioned for a reservation of forty thousand acres, claiming that he could induce a hundred families to come over from Scotland.[32] His petition was necessarily postponed and it seems that he never again attempted to put his project into operation.

But circumstances in the northern colonies, of which the people of West Florida were hardly aware, were about to bring about a resumption of land granting which the circular instruction of 1773 had interrupted in such an untimely manner. In these colonies the smoldering fire of opposition to British policies, sedulously fanned by a zealous minority, was on the point of bursting into the flame of revolution. Opinion was by no means unanimous that there should be a break with the mother country and the English ministry was anxious to protect and reward those persons who remained loyal in spite of the contumely which was heaped upon them by their more patriotic (or rebellious) neighbors. On July 5, 1775, Dartmouth wrote Chester "upon the subject of the unnatural rebellion which has broke out in many parts of North America." The king wished to afford every possible protection to such of his subjects in the colonies in rebellion as were too weak to resist the violence of the times and too loyal to take part in any opposition to the government. Therefore, it was to be hoped that West Florida would become an asylum for distressed friends of England. It was the king's pleasure not only that the execution of the instruction forbidding the granting of land be suspended, but also that all reservations and restrictions be relaxed and that gratuitous grants, exempt from quit-rents for a period of ten years, be made to all persons from the other colonies who sought asylum in West Florida, provided, of course, they gave proof that they were friends of the mother country. The governor was also advised to give aid, from the contingent fund, sparingly to be sure, to such of these as were with-

32. *Ibid.*, June 13, 1774. Chrystie later won fame by his defeat of some of the Willing raiders at Manchac in 1778.

out means of support.[33] The parliamentary support fund
for 1776–1777 carried an additional appropriation for
this purpose.[34]

On receipt of this letter from Dartmouth, Chester issued
a proclamation setting forth the availability of West
Florida as a place of refuge, and made plans to have copies
distributed throughout the disaffected colonies.[35] Thus the
granting of land was resumed on a larger and more reck-
less scale than before. Those who had occupied lands on
authority of the council minute of October 16, 1773, now
took out regular grants, and the loyalists, who flocked
to the colony from practically every one of the seaboard
colonies, received not only grants on family right, but
also tracts as bounties which varied in size according to
the prominence of the grantee and the losses he had suffered because of his support of the king. The boom of
westward expansion, which had suffered a temporary
check, was revived with added impetus.

The effect of the lifting of the embargo on the granting
of land was felt immediately. The news was received at
Pensacola in early November, 1775. On November 13, the
council ordered that the town of Dartmouth be laid out
at the junction of the Iberville and the Amite rivers. The
lots there were to be sold for sixteen or thirty dollars each,
according to the location, and the proceeds were to be used
to clear the streets and to build a levee. The quit-rent and
terms of improvement were similar to those prescribed for
lots in Pensacola and Mobile.[36] Apparently this town was
never formally erected. In the following February, Chester
announced to the council that he had ordered the surveyor
to lay off a town at Natchez.[37] And in August the council
directed that the long-discussed town of Harwich be
marked out just above Manchac, and that lots be sold un-

33. C.O.5: 619, pp. 129–131.
34. William Knox to Chester, March 5, 1777, *ibid.*, pp. 158–159.
35. Minutes of Council, Nov. 11, 1775, C.O.5: 634.
36. *Ibid.*
37. *Ibid.*, Feb. 27, 1776, C.O.5: 631.

der conditions similar to those prescribed for Dartmouth.[38] In January of the following year, a committee was appointed to supervise the expenditure of the five or six hundred dollars which had been collected from the sale of lots in this town.[39] Between 1777 and 1779, fifty-eight lots were granted in Harwich. The fact that eight of these were granted to Elihu Hall Bay, ten to Alexander Ma'Cullagh, and thirteen to Philip Livingston, Junior, all provincial officials, is a pertinent commentary.[40] It might be noted parenthetically that the average settler or plantation owner was not interested in town lots, but in tracts ranging in size from a hundred to several thousand acres. In November, 1776, the council directed the register to appoint a deputy at Natchez in order that the inhabitants might make affidavits with greater ease.[41] The following spring, one Harry Alexander, writing from British Point Coupée (opposite the thriving French settlement of Point Coupée), urged on Lord George Germain the advantages of moving the seat of government from Pensacola to some point on the Mississippi.[42] The next year, when writs were issued for the election of an assembly, four representatives each were allotted to the districts of Manchac and Natchez. All of these events indicate the drift toward the Mississippi region.

In the forefront of the new settlers in the western regions were the immigrants who flowed into the province as a result of the disorders in the older colonies. The minutes of the council contain an interesting record of the petitions of those who came to the province during the period of the Revolution. All came pledging allegiance to the crown; some had numerous slaves, white servants, and cattle; others were without property, a condition which they usually asserted had been brought on by their

38. *Ibid.*, Aug. 6, 1776.
39. *Ibid.*, Jan. 14, 1777, C.O.5: 634.
40. C.O.5: 610 contains fifty-eight patents.
41. Minutes of Council, Nov. 8, 1776, C.O.5: 631.
42. Harry Alexander to Lord George Germain, April 25, 1777, C.O.5: 155, not paged, Florida State Historical Society photostats.

loyalty to England. Though most of the colonies were represented, the majority of the refugees were from Georgia, South Carolina, and Virginia, and practically all requested land in the western part of the province.

The names of these loyalists are too numerous to mention, but a few may be recorded as indicative of the whole. Bernard Lintot came from Connecticut with his wife, seven children, two indentured servants, and seven Negroes.[43] Thomas Bassett arrived from Georgia with his family and fourteen Negroes, and William Webb with five Negroes, from the same colony.[44] Alexander Grayden, a carpenter with two apprentices, came from South Carolina[45] as did William Marshall, Junior, and David Holmes, with twenty and twenty-two Negroes, respectively.[46] In 1779, John Turner stated that he had led a number of families from the same colony to the region around Natchez.[47] Apparently loyalists from Virginia formed quite a settlement on the Pearl, for on December 26, 1776, James Donald, John Mitchell, Robert Donald, and John Gordon, all from the Old Dominion and possessing from one to ten slaves each, petitioned for land on the east branch of that stream.[48] In 1779 Thomas Taylor Byrd informed the council that he was the son and heir of the late Colonel William Byrd of Virginia, that he had been deprived of a large fortune because of the loyalty of his father, and that he had come to West Florida in order to engage in planting. The board advised that he be granted a hundred acres on family right and a thousand as bounty.[49] William Hiorn[50] and Christian Buckler,[51]

43. Minutes of Council, Jan. 8, 1776, C.O.5: 631.
44. *Ibid.*, June 21 and July 10, 1776.
45. *Ibid.*, July 8, 1776.
46. *Ibid.*, Aug. 29, 1777.
47. *Ibid.*, Jan. 7, 1779, C.O.5: 635. This was doubtless the party of forty whites and five hundred slaves mentioned by Chester to Germain in his letter of Nov. 27, 1778. C.O.5: 595, pp. 461–464, Miss. Trans.
48. Minutes of Council, Dec. 26, 1776, C.O.5: 634.
49. *Ibid.*, May 17, 1779, C.O.5: 635.
50. *Ibid.*, Nov. 6, 1776, C.O.5: 631.
51. *Ibid.*, Dec. 26, 1776, C.O.5: 634.

owning nineteen Negroes together, were from Pennsylvania, as was William Dunbar, a native of Scotland, who has left an interesting account of life on his plantation near Baton Rouge.[52] James Baird, from North Carolina, arrived with twelve slaves, a mandamus for membership in the council, and an account of losses suffered because of his failure to join the opponents of the king. A warrant for 1,900 acres was issued to him.[53]

Nor were all the refugees from the continental colonies. In 1776 several gentlemen arrived from St. Vincent. They stated that the war in the northern colonies had caused such a scarcity of provisions on that island that they were determined to settle in West Florida. Among the leaders of these were William Walker, who had brought with him an overseer, one free Negro, and thirty-seven slaves, and Levi Porter, who had two white servants and six slaves. All these men were offered generous encouragement.[54] In the fall of 1777 Robert Tait reported to the council that because of scarcity of provisions he had come from Grenada to West Florida and that he had with him nine slaves. The council ordered that he be granted land on the Escambia River.[55]

The raid led by James Willing in the spring of 1778,[56] emphasizing as it did the exposed position of the Mississippi region and the need for protection, undoubtedly gave pause to the westward movement. The British, however, were soon able to reëstablish control and the sending of military garrisons to Manchac and Natchez probably had a reassuring effect. The granting of land along the Mississippi continued until the fall of this part of the province to Spain in the latter part of 1779.

It is difficult to determine accurately the population of the western part of the province. In 1771 Durnford said

52. *Ibid.*, Sept. 16, 1777, C.O.5: 631; Mrs. Dunbar Rowland, *Life, Letters, and Papers of William Dunbar.*
53. Minutes of Council, Jan. 13, 1780, C.O.5: 635.
54. *Ibid.*, Dec. 26, 1776, C.O.5: 634.
55. *Ibid.*, Oct. 22, 1777, C.O.5: 631.
56. See pp. 208–209 below.

that there were few settlements on the Mississippi, but in 1774 he estimated the population of the region at 2,500 whites and 600 slaves.[57] With the continued immigration from the older colonies, and especially with the coming of the loyalists, it is not improbable that the population doubled in the succeeding five years. Slaves were imported by the ship load. All evidence indicates that both settlers and speculators made the Mississippi region a beehive of activity.

In conclusion, then, it is evident that a number of factors caused the province to face west. An appreciable stream of immigration began about 1770 to flow toward the Mississippi region from the back country of the seaboard colonies. This increased steadily until it suffered a temporary check from the order in council of 1773, which directed the governor to cease granting land save on royal order and to reduced officers. However, the designation of West Florida as an asylum for loyalists in 1775 provided an additional stimulus to immigration, and settlers in large numbers from the colonies in rebellion and from the West Indies sought refuge, particularly in the Mississippi region of the province.

57. A Description of West Florida, enclosed in Durnford to Dartmouth, Jan. 15, 1774, C.O.5: 591, pp. 9–32, Miss. Trans.

VII

LIFE AND LABOR

WEST FLORIDA, in the period under consideration, was primarily a frontier province and all attempts to explain social, economic, and religious
conditions therein must be made with this fact in mind if
a discerning interpretation is to be given. Though the
British, when they assumed control, found settlements of
long standing at Pensacola, Mobile, and Biloxi, these were
not advanced enough in development or of sufficient importance to keep the colony from being frontier in character. Conditions in West Florida from 1763 to 1781
show a marked similarity to those in Georgia a genera-
tion earlier and in the Carolinas in the first part of the
century. The land-hungry, adventurous pioneer, anxious
to improve his fortune by attaching himself to the new
government, by engaging in trade with the Spanish or
Indians, or by cultivating the fertile lands on the banks
of the Mississippi or the Pearl, was characteristic of the
times. The refinements of the older colonies were either
lacking altogether or were so unusual as to attract comment when they appeared.

The Europeans in the province were largely Spanish,
French, German, and English, with the French and English the most numerous. The Spanish had occupied Pensacola since the latter part of the seventeenth century, but
the town was little more than a military post, and when the
English took possession the inhabitants sold their holdings
to speculators and apparently left practically without exception. English records are almost devoid of references
to Spaniards. The town itself was in such wretched repair
that shortly after the arrival of Governor Johnstone it was

laid out anew by Surveyor General Elias Durnford, and little remained to remind one of the former residents.

The influence of the French was less ephemeral. They had made a settlement at Biloxi in 1699; but by 1763 Mobile, founded in 1710, was much more important. The French were not pleased at the transfer to British dominion and doubtless did not relish the prospect of rule by their traditional enemies. It was thought at first that most of them would migrate across the river to the part of Louisiana which remained to France. The news, however, that this territory had been ceded to Spain fundamentally altered the situation and throughout the period of English control Mobile and the surrounding country remained strongly French. To induce the French across the Mississippi who were dissatisfied with Spanish rule to come into the colony was a favorite project of West Florida governors, but failure to provide adequate protection for the western part of the province discouraged this prospective immigration. The efforts to attract some Germans who had established a settlement and built a church on the river just above New Orleans failed for the same reason.

French colonists from another source for several years demanded the frequent attention of the authorities. In January, 1766, Lieutenant Governor Montfort Browne arrived in the colony with forty-six French Protestants who had been sent over at the expense of the home government for the purpose of encouraging the culture of silk and the cultivation of vineyards.[1] These people with their pastor and teacher, Peter Levrier, were located in a township east of Pensacola on the west bank of the Escambia River and their village was called Campbell Town. For a while they were maintained by an allowance from the governor's contingent fund. The results of the settlement, however, were disappointing. The location was unhealthful and the "French emigrants," as they were called, suffered much from sickness. Levrier apparently was not a

1. Minutes of Council, Jan. 20, 1766, C.O.5: 632.

responsible leader; before leaving London he assigned his salary of one hundred pounds a year to a man to whom he was in debt, but he continued to draw on it in favor of others.[2] In 1770 Lieutenant Governor Durnford, who as surveyor general had laid out the township, reported that Campbell Town was deserted except for two or three inhabitants and that the other emigrants had either died or left the province.[3]

A single reference to another group of foreigners piques the curiosity, but a careful search of the records fails to yield further information. An indenture or contract of May 1, 1766, sets forth at length an agreement between Jeremiah Terry and Company and a band of "German emigrants" who had been brought at great expense from Rotterdam, by way of Charles Town, to Pensacola. In the group there were fourteen families and six single men, a total of forty-five people. The indenture provided that the adults should serve Terry and Company for a period of four years and that those under twenty-one should serve until they became of age; Terry and Company on their part agreed to supply clothes and food according to the custom of the time.[4] But here the record ends. Terry was

2. Representation of John Ellis, agent of West Florida, to Lord Shelburne, Oct. 24, 1766, *Miss. Prov. Arch.*, I, 533–535.

3. Minutes of Council, March 6, 1770. Levrier apparently went to Charles Town. An advertisement in the *South Carolina Gazette*, Sept. 26, 1774, stated that Peter Levrier, pastor of the Huguenot Church, decrying the decline thereof, was offering to teach French.

The adventures and misfortunes of the French Protestants parallel somewhat those of the Palatines who about 1710 came to North Carolina and New York. Both groups were sent over by the mother country with the intention of aiding the provinces by supplying them with skilled workers. Both efforts failed because of misfortune and bad management. An even closer parallel is the case of the two hundred Huguenots who were sent to South Carolina in 1764 and located in the Abbeville District. They were temporarily supported by a grant of £500 from the provincial legislature and were settled in villages which were called Hillsborough and New Bordeaux. W. N. Sainsbury, "The French Protestants of Abbeville District of S. C.," in *Collections* of the Historical Society of South Carolina, II, 75–103. There is a brief explanation with an abstract of documents.

4. C.O.5: 602, pp. 182–183.

a prominent merchant of Pensacola and in July of the same year was made a member of the council.[5] He owned at least 2,600 acres of land near Pensacola and the Germans may have been settled there.[6] Yet it seems impossible that such a considerable group should have settled in the province and escaped the watchful eye of Bartram, Romans, and Hutchins, who wrote of the province in such a discerning way. Romans, indeed, has an indefinite reference to some Germans on the Pascagoula River but it is difficult to identify them with those imported by Terry and Company.[7] Of course it is possible that they were settled in another colony in which Terry and Company were interested, but in that case one wonders why they should have been carried from Charles Town to Pensacola.

The English naturally were the predominating people in the province. Some, like Philip Livingston, Junior, came for the purpose of profiting from participation in the government. Others, such as David Hodge, sought to find gain in the dangerous but remunerative Spanish trade. Still others sold the Indians English goods for valuable deerskins. The vast majority, however, especially after 1770, came from the older and comparatively crowded colonies of the Atlantic seaboard for the purpose of occupying the fertile lands which had been opened to settlement by the Proclamation of 1763. After 1776 this stream of immigrants was composed largely of loyalists who were seeking asylum in a province which had not thrown off its allegiance to the crown. It is significant that practically every one of the older colonies was represented in this movement. The English settlers reached the province by various routes. Some came by way of the Ohio and the Mississippi; others, especially those from New Eng-

5. Minutes of Council, July 28, 1766, C.O.5: 632.
6. List of grants in West Florida, enclosed in letter, Browne to Shelburne, June 8, 1767, Miss. Trans., vol. X. It is interesting to note that two thousand acres of this land were granted to Terry soon after the arrival of the Germans.
7. Bernard Romans, *A Concise Natural History of East and West Florida*, pp. 4–7.

land, came by boat down the Atlantic and through the Gulf of Mexico.[8] Many from the southern colonies came overland bringing their effects and belongings on pack horses, though the surly Creeks did not encourage passage through their lands.[9] There was frequent though irregular communication between Charles Town and Pensacola by water. The English as a whole appear to have been of good pioneer stock, though the frontier character of the province naturally attracted a rowdy element, and the delay in extending the authority of the civil government to the banks of the Mississippi and the almost prohibitive expense of punishing malefactors for crimes committed there, encouraged lawlessness in the western part of the colony.[10]

Though a frontier tends to minimize social and class distinctions, several groups may be more or less clearly differentiated in West Florida. The most influential class was probably the provincial bureaucracy composed of men who had come to the colony primarily for the purpose of holding office and profiting therefrom. The merchants who were interested in the Indian trade and commerce with the Spanish colonies constituted another important group. They were frequently able to bring pressure to bear upon the local administration and even, on occasion, upon the home government. The planter class was much in evidence after 1774, especially in the western part of the province. The small landowners composed a large part of the population. They took out from two hundred to five hundred acres of land and settled in various parts of the province, though the tendency was to gravitate toward the fertile lands in the west. There were a few artisans and a small number of indentured servants. It is not to be assumed that these classes were separated by hard and fast lines. The government officials were frequently interested

8. A Description of West Florida, etc., enclosed in letter, Durnford to Dartmouth, Jan. 15, 1774, C.O.5: 591, pp. 9–32, Miss. Trans.
9. William Bartram, *Travels through North and South Carolina, Georgia, East and West Florida*, pp. 443–446.
10. Durnford's Description, C.O.5: 591, pp. 9–32, Miss. Trans.

in commerce, and both officials and merchants received grants of land. A planter on the Mississippi might be engaged in trade, a small landowner might by the accumulation of slaves and land raise himself to the planter class, and an indentured servant at the conclusion of his term might become a small landowner. The slaves, at the foot of the social order, had no chance of improving their condition except by manumission. It is impossible to give a definite statement as to the population of the province. In 1774 Durnford estimated that there were 4,900 people in the colony distributed as follows: 2,500 whites and 600 slaves on the Mississippi and in adjacent regions; 1,200 whites and 600 slaves east of Lake Pontchartrain.[11] Immigration during the next five years was heavy and the population increased rapidly.

The four principal centers of settlement were Pensacola, Mobile, Manchac, and Natchez. A town government, apparently, was not erected during the period of British control. None of the settlements was more than a village.

Pensacola, the seat of civil government and during parts of the period headquarters of the southern military department of North America, was, by virtue of its official importance and its fine harbor and favorable location for the Spanish trade, the administrative and commercial center of the province. It was located on the sandy shore of the Gulf of Mexico, with the land immediately surrounding it suitable only for raising vegetables. The tenacity with which the Creeks held to their lands prevented expansion in the fertile river valleys to the north. Thomas Hutchins, a military officer who served in West Florida, gave the following description: "The town of Pensacola is of an oblong form and lies almost parallel to the beach. It is about a mile in length, and a quarter mile in breadth, but contracts at both ends. At the west end is a fine rivulet from which vessels are supplied with water. The present fort was built by the writer of this narrative in 1775 with

11. *Ibid.*

cedar pickets, with four block houses at proper distances.
. . . It takes up a large space of ground in the middle of
the town, which it divides in a manner into two separate
towns, and can be of no great service toward the defense
of the place, in case an attack be made on it, either by the
natives or a civilized enemy." [12] Pensacola, in contrast to
Mobile, was noted for its healthful location.

Mobile, at the head of Mobile Bay and at the mouth of
the Mobile River just below the confluence of the Alabama
and Tombigbee, was the center of French influence. Its
harbor was not as good as that of Pensacola and, according to Hutchins, large vessels could not go within seven
miles of the town. [13] Bartram, who visited the settlement in
1777, said that Mobile was situated on a rising bank extending nearly half a mile back. At one time the town had
been nearly a mile in length but at the time of his visit
many of the houses were vacant and in ruins, with the few
good buildings occupied by French gentlemen and English, Scottish, and Irish emigrants from the northern British colonies. The Indian trade, Bartram said, was in the
hands of Messrs. Swanson and McGillivray, who had made
extraordinary improvements in the buildings. [14] A military
post was maintained there. Although Mobile and Pensacola were the only ports of entry, a large amount of goods
was undoubtedly brought into the colony by way of the
Mississippi.

Manchac, located approximately one hundred miles
above New Orleans, [15] was of interest as a trading and

12. Thomas Hutchins, *An Historical Narrative and Topographical
Description of Louisiana and West Florida*, p. 77. Durnford gives a
similar account in his Description of West Florida. A manuscript map
in the Gage Papers entitled Plan of the Siege of Fort George and the
Works Adjacent at Pensacola in West Florida, 1781, by Captain-
Lieutenant Henry Heldring, gives an idea of the layout of the town.
13. Hutchins, *Louisiana and West Florida*, pp. 69–70.
14. Bartram, *Travels*, p. 404. Of course, the best description of Mobile
in this period will be found in the delightful volume of Peter J. Hamilton, *Colonial Mobile*.
15. Manchac was located at the point where the Iberville flowed out
of the Mississippi. "The Mississippi is the source of the Iberville, when

military post. Mention has already been made of the suggestion of Chester and others that it might be advisable to move the seat of government to this place. Bartram remarks on the few large warehouses and commodious buildings, particularly those of Messrs. Swanson and Company, Indian traders and merchants. The town of Harwich was laid out just north of Manchac but the conquest of the province by Spain prevented its development. Just across the Iberville there was a small Spanish military post connected with the English side by a slender wooden bridge.[16] Baton Rouge, some twelve miles above Manchac, was more a neighborhood of plantations than a compact settlement.

Natchez or "The Natches," as it was called during this period, was near the Mississippi on the site of the old French Fort Rosalie, about 140 miles above Manchac. The land surrounding the old fort was very fertile and Natchez was a populous rural community rather than a town, though its nucleus was a trading post. Browne's engaging description of Natchez has already been noted.[17] Hutchins was scarcely less enthusiastic. "The soil at this place," he wrote, "is superior to any of the lands on the borders of the river Mississippi for the production of many articles. . . . [It] produces in equal abundance Indian corn, rice, hemp, flax, indigo, cotton, pot-herbs, pulse of every kind, and pasturage; and the tobacco made here is esteemed preferable to any cultivated in other parts of America. . . . The elevated, open, airy, situation of the country renders it less liable to fevers and agues." [18] Both Hutchins and Durnford spoke of the rapid influx of settlers from the northern colonies to this district during the latter years of English control.

raised high enough to run into it, and occasions what is erroneously called the island of Orleans to be then an island in fact, but at any other time it is not environed with water." Hutchins, *Louisiana and West Florida*, pp. 60–61.

16. Bartram, *Travels*, pp. 427–428.

17. See pp. 64–65 above.

18. Hutchins, *Louisiana and West Florida*, pp. 49–52. An interesting account of Natchez in this period is found in Theodora Britton Marshall and Gladys Crail Evans, *They Found It in Natchez*.

There were several other settlements of minor importance. Fort Crofton, above Mobile, was a place of retreat for the sick soldiers. Biloxi was in the British period occupied by only a few families, "the offspring of the original settlers," who were chiefly employed in raising cattle and stock and making pitch and tar.[19] There were French families on the Mobile River and on the shores of Lake Pontchartrain, and an ever-increasing number of English families on the Pearl, the Pascagoula, the Alabama, the Tombigbee, the Amite, and the Mississippi.

Point Coupée was a thriving French community on the Spanish side of the Mississippi about thirty-five miles north of Manchac.[20] To the English frontiersman it was at once an example of what English settlements might become, and a source from which he could purchase food and livestock. Hutchins estimated that the Point Coupée district, which extended about ten miles along the river, contained two thousand whites and seven thousand slaves, but this figure is probably too large. The agricultural products, according to the same authority, were tobacco, indigo, and Indian corn, and vast quantities of poultry raised for the New Orleans market. Much timber was squared and many staves were rived, and these were conveyed by rafts to New Orleans.[21] Bartram gave a pleasing picture of the character and condition of the inhabitants: "The French here are able, ingenious, and industrious planters; they live easily, plentifully and are far more regular and commendable in the enjoyment of their earnings than their neighbors, the English; their dress [is] of their own manufacture well wrought and neatly made up, yet not extravagant or foppish; manners and conversation [are] easy, moral, and entertaining." [22] The French of Point Coupée were on excellent terms with the English

19. Hutchins, *Louisiana and West Florida*, p. 63.

20. Tables of distances on the Mississippi River may be found in *ibid.*, p. 95, and in "Harry Gordon's Journal," *Collections* of the Illinois State Historical Library, XI, 311.

21. Hutchins, *Louisiana and West Florida*, p. 44.

22. Bartram, *Travels*, pp. 431–437.

settlers and it is unlikely that the international boundary was much of a check on their social and commercial intercourse. Dunbar wrote on several occasions of buying supplies at that place for his plantation on the English side of the river. And John Fitzpatrick, an English merchant of Manchac, makes frequent mention in his letterbook of business transactions with inhabitants of the Point Coupée region.[23]

Information in regard to social life and conditions in West Florida is not plentiful, but what is available indicates that in most respects the colony did not differ essentially from the back country of her sister provinces on the Atlantic seaboard on which she drew for precedent, custom, and population. Of course, life was rougher in West Florida and conveniences of living were fewer. Romans, doubtless having in mind the more settled portions of the older colonies, was struck by the frontier simplicity which he found. "The manners and way of life of the white people in Florida," he wrote, "differ very greatly from those in the other provinces, particularly in respect to clothing; they are very plain, their dress consists of a slight waistcoat of cotton, a pair of trousers of the same and often no coat; if any, it is a short one of some slight stuff; in winter a kind of surtout, made of a blanket, and a pair of Indian boots is all the addition; the women also dress light and are not very expensive; happy frugality! May the inhabitants of this blessed climate long continue to cherish thee as their greatest temporary blessing!" [24] The clothes of slaves were very simple. Dunbar gave to each of his Negro men a pair of shoes, trousers, and a jacket and to each of his women slaves a pair of shoes, a petticoat, and a jacket.[25] One is inclined to doubt whether the generality of slaves was clothed as well as those belonging to Dunbar. The mildness of the climate, save in the

23. Rowland, *William Dunbar*, p. 36. The Fitzpatrick letterbook is in the New York Public Library.
24. Romans, *Florida*, p. 112.
25. Rowland, *William Dunbar*, p. 67.

dead of winter, encouraged simplicity in wearing apparel. "Happy climate," Romans observed, "where all the seasons of the year, the inestimable gifts of *Flora* and *Pomona* are common, where snow or ice are seldom seen, and where the cruel necessity of roasting one's self before a fire is utterly unknown." [26] Yet on one occasion, in February, 1780, Dunbar records, the weather was "excessively cold" and the Mississippi River was filled with ice and entirely frozen over in places. His slaves were sickly as a result of these unusual conditions.[27]

Alcoholic beverages were consumed in greater or less moderation. These might be procured from the taverns, which, as in other colonies, were regulated by legislative enactments. Drink, among the English inhabitants, according to Romans, was water, tempered with a moderate quantity of West Indian rum. Among the higher classes Portuguese and Spanish wines were consumed, while New England rum, "that bane of health and happiness," was drunk by the lower classes.[28] The planters and stavemakers on the Mississippi served wine on social occasions. Dunbar, who is our chief source for this region, frequently made a brief note of social gatherings. The following is typical and suggestive of the character of these occasions: "Yesterday being New Year's day, the gentlemen of the settlement dined with me and celebrated the day with mirth and good humor, our spirits being elevated by the moderate use of good Madiera wine and claret." [29]

Several disconnected references, found in the official records, give a touch of human interest to the general study of social conditions and help to make clearer a rather indistinct picture of life in the province. Pensacola, with visiting Indians, itinerant seamen, and loitering soldiers, must have had some of the characteristics of the later fron-

26. Romans, *Florida,* pp. 115–116.
27. Rowland, *William Dunbar,* p. 71.
28. Romans, *Florida,* p. 116.
29. Rowland, *William Dunbar,* pp. 56–57. John Fitzpatrick refers occasionally to sums won or lost at cards. Fitzpatrick to I. I. Graham, July 13, 1780, for example.

tier towns of the far west. In 1772 the attention of the
council was called to the evil custom of firing "musquets"
and fuses in the streets, which had of late become very
prevalent, to the great danger of the lives of many of his
Majesty's subjects. His Excellency was therefore pleased
to order the clerk to give notice that any one who engaged
in such a practice (except in his own defense) would be
prosecuted according to law.[30]

Fires were a dreaded danger and determined efforts
were made to cope with them. On November 5, 1771, the
council stated that two recent accidents of fire, and especially the alarming fire of the preceding night, had shown
the necessity of another fire engine and the need for an additional number of buckets. The governor, therefore, was
requested to apply for another fire engine, to be paid for
from the contingent fund, and to order twelve fire hooks
and one hundred "canvass tarred buckets" to be made.[31]
In the following July the council ordered that Andrew
Alsopp be paid thirty dollars for repairing the fire engine.[32]

Provisions were made to insure payment of obligations
and, in case of default, punishments were inflicted. In
1766 Nathaniel Thompson was authorized by the council
to dispose of his house at a public lottery in order to
satisfy his creditors.[33] By 1768, however, the official con-
science had been awakened (no doubt by an additional
instruction which was issued on the subject) and this
privilege was denied a petitioner on the ground that such
a practice was contrary to law and conducive to idleness

30. Minutes of Council, Oct. 7, 1772, C.O.5: 630.
31. Minutes of Council, Nov. 5, 1771.
32. *Ibid.,* July 9, 1772, C.O.5: 630. "The engine of that day was an
oblong affair and rather small. It was placed on heavy metal wheels
and drawn by hand. Water was poured into the forward end by several
bucket men, and on each side several men worked a handle which gen-
erated force sufficient to drive the water through a large pipe, by means
of which the stream was played upon the burning building. G. W. Ed-
wards, *New York as an Eighteenth Century Municipality,* pp. 131–132.
33. Minutes of Council, April 20, 1766, C.O.5: 632.

among the people.[34] The imprisoning of debtors was prac-
ticed. Furthermore, a law to prevent the escape of these
unfortunates was passed, which forbade ship captains to
carry from the province any person who did not have a
permit from the governor. On several occasions inmates of
the debtors' prison petitioned the council for relief.[35] A
law eventually enacted provided that with the consent of
the creditor, a debtor might be allowed, under certain conditions, to work out his indebtedness; and if the creditor
refused to consent he was required to contribute toward
supplying the food of the debtor.[36]

Punishments, in accordance with the current practices,
were severe. In 1769 one Marshall was paid thirty dollars
for the erection of a pillory.[37] Dunbar told of a Negro
girl, who, convicted of murdering a white girl, was sentenced to have her hand cut off and then to be hanged.[38]
The governor had the power of pardon and he used it
rather freely, frequently on condition that the person
pardoned leave the province. On January 31, 1775, for example, Chester pardoned on this condition two men who
had been sentenced to death for burglary.[39] An old English custom was reflected in a resolve of the council, that
"a scandalous, infamous and mean libel," published at
Charles Town against his Honor, Lieutenant Governor
Browne, be burned by the common hangman.[40]

On May 26, 1769, Dugald and Mary Campbell appeared before two justices of the peace in Mobile and declared that for reasons best known to themselves they
wished to cease living together. Dugald was not, from this
time forward, to be responsible for any debts contracted
by Mary. To her he gave certain household goods and
promised to pay ten pounds annually, in quarterly instal-
ments, as long as he or she lived. He gave her ten pounds

34. *Ibid.,* Feb. 16, 1768.
35. *Ibid.,* Jan. 30, 1769.
36. See p. 112 above.
37. Minutes of Council, Feb. 7, 1769, C.O.5: 632.
38. Rowland, *William Dunbar,* p. 72.
39. Minutes of Council, Jan. 31, 1775, C.O.5: 634.
40. *Ibid.,* Nov. 6, 1767, C.O.5: 632.

to pay her passage to any other province or to any place
to which she might wish to go.[41] This was a civil separa-
tion and was not a divorce in the modern usage of the term.

Religious conditions within the colony further illustrate
its frontier character. The instructions to the governors
gave ample directions for the maintenance of public moral-
ity and the establishing of the Church of England. The
governor was to take especial care that "God Almighty be
devoutly worshipped," that the Book of Common Prayer
be read on Sundays and holidays, and that the Blessed
Sacrament be administered according to the rites of the
Anglican Church. He was further instructed not to recognize any foreign ecclesiastical jurisdiction and to encourage that of the Bishop of London, save in matters of
collating ministers to benefices, issuing licenses for mar-
riages, and the probating of wills—matters which were
reserved to the governor himself. Lands were to be set aside
for the support of glebes and Protestant schools, but no
minister was to be collated and no schoolmaster was to be
permitted to keep a school unless he had a certificate of
orthodoxy and character from the Bishop of London.[42]
On March 29, 1765, an order in council, based on a representation of the Board of Trade of March 25, was issued
providing that the Earl of Halifax, a principal secretary
of state, be empowered to appoint to the Floridas such
ministers as had been recommended by "the Right Reverend Father in God, the Lord Bishop of London"; and
the governors were to collate these appointees to their
benefices.[43] The annual grant from Parliament contained
two appropriations of one hundred pounds each for the
support of ministers at Pensacola and Mobile and two
items of twenty-five pounds each for the support of school-

41. C.O.5: 605 (not paged).

42. Instructions to Johnstone dated Dec. 7, 1763 (Nos. 28–40), C.O.5:
201, pp. 131–177.

43. C.O.5: 23, p. 493. This and many of the following references are
found in the Pennington manuscripts which have been collected by Mr.
Edgar Legare Pennington for the Florida State Historical Society. The
present writer found some of the documents by independent research
but is indebted to Mr. Pennington for others.

masters at the same places. The intentions of the English government, theoretically at least, were good.

The first Anglican ministers who served in West Florida were the Rev. William Dawson at Pensacola and the Rev. Samuel Hart at Mobile. These clergymen, discouraged by the conditions which they found and unable to make ends meet on their meager salaries, early left their stations and went to South Carolina, where Hart soon died and Dawson became prominent in church circles. William Gordon and Nathaniel Cotten soon appeared and labored in Mobile and Pensacola, respectively. Apparently they received additional remuneration for services as chaplains of the military detachments in their particular districts and in this way they were able to maintain a better standard of living than would otherwise have been possible.[44] These men seem to have worked conscientiously at their tasks.

Cotten, a graduate of Jesus College, Cambridge, was appointed in February, 1768.[45] By June 28 of the same year he had reached the province and on November 30, was writing Hillsborough of the need of Bibles and prayer books and requesting that he be allowed thirty pounds annually as rent until a glebe house was built.[46] On December 15, he wrote the Bishop of London that the people were inclined to attend worship and commented on the large number of Presbyterians. He again emphasized the great need for Bibles and prayer books as well as for a church and a glebe house.[47] A similar letter to Hillsborough on June 9, 1770, reiterated these needs, but it is interesting to note that while prayer books were requested for members of the council, a "lesser sort" for the other people was thought adequate.[48] His earlier petitions, however, had not been in vain for on the next day he wrote the Bishop of London, thanking him for a box of books, Bibles, prayer books, Testaments, and tracts which, he

44. Chester to Hillsborough, Aug. 25, 1771. Pennington MSS.
45. C.O.5: 324, vol. 51, p. 342. Pennington MSS.
46. C.O.5: 586, pp. 4–42.
47. Pennington MSS.
48. C.O.5: 587, pp. 365–366.

said, had been distributed to a good advantage. He also took the opportunity to urge that supplies of this kind be sent at regular intervals.[49] In July the provincial council petitioned Hillsborough for an appropriation for a church building, since not over a third of the people, it was stated, could get into the largest house in Pensacola.[50] This request was not granted, and the church services were usually held in the building which was used for official purposes. Cotten kept a careful record of births and deaths in the town and garrison of Pensacola and this record was, from time to time, transmitted to the home government, Lieutenant Governor Durnford sending one to Hillsborough on June 9, 1770. In the two year period, from June, 1768, until June, 1770, sixty-three people died, some twenty-four of whom were soldiers of the garrison, and eighty-two children were born, three of whom were characterized as "natural." [51]

Cotten died in the summer of 1771 from "dropsy and complication of disorders." [52] On April 26, 1773, George Chapman was appointed to Pensacola, but as he said, having had a bad report of the climate and having a "young family" and a weak constitution, he, with evident embarrassment, declined the office.[53] The place had not been filled by 1777, for in March of that year Chester wrote Germain asking that a minister be appointed but requesting that one David Gillies who had been recommended from Pensacola to the Bishop of London not be selected as he was "a man of immoral character and not ordained in the Church of England." [54] On July 5, 1780, James Brown presented a royal mandamus directing Chester to appoint him to the church and parish of Pensacola.[55] We have no

49. Pennington MSS.
50. C.O.5: 587, pp. 377–380, Miss. Trans.
51. *Ibid.,* pp. 319–330.
52. Chester to Hillsborough, Aug. 25, 1771. Pennington MSS.
53. George Chapman to J. J. Majendie; warrant for appointment in C.O.5: 324, vol. 51, p. 313. Pennington MSS.
54. March 6, 1777, C.O.5: 593, pp. 241–244, Miss. Trans.
55. West Florida Commissions, p. 161.

account of Brown's work, though his ministry was doubtless cut short by the conquest of Pensacola in the following May. Gordon continued at Mobile until the end of the
English period and after the death of Cotten preached at
intervals at Pensacola.

One act of the provincial legislature was devoted to regulating the organization of the local Anglican churches.
On June 29, 1769, there was passed "An Act for Appointing Vestries and Parish Officers for the Towns of Pensacola and Mobile." This law directed that the freeholders
and householders of these places should meet annually for
the election of two church wardens, two overseers of the
poor, two lay wardens, and two appraisers. Each vestry
was authorized to elect the parish clerk and the sexton and
to set the church and poor rates, which were not to exceed
thirty pounds for Pensacola and ten pounds for Mobile.
Any man who was elected to the vestry and refused to serve
should forfeit five pounds to the poor, but no one should
be required to serve two years in succession. Persons of a
persuasion other than the Church of England, who should
procure for themselves a house of worship and care for
their own poor, should not be liable for rates of the
Anglican Church.[56] It is difficult to say to what extent the
provisions of the act were put into operation.

An Anglican church building was apparently never
erected in the colony. On January 17, 1778, Governor
Chester wrote Lord George Germain that the General
Court of Pleas had paid into his hands 1,200 dollars or
£280 which had been collected as fines, with the recommendation that this amount be used to build a church. He
added that the principal inhabitants had indorsed the
plan, and requested that the sum be used for this purpose.[57] On May 15, Germain wrote that he approved the
plan and would recommend to the Lords of the Treasury
that they allow the money to be spent in this way,[58] and

56. Transcripts of laws of West Florida in Alabama State Department of Archives and History; photostats are in Library of Congress.
57. C.O.5: 594, pp. 267–270, Miss. Trans.
58. *Ibid.*, pp. 287–290.

on November 4, he enclosed to Chester a warrant authorizing the expenditure.[59] The conquest of the province by Spain doubtless prevented the execution of the plan.

The Church of England was the dominant ecclesiastical body but ministers of other denominations occasionally appeared. In 1773 Chester wrote Dartmouth of a New Jersey clergyman who with a number of his parishioners had gone to take up lands near Natchez.[60] This was doubtless the Rev. Samuel Sweesy, who, on April 19, had stated in a petition to the council that he had recently come into the province with his wife, five children, and two apprentices. He stated further that some settlers had come with him and that he planned to bring others. Twenty-five thousand acres were reserved for him near Natchez,[61] but a careful search of the records fails to give additional information as to his activities.

One other religious group remains to be mentioned. The Treaty of Paris had guaranteed freedom of worship to the Spanish and French who elected to remain in the province. The French at Mobile maintained the Roman Catholic service, and a memorial of 1768 stated that the church building there was the only one in the province.[62] In 1772 the Roman Catholic inhabitants of that place in a petition stated that they had heard that the British government was aiding in paying the salaries of priests in Canada, and asked that this favor be extended to West Florida. Chester referred the matter to Hillsborough[63] who replied that no such aid was being allowed in Canada and that none could be given in West Florida.[64] The relations between Catholics and Protestants were quite peaceful. The colonial assembly was more tolerant, however,

59. *Ibid.*, pp. 669–672.
60. Chester to Dartmouth, May 16, 1773, C.O.5: 579, pp. 357–359.
61. Minutes of Council, April 19, 1773, C.O.5: 630.
62. C.O.5: 577, pp. 37–39.
63. Chester to Hillsborough, Feb. 21, 1772, C.O.5: 579, p. 9. Pennington MSS.
64. June 6, 1772, C.O.5: 579, p. 237. Pennington MSS. However, by the Quebec Act of the following year, Catholic clergy in Canada were allowed to collect tithes.

than the English home authorities, for a naturalization act was disallowed by the Privy Council because it offered too great inducements to Catholics to come into the province.[65]

There is little information concerning formal education in West Florida. The appropriations which were made in the parliamentary support fund for schoolmasters in Pensacola and Mobile have already been noted.[66] The petition of John Firby, schoolmaster at Pensacola, to the council on March 3, 1772, is a sad commentary on the way the province failed to coöperate with the mother country in this matter, and at the same time it is a brief history of education in Pensacola. Firby, according to the petition, had been appointed by the Bishop of London and informed that he should have a dwelling house and a school erected at the expense of the province. He had been instructed to demand two hundred acres of land for the support of the school and had arrived in Pensacola in 1765 and assumed his duties. Governor Johnstone had promised the land but said that the town was not able to build a school and that Firby ought to have an allowance for a house. Lieutenant Governor Browne had put him off until the arrival of a full governor. Firby next appealed to the vestry who said that the house and school ought to be built but that they could not raise the money. By this time he had been in the province for six and a half years and had received no allowance for rent. He requested, therefore, that the land be laid out and that an allowance be made for rent in order that he might be able "to take all the children belonging [to] the poor and use his best endeavors to teach them religion and virtue." The council was piously of the opinion that two hundred acres should be immediately run out for the use of the school and that the governor should recommend to his Majesty that a reasonable amount be allowed the schoolmaster for rent.[67]

There was little in the life of the province to suggest

65. See p. 113 above.
66. See p. 21 above.
67. Minutes of Council, March 3, 1772.

intellectual activity, though it is dangerous to generalize when evidence is scanty. Governor Johnstone, MacPherson, Nathaniel Cotten, William Dunbar, and a few others were people of culture, but these were exceptions. Among the few books mentioned in the British records are Bibles, prayer books, and those volumes which were sent over by the home government to explain the Swedish process for the manufacture of naval stores. An inventory of the effects of John Blommart of the Natchez region, whose goods were confiscated after he had led a counter movement against the Spanish in 1781, shows that he had a library of about a hundred and fifty volumes.[68] And the letters of John Fitzpatrick, the Manchac merchant, though largely concerned with commercial matters, indicate that he and his friends were not without interest in books. On one occasion he mentioned owning "a pretty assortment of English books" which he valued at two hundred and fifty dollars.[69] There were no printing presses and of course no newspapers. But then it must be remembered that West Florida was a frontier province, where the struggle for existence left little time for cultural pursuits.

Contemporary writers gave enthusiastic accounts of the agricultural products and possibilities of West Florida. Bartram mentioned corn, indigo, potatoes, beans, peas, cotton, tobacco, and almost every sort of "esculent vegetable," as well as pears, peaches, grapes, and plums.[70] Mease commented on the oranges, Chickasaw plums, and white and blue figs in the vicinity of Mobile. The blue figs, he said, grew luxuriantly in all parts of the country

68. Translation of Spanish Records in Office of Chancery Clerk, Natchez, Mississippi, vol. A, pp. 24–43. Other items in the inventory which suggest culture and affluence were: two large pictures, thirteen silver table spoons, eight tea spoons, a soup ladle, a medallion of the Free Mason Society, and a corner cupboard with glazed doors. The inventory amounted to nearly 12,000 Spanish dollars including notes due Blommart.

69. Fitzpatrick to Gregory French, June 22, 1781. Fitzpatrick letterbook.

70. Bartram, *Travels*, pp. 422–423.

and almost without cultivation.[71] References to an abundance of poultry are frequent. Almost all writers spoke of the herds of "black cattle" around Mobile and Biloxi. Captain Harry Gordon said that Pierre Rochon who lived near Mobile was reputed to have a thousand head.[72] Lieutenant Governor Durnford valued his 1400 head of neat cattle and horses, which he lost at the time of the fall of the province, at £5,600.[73] Hogs and pigs were numerous around Natchez and one planter in this region had a flock of seventy sheep.[74]

In spite of these optimistic accounts of the productivity of the province, West Florida, during the short period of its existence under British rule, did not produce a staple or money crop of any great importance. The region immediately surrounding Pensacola was, as has been noted, sandy and not suited to agriculture, though in the latter part of the English period several successful attempts were made to produce rice. Around Mobile the old French families raised cattle and Indian corn in a rather indolent fashion. The fertile areas in the western part of the province were just being opened when the English period ended. It was in this section, however, that agriculture reached its most advanced stage, and it is a happy circumstance that the diary of William Dunbar, a well-educated Scotsman, who owned a plantation just north of Manchac, has been preserved.[75] The diary covers the period from

71. Journey Made by Edward Mease to Natchez and Several Parts of the Province of West Florida, Nov. 4, 1770–Apr. 1, 1771, C.O.5: 588, pp. 331–334, Miss. Trans. I know from personal experience that these figs are still produced in abundance and that they are delicious beyond description.

72. "Gordon's Journal," *Collections* of the Illinois State Historical Library, XI, 306. The black cattle of West Florida were doubtless of a similar breed to those of South Carolina, the fecundity of which in the early part of the eighteenth century necessitated legislation providing for their control and wholesale destruction. E. McCrady, *The History of South Carolina under the Proprietary Government*, p. 351.

73. Statement of losses incurred by Lieut. Gov. Durnford, C.O.5: 581, p. 23.

74. Translation of Spanish Records in Natchez, vol. A, pp. 1–43.

75. Rowland, *William Dunbar*. Dunbar is an extraordinary character. He was associated with Andrew Ellicot in surveying the Florida bound-

May 22, 1776, to June 24, 1780, and is a mine of information in regard to agriculture, slavery, plantation life, and stave-making.

Dunbar resided on his plantation with his overseer, a carpenter, and about twenty-five slaves. The number of slaves varied from time to time due to purchases, sales, births, and deaths. The principal crops raised by Dunbar were corn, rice, indigo, and tobacco; vegetables mentioned were peas, pumpkins, cabbages, and potatoes. In 1776 his corn crop amounted to four hundred barrels,[76] most of which was probably consumed on the plantation or disposed of to neighbors. In the following fall he recorded that he had "made and completed a corn mill upon a new construction to go by horse, with a mill house." [77] Cornbread, it will be remembered, was a regular part of the slave diet. Rice was cultivated in 1776 to a considerable extent. There are frequent references to Negroes—sometimes as many as seventeen—hoeing, cutting, and threshing rice. On one occasion, for example, "Today, promising to be fair, we begun all hands to cut the great rice field." [78] Indigo was produced on a small scale, for in the spring of 1776 Dunbar wrote of planting a little indigo and in August of the same year of beating the indigo and filling two small vats. In the fall of 1777, indigo seed in the pod amounted to ten barrels.[79] Dunbar wrote little of the cultivation of tobacco, but on one day in 1780 he offered 723 "carrots" of this commodity for sale.[80] Cotton was raised

ary and later became a correspondent of Thomas Jefferson at whose suggestion he was elected a member of the American Philosophical Society, the leading American scientific group of the time. The publications of the society contain fifteen contributions from Dunbar. His articles indicate a wide range of interest and an inquiring mind. F. L. Riley, "Sir William Dunbar—the Pioneer Scientist of Mississippi," *Publications* of the Mississippi Historical Society, II, 85–111.

76. Rowland, *William Dunbar*, p. 38.

77. *Ibid.*, p. 52.

78. *Ibid.*, p. 33.

79. *Ibid.*, pp. 23, 31, 54.

80. *Ibid.*, p. 73. To Romans we are indebted for the information that in West Florida tobacco leaves were made up into close-packed bundles called "carrots." Romans, *Florida*, p. 149. It is interesting to observe

in the province in a small way, but the amount exported
was negligible. Dunbar apparently did not raise any during the period of his diary, though in the early part of the
next century he was to produce it in great quantities and
to operate a gin and presses.[81]

Dunbar used slave labor almost exclusively. His treatment of his slaves was, on the whole, humane, though he
maintained stern discipline and punished runaways most
severely. This attitude was dictated to a certain extent by
self-interest, but he was a person of fine sensibilities. He
did not require regular Sunday work though the Negroes
were sometimes employed around their cabins on this day.
On one occasion, at least, he rewarded "a few of the boys"
with handkerchiefs for extra Sunday work.[82] The diary
does not indicate that he took any interest in his slaves'
spiritual welfare—or in his own for that matter. From
various references to clothes and cabins it is evident that
his slaves were quite well cared for. In 1780 he recorded
that two days were allowed "the Negroes to work in their
own fields." [83] This probably refers to individual vegetable
patches which were found on many plantations during a
later period, or perhaps to plots which the slaves were
allowed to till for their own profit.[84] Some of Dunbar's
Negroes occasionally ran away. These were usually apprehended, or, as in the case of one Ketty, "came home . . .
of herself finding it uncomfortable lodging in the woods."
Bessy, who ran away at the same time and who did not
return of her own accord, was when apprehended kept in
irons for four days and given "twenty-five lashes with a
cowskin as a punishment and example to the rest." A similar incident gives an insight into Dunbar's attitude toward the slaves. "Two Negroes," he wrote, "ran away but
were catched and brought back . . . condemned them to

that this word survives today in Webster's *New International Dictionary*.

81. Rowland, *William Dunbar*, p. 349.
82. *Ibid.*, p. 39.
83. *Ibid.*, p. 72.
84. U. B. Phillips, *Life and Labor in the Old South*, p. 253.

receive five hundred lashes each at five different times and
to carry a chain and log fixt to the ankle. Poor ignorant
devils, for what do they run away? They are well clothed,
work easy and have all kinds of plantation produce at no
allowance. After a slighter chastisement than was intended
they were again set at liberty and behave well." [85]

The planters on the Mississippi, as in all areas where
slaves composed a large proportion of the population, were
very apprehensive of a slave insurrection. Dunbar described feelingly his horror on learning that such a rebellion was being plotted in his neighborhood and that
some of his slaves were among the ringleaders. "Judge my
surprise!" he exclaimed. "Of what avail is kindness and
good usage when rewarded by such ingratitude; 'tis true
indeed they were kept in due subordination and obliged
to do their duty in respect to plantation work, but two of
the three had behaved so well that they had never once
received the stroke of the whip." An immediate investigation was made. One of Dunbar's slaves, "stung with the
heghnousness [*sic*] of his guilt, ashamed perhaps to look
a master in the face against whom he could urge no plea
to paliate his intended diabolical plan," committed suicide
by throwing himself, while his arms were bound, from a
boat into the river. The other conspirators were tried
according to the law of the province and three were hanged
within less than ten days after the discovery of the plot.[86]

The provincial laws for governing slaves and the regulation of slavery were strict and showed the influence of
Georgia and South Carolina and of the sugar colonies. The
first law of this kind was enacted on December 20, 1766,
at the first meeting of the assembly. This was repealed the
following June by the passage of another law entitled "An
Act for the Order and Government of Slaves," but this
was disallowed by the Privy Council on January 15, 1772,
and the first law (the repeal of which had been a part of
the second) was declared in force again. It is difficult to

85. Rowland, *William Dunbar*, pp. 38–39, 46–47.
86. *Ibid.*, pp. 26–28.

tell to what extent the regulations were enforced, but they indicate, to a certain extent at least, the current attitude toward slaves and slavery. An examination of the act of 1766 is enlightening.[87] A slave might be emancipated if security of one hundred pounds sterling was given at the secretary's office to guarantee that the freed Negro would not become a burden to the province. A slave was not allowed to go more than two miles from the premises or plantation of his master without a ticket or pass; the penalty for violation was to be corporal punishment at the discretion of the master, but not to exceed twenty lashes on the bare back. A punishment was provided for those who, without sufficient provocation or lawful authority, beat, bruised, or disabled slaves. A slave who offered violence to a white person was to be tried by two justices of the peace and three freeholders. The penalties for the first and second such offenses were to be fixed by the judges; on the third offense the punishment was death, though this might be administered on the first if the white person had been "grievously wounded or maimed." Slaves accused of capital crimes were to be tried in a similar way and the judges were authorized to give "death sentence and to cause its execution." In the trial of slaves, free Negroes, mustees,[88] and Indians (except those Indians in amity with the British government who were tried by their own laws), the testimony of slaves, free Negroes, mustees, and Indians, taken in the most solemn manner and without oath, was to be allowed, but the weight of this evidence was left to the consideration of the justices and freeholders who tried the case.

The owner of a slave who was executed in a legal way was to be reimbursed by an appropriation from the assembly; there is evidence to show that this provision was carried out on several occasions.[89] The murder of a slave was a

87. Transcripts of laws of West Florida in Alabama State Department of Archives and History; photostats in Library of Congress.

88. Correctly speaking, a mustee is the offspring of a quadroon and a white person. Here it doubtless means mulatto.

89. See, for example, revenue act of Jan. 6, 1768, section 36.

felony punishable by the forfeiture of one hundred pounds for the first offence; and for the second, the offender would be considered guilty of a felony "without benefit of clergy." The stealing of a slave, it is interesting to note by way of comparison, was punishable by death. The penalty for harboring runaways was a fine of forty shillings for the first day and nine for each additional day. Tavern keepers were forbidden to sell a slave spirituous liquor without the consent of his master. A slave was not to engage in business on his own account or keep hogs, cattle, or poultry. He was forbidden to carry firearms beyond the cleared grounds of his owner. A master was required to furnish sufficient summer and winter clothing and wholesome food for his slaves.

The law of 1767 was similar to that of 1766 but it had a few interesting variations. A court for the trial of slaves was given authority to pass sentence of death, transportation, dismembering, or any other punishment which it saw fit, and to direct the provost marshal to cause immediate execution of these orders, except that a pregnant woman should be reprieved until after delivery. A slave convicted of gaming with dice or cards was to be whipped through the streets. No slave was to be made free by the act of accepting the Christian faith.

The petitions for land indicate that most of the families did not own slaves, and that the greater part of those that did owned only from three to eight. Nevertheless, there are several instances on record where larger numbers were owned, and the influx of loyalists after the outbreak of the Revolution brought several families who had more than fifty. In 1770 the firm of McGillivray and Struthers stated that it owned forty.[90] Attorney General Wegg claimed in 1772 to have twenty-two; and Reni Harpan de Lâgâwtrois, evidently one of the old French inhabitants, applied for a grant of land that he had already cultivated on the Pearl on the ground that he possessed twenty

90. Minutes of Council, May 1, 1770.

slaves.[91] Simon Hancock in 1776 claimed forty-five,[92] and in the following year Stephen Watts and Dr. Samuel Flower, Dunbar's neighbors near Baton Rouge, were said to own a total of sixty-four.[93] The largest number on record is eighty-one, belonging to one Richard Ellis.[94]

West Florida was a semi-tropical frontier province; climate and conditions, especially in the western part of the province, favored the introduction of slaves and it is not surprising to note that the slave trade flourished. Probably a great volume of this trade was carried on from boats on the Mississippi River, but records regarding the business are meager. It is only when English traders came to grief that the details are available. In 1769 Richard Nichols, master of a schooner, complained to Lieutenant Governor Browne that the Spanish governor of Louisiana, General O'Reilly, interfered with his attempt to sell twenty Negroes on the Mississippi.[95] And in 1778 the Americans seized a schooner belonging to David Ross and Company, English merchants in the Mississippi; the vessel contained fifty picked Negroes valued at three hundred dollars each.[96] It is natural to suppose, indeed the evidence very strongly indicates, that the English traders disposed of their slaves as well as other merchandise on both the English and the Spanish sides of the river.

It is difficult, because of the limited number of examples and the varied circumstances, to generalize satisfactorily regarding the average prices paid for slaves in West Florida. The archives of the province contain some bills of sale of slaves which give specific prices in individual cases,[97] and Dunbar occasionally records a sale and the amount received. On March 2, 1772, Patrick Morgan paid £45

91. *Ibid.*, June 28, 1772.
92. *Ibid.*, Nov. 5, 1776, C.O.5: 631.
93. *Ibid.*, Sept. 16, 1777.
94. *Ibid.*, April 20, 1776.
95. Nichols to Browne, Oct. 14, 1769, C.O.5: 577, pp. 225–227.
96. Minutes of Council, April 25, 1778, C.O.5: 631.
97. C.O.5: 613.

18*s.* 4*d.* sterling for two Negro girls, Sarah and Diana,[98] but in the following April William Ogelvie paid five hundred Spanish milled dollars for Tonette, "a mulatto wench." [99] This was the highest recorded price paid for a slave in the English period in West Florida; it is possible that Tonette's ability to perform manual labor was not her only recommendation. Thomas Augston received ninety-five pounds sterling for a mulatto man.[100] Dunbar, in commenting on the death of his favorite Negro, Cato, declared that the latter would have brought one hundred pounds sterling at market.[101] But these prices were unusual. On one occasion Dunbar sold five Negro men for 260 Spanish dollars each, and sometime later he sold a Negro girl for 220 dollars.[102] John Stuart, probably the Indian agent, bought a man and woman, Prince and Princess, for 625 dollars, while Attorney General Wegg received only 520 dollars for Jack and Lizette.[103] Jacob Blackwell, collector of the customs at Mobile, sold a group of ten slaves—men, women, and children—for 2,260 dollars.[104] From these figures it would appear that the average male slave would sell for 250 to 300 Spanish dollars and the average female slave for about fifty dollars less.

In commenting on the institution of slavery in West Florida, Romans said that a Negro on the Mississippi was reckoned to bring his master a hundred dollars a year, besides his share toward all the provisions consumed on the plantation. Generally speaking, he said, Negroes were better treated there than in Carolina.[105]

Manumission was not unusual and the evidence does not indicate that the provision of the law requiring the posting

98. *Ibid.,* p. 52.
99. *Ibid.,* pp. 67–70.
100. *Ibid.,* pp. 62–63.
101. Rowland, *William Dunbar,* p. 71.
102. *Ibid.,* pp. 23, 40.
103. C.O.5: 613, pp. 147–148, 276–278.
104. *Ibid.,* pp. 67–70.
105. Romans, *Florida,* p. 111.

of security to prevent the freed person from becoming a public charge was observed. James Germany, an Indian trader, freed his man, Gloucester, because of long and faithful service.[106] Charles Parent of Mobile, in consideration of faithful service and other good causes, gave freedom to a mulatto woman, Juliet Vilars, who was to receive all of the cattle marked "IVi" in his herd and all of her clothing.[107] Mary Anne, a "creole" Negro of Mobile, purchased her freedom with eighty dollars which she had earned while in her master's service.[108]

Social conditions characteristic of the institution of slavery were bound to exist. Louis Fornent of Mobile freed his Negro woman, Mary, with her three mulatto children and provided thirty head of cattle for their maintenance. He reserved for himself the right to dispose of the cattle for their support and stipulated that the mother and children should live with him and obey him during the remainder of his natural life; "and," the remarkable paper concluded, "should the above named Negro woman hereafter have other mulatto children by me, during my natural lifetime, said children shall be equally entitled to a share of the aforementioned cattle with the mother and children now or then in being." [109] Pierre Rochon of Charlotte County (the district around Mobile), "being moved by paternal affection," freed his six mulatto children and directed that their mother should be free after his death; a heifer was provided for the support of each child. It was specified that the children should remain with him until his death, after which they were to be advised by a certain René Roi.[110] Dunbar mentions the birth of a mulatto baby on his plantation, but he does not give any suggestion as to its paternity.[111]

106. C.O.5: 613, pp. 401–402.
107. *Ibid.*, pp. 163–164.
108. *Ibid.*, pp. 58–59. Creole, as used here, probably meant native-born as distinguished from one brought in from Africa.
109. *Ibid.*, pp. 362–363.
110. *Ibid.*, pp. 14–16.
111. Rowland, *William Dunbar,* p. 68.

There is an occasional reference to Indian slaves, but these were the exception and not the rule. The English government was anxious to hold the friendship of the neighboring tribes, and the kidnaping of Indians for the purpose of selling them into slavery, a practice common in the Carolinas during the frontier period in those provinces, would have made impossible the good-will policy of the mother country and would have driven the natives into the hands of the Spaniards, who were constantly suspected of tampering with them.

White servitude existed in the colony but indentured servants were not nearly so numerous as slaves. An early law was entitled "An Act for the Regulation of Servants." It contained a number of provisions calculated to govern the relationship of master and servant and was distinctly mild in character. No servant was to be sold out of the province without his consent, and all sales of servants were to be made in the presence of a justice of the peace. A servant who had served at least four years was to be given a new suit of apparel and thirty shillings sterling on the expiration of his term. A bargain made with a servant during the period of his indenture to increase his term of service was not binding. The master was to provide his servant with sufficient meat and drink, and was not to burden him beyond his strength or immoderately to correct him. Nor was the master to cast adrift a servant who was ill with a disease contracted during his period of servitude.

On the other hand, a servant who absented himself without the consent of his master was to make up the time lost at the rate of five days for one. A servant who clandestinely disposed of the goods of his master was required to restore three-fold. A servant convicted before two justices of the peace for insolence to his master might be whipped by order of the court, but the punishment should not exceed thirty-nine lashes. A dispute between a master and a servant was to be tried in a summary way before two justices, but an appeal was allowed to the court of quarter sessions, though a penalty might be levied on persons who made vexatious or unreasonable appeals.[112] In many of the older colonies provision was made for grants of land to servants at the expiration of their servitude, but no such arrangement was made by legislative enactment in West Florida. As land was freely granted anyway, perhaps such a provision was thought to be unnecessary.

Few of the actual indentures are available. The contract between Jeremiah Terry and Company and the "German emigrants" has already been discussed.[113] An indenture of September 4, 1764, between Terry and John Grant states that the former has paid one hundred dollars to Captain Thomas Fisher of the sloop *Sally* who has advanced this amount to Grant at New Providence. In consideration of this payment Grant agrees to serve Terry or his heirs or assigns for a period of two years, and to make up lost time, day for day. Terry agrees to provide Grant with food, lodging, and clothing, according to "the custom of the place." [114] One other item of interest is at hand in regard to Terry. In 1768 his firm purchased two "free but apprenticed" Negroes from Nathaniel Reason.[115] The number of indentured servants owned by one person was usually one or two, and the total number of such servants in the province could not have been great, for they are only occasionally mentioned, even in petitions for grants of land, where it behooved the petitioner to enumerate his dependents in detail.

The number of apprentices who were brought into the province by immigrants indicates the extent to which this combined system of charity, labor, and education was in vogue in the colonies at this time. It is interesting to observe that a single apprentice was rarely found in a family; the number was usually two and sometimes three.[116] A number of minors were apprenticed in West

112. Act of Dec. 20, 1766.
113. See pp. 152–153 above.
114. C.O.5: 601, p. 35.
115. C.O.5: 606, pp. 75–77.
116. Of the nine cases gleaned from Minutes of Council 1772–1779, seven families possessed two, and two families three.

Florida. In 1764, Thomas Dobbins was bound for a period
of three years to Samuel Carr, pilot of the port of Mobile.
The indenture was in the usual form. Thomas promises
to keep the secrets of his master, to do his commands
gladly, to do or see no damage done to him, not to waste
his goods or to lend them unlawfully. He further agrees
"not to commit matrimony or fornication" during his
service, not to play at cards, dice, or tables, not to haunt
the taverns or the playhouses, nor to absent himself from
his master's service without leave. Carr promises to instruct Thomas in "his art," to furnish him with meat,
drink, and lodging, according to custom and to give him
a new suit of clothes at the expiration of his service.[117]
A similar indenture was executed between Thomas Hurd
and John Ames, a carpenter.[118] Donald McPherson was
apprenticed for five years to Alexander McPherson, a
member of the provincial bureaucracy, to learn the
"science of law." During the first two years he was to
receive his upkeep only, whereas during the third, fourth,
and fifth years he was to receive twenty, twenty-five, and
thirty pounds, respectively, but was to support himself.[119]
Sarah Forward, described as a poor orphan of nine, was
apprenticed by the overseers of the poor and the church
wardens, with the consent of two justices of the peace,
to Andrew Allsopp and his wife for a period of seven
years.[120]

With land so plentiful and so easily available, free
laborers were not present in large numbers. "An Act to
Restrain Drunkenness and to Promote Industry" was for
the purpose of regulating this element of the population.
A work day was defined as nine hours, and one shilling
should be deducted for every hour that the workman was
absent. No person who was hired by the day, the act recited, should be entitled to receive wages on the day or days

117. C.O.5: 601, p. 22.
118. C.O.5: 613, pp. 133–135.
119. *Ibid.*, pp. 141–143.
120. *Ibid.*, pp. 241–243.

when he was drunk. A memorandum should be made of all engagements between tradesmen and employers, and wages should be paid according to the terms of the agreement; no workman should quit any work for which he had been engaged until he had completed it.[121] This law was probably not strictly enforced—indeed, it is doubtful whether any of the provincial laws were. The records occasionally mention a skilled artisan, a carpenter, a blacksmith, and perhaps a cooper. William Dunbar employed a carpenter to whom he paid twelve dollars a month.[122] He also mentions a blacksmith, but it is possible that this worker was one of his slaves.[123] The lack of skilled workmen was one of the complaints of General Campbell when he was attempting to put the colony in a state of defense in 1779.

Except in the two industries of stave-making and the production of naval stores, goods were not manufactured for export in appreciable quantities. However, many articles were made for domestic use and several mechanical contrivances are mentioned. In the council minutes there are references to "the brick kilns on the other side of the lagoon" from Pensacola.[124] Grants of land were sometimes made on the condition that the grantees erect saw mills.[125] A grant to Henry Driscoll and Henry Lezars, located "near the flood-gates of their saw mill" indicates that at least one water-powered mill was in operation.[126] Dunbar's corn mill, which was run by horse power, has already been mentioned. John Blommart owned two stills, one of sixty and the other of a hundred and sixty gallons capacity.[127]

Romans mentions a cotton mill which was owned by a Mr. Krebs who lived on a plantation on the Pasca Oocooloo [Pascagoula]. The French, he says, had improved this mill to such an extent that two Negroes were employed in

121. Act of Dec. 26, 1766.
122. Rowland, *William Dunbar*, p. 38.
123. *Ibid.*, p. 57.
124. Aug. 13, 1765, Jan. 7, 1766, C.O.5: 532.
125. Minutes of Council, Jan. 20, March 1, July 28, 1766, C.O.5: 632.
126. *Ibid.*, Oct. 13, 1766.
127. Translation of Spanish Records in Natchez, vol. A, pp. 24–43.

removing from the mill the seed which were separated from the cotton.[128] Though the estimate of the efficiency of the machine was based on hearsay and is doubtless exaggerated, nevertheless it is interesting that this account was written almost twenty years before Whitney's invention of the cotton gin.

The production of naval stores in America was a matter of concern to the English government throughout the colonial period. It did not please the mercantilists that England, a great sea power, should be dependent on foreign nations for her essential naval supplies. Therefore, it is not surprising that the home government made great efforts to encourage production of these materials by offers of bounties and preferential tariffs. In West Florida the cultivation of a certain acreage of hemp, if the land were at all suitable, was one of the conditions of the grants made by mandamus; this was true of similar grants made about this time in other colonies. Yet there is no indication that hemp was produced in West Florida in merchantable quantities.

The long-leaf, yellow pine which grew in large quantities in most parts of the province was rich in the resin from which pitch and tar are derived, and the production of naval stores was a natural industry.[129] In 1771 Governor Chester acknowledged receipt of twelve copies of a book containing an account of the process used in Sweden in the manufacture of pitch and tar. These had been sent by John Pownall, secretary of the Board of Trade. Chester promised that they should be made public and distributed to the best advantage.[130] The French, who lived near Biloxi and on the east shore of Lake Pontchartrain, produced naval stores in commercial quantities and smuggled them across the lake to New Orleans, where they found a ready

128. Romans, *Florida,* p. 140; Hamilton, *Colonial Mobile,* pp. 230–232.
129. Even today after a lapse of a hundred and fifty years and the ravages of a most wasteful system of lumber production, this region still produces a large amount of naval stores.
130. Chester to Hillsborough, Aug. 24, 1771, C.O.5: 588, pp. 301–304, Miss. Trans.

market. This illicit trade was noted by several travellers and officials, but the volume of it, for obvious reasons, is uncertain. Captain Harry Gordon, in 1766, reported that three large schooners were constantly employed in carrying tar across Lake Pontchartrain. One Crips, he said, worked a dozen Negroes in this business; Pierre Rochon, who lived near Mobile, had a number of Negroes whom he employed chiefly in a "tar and lumber way." [131] Edward Mease mentions one Favre, near the mouth of the Pearl, who made a good quantity of tar and sold it in New Orleans.[132] The English were rather tolerant of this smuggling until 1777, when they seized three small Spanish vessels which were engaged in carrying naval stores across the lake. The repercussions of this action will be mentioned later.[133]

The making of staves for the West Indian colonies was an industry which thrived on the Mississippi. The West Indies, small in area and fertile, had been dependent on the continental colonies since the beginning of the century for provisions and lumber. It is not surprising that the forests on the banks of the Mississippi River should have been utilized as a source of supply for barrel and hogshead staves and headings. William Dunbar usually employed a gang of about eighteen Negroes, including "fallers," "sawers," "rivers," "bolters," and "carters" producing these articles. On one occasion he recorded having 60,000 barrel and 40,000 hogshead staves on the river bank ready for shipment.[134] He sometimes made more than 5,000 staves in a week.

Means of transportation in the colony were primitive. Governor Chester's chariot was so unique as to be com-

131. "Gordon's Journal," *Collections* of the Illinois State Historical Library, XI, 306.
132. Journey Made by Edward Mease to Natchez, etc., Nov. 4, 1770–April 1, 1771. C.O.5: 588, pp. 331–334, Miss Trans.
133. See pp. 196–197 below.
134. Rowland, *William Dunbar*, pp. 52, 57. A bolter was one who cut the timber into proper lengths for splitting or riving.

mented on by one observer.[135] Pack-horses were frequently
used by Indian traders, and these animals were common
if not plentiful. Dunbar imported oxen from Point Coupée
and used ox carts on his plantation.[136] There was a road
between Pensacola and Mobile [137] and a ferry over the
Perdido River which was the largest stream between these
two towns. Bartram comments on the "straight, spacious,
and perfectly level" road between the forks of the Amite
and Iberville rivers and Manchac.[138] This highway was an
important link in the inland water route by way of
Rigolets, Lakes Pontchartrain and Maurepas, and the
Amite and Iberville rivers, to the western part of the
province. Dunbar, who lived about 125 miles south of
Natchez, mentions the "Natchez road" but this was probably hardly more than a trail.[139]

Roads were not of great importance because there were
ample means of water communication. A number of rivers
cut the province like so many meridians of longitude.
These extended far inland and navigation was not interrupted by a fall line or rapids, since most of the settled
part of the province was within the coastal plain. The
Alabama, the Tombigbee, the Pascagoula, the Pearl, and
their tributaries were natural highways for trade and
settlement. The Gulf of Mexico, with a sheltering row of
islands along the coast, was the means for connecting these
streams as well as Pensacola, Mobile, and Biloxi. Lakes
Maurepas and Pontchartrain, as has already been pointed
out, were valuable links of communication. The Mississippi
River, the western boundary of the province for a distance
of about two hundred miles, was a natural highway for
that part of the province as well as an artery which led
into the heart of the continent. When one considers the

135. A chariot, in the eighteenth century, was a four-wheeled carriage
which contained a driver's box.
136. Rowland, *William Dunbar,* pp. 56–57.
137. Minutes of Council, Oct. 1, 1771.
138. Bartram, *Travels,* pp. 427–428.
139. Rowland, *William Dunbar,* p. 56.

availability of water routes and the difficulties of making roads through swamps and the luxuriant semi-tropical vegetation, it is not difficult to understand why boats were so widely used.

Travel within the provincial waters was, of course, by small craft. Brigs and sloops were used on the coast and on the lakes; rowboats or bateaux were found on the rivers, especially the Mississippi. Piraguas are sometimes mentioned especially around Lake Pontchartrain. The Mississippi was of two-fold significance, as a vital part of the intra-colonial communication system and as the connecting link between West Florida and the British posts in the Illinois country. The means of navigation on this river, therefore, are of especial importance and interest. The progress of a sailing vessel up this stream was slow and laborious on account of the bends in the river and the uncertainty of the wind. When the wind was not favorable, five or ten miles a day was made by "warping." [140] The trip from the mouth of the river to New Orleans, a distance of about eighty miles, was never accomplished in less than a week or ten days and sometimes a month was required. For the journey from New Orleans to the Illinois country large boats of from ten to twenty tons' burden were used. These were propelled by oarsmen, ten to twenty-four in number according to the size of the boat. Such a trip, approximately fifteen hundred miles in length, was accomplished in about seventy days. The return journey, downstream, required only fourteen to sixteen days.[141] Flat boats and rafts were also used in bringing skins, staves, and other materials down the river.

With a colony so dependent on transportation by water and with naval stores and suitable timber available in such large quantities, it is not surprising that vessels were

140. Warping was the process of propelling a vessel upstream by attaching a rope to a tree, pulling the vessel up to the tree, then repeating the procedure.

141. Hutchins Papers, III, 59, in Pennsylvania Historical Society; "Gordon's Journal," *Collections* of the Illinois State Historical Library, XI, 302.

built in the province. The references to shipbuilding, however, are few and indicate that this industry was carried on only for the purpose of meeting local needs. The papers of the "square sterned schooner" *Mobile* state that it was built in the province in 1765.[142] Edward Mease, on his trip to the western part of the province in 1770 and 1771, came in contact with a Captain Jerome who was building a schooner for the Pensacola trade.[143] Durnford, in the account of the province which he wrote for Dartmouth, mentions a vessel of about "25 tons burthen which was lately built" on the Pascagoula River.[144] It is quite probable that a number of small vessels were constructed during the period of British occupation.

Most of the commerce of the colony comes under three heads: the Spanish trade, the Indian trade and the export of deerskins, and the trade on the Mississippi River. At the time the province was established it was thought that Pensacola would become a commercial center from which goods of British manufacture might be distributed to the Spanish settlements in Mexico and Central America in exchange for silver and gold and valuable tropical commodities which did not compete with the products of the English colonies. A large quantity of goods was shipped to Pensacola. The efforts of Johnstone and Browne to induce Spanish ships to come to Pensacola for the goods have already been recounted. Such trade was in violation of the provision of the navigation act of 1660 which required that ships carrying the produce of Asia, Africa, or America to England or the colonies should be of English ownership, commanded by an English master, and manned by a crew three-fourths of whom were subjects of the English king. For infringement of this regulation, the officers of the navy were at first inclined to seize the Spanish ships. The home government, however, evidently came to the conclusion that a commerce which entailed

142. C.O.5: 601, p. 115.
143. C.O.5: 588, pp. 331-334.
144. C.O.5: 591, pp. 9-32, Miss. Trans.

the exchange of British goods for gold, silver, and desirable raw materials, and which employed English shipping in carrying the goods from England to the place of exchange and the raw materials from this place to England, was desirable even though it did technically infringe upon a provision of the venerable acts of trade. An act of Parliament of 1765 legalized this trade in certain ports of Jamaica and, though the permission to engage in this commerce was never officially extended to Pensacola and Mobile, Hillsborough, by implication at least, made it clear that in this particular a strict enforcement of the navigation acts was not expected.[145] The sale of British merchandise to the Spaniards was a matter of interest not only to the merchants of London, Liverpool, and Pensacola, who expected to profit from it, and to provincial officials, who hoped to see the colony prosper, but also to General Gage, the British commander-in-chief for North America, who received accounts of it from subordinate officers and commented on it in his reports to England.[146]

Several Spanish ships visited Pensacola in the period before 1770, and for a short time the trade flourished. Then, for reasons that are not quite clear, it was interrupted and apparently was never resumed in appreciable proportions. Hutchins says, rather tersely, that the hopes of the Spanish trade induced many people to settle in Pensacola at great expense, but that the results did not come up to their expectations.[147] Romans remarks on the disappointments of this trade, "the deceitful appearance of which has led many to ruin" and blames the perfidy of the Spanish, the decline in prices, underselling by the Dutch and French, and overstocking on the part of the English merchants. He speaks also of the hazards of at-

145. See Chaps. II and III above.

146. Gage to Shelburne, April 24, 1768, C. E. Carter, *The Correspondence of General Thomas Gage,* I, 169.

147. Hutchins, *Louisiana and West Florida,* p. 77.

tempting to deliver the goods to the Hispanic colonies, an unwise practice which put English merchants at the mercy of the Spanish.[148] It is probable that the government of Spain, with a characteristic policy of preserving commercial advantages in her colonies for herself and her subjects, took steps to prevent the English from enjoying this lucrative trade. Browne is the last of the West Florida governors to comment with any degree of enthusiasm on the trade or its possibilities. Chester mentions it but rarely. Elias Durnford, in his account of the province, written in 1774, states that Pensacola, because of the proximity of the Spanish settlements, would have been in a flourishing state had not this commerce received a check in the infancy of the settlement, from which it had never recovered. Unfortunately he does not go into detail.[149] Whatever the cause, the trade languished and Pensacola, deprived of commercial support and from this time important mainly because it was the center of government, went through a period of deflation.

The fur and skin trade from earliest colonial times had been a source of wealth to English merchants. The Dutch had carried on a profitable trade in these commodities with the Iroquois in the Hudson and Mohawk valleys until New Netherland was conquered by the English in 1664, and this commerce was taken over by the victors. The French, settling as they did on two great navigable rivers which led into the interior of the continent, were from the first more interested in the fur trade than in colonization and settlement. As the English traders pushed westward and the French traders established posts in the Great Lakes region and in the Ohio and Mississippi valleys, there was an inevitable clash of interests. The rivalry over the fur trade was one of the factors which made it impossible for France and England to possess in peace adjoining colonial empires in North America. With the Treaty of Paris in

148. Romans, *Florida*, p. 213.
149. C.O.5: 591, pp. 9–32, Miss. Trans.

1763 England fell heir to the trade of the French in Canada and became joint heir with Spain to the trade of the Mississippi valley. During the early part of the eighteenth century Charles Town was the largest British center of this commerce in the south and in 1748 exported 160,000 deerskins.[150] With the extension of the frontier by the founding of Georgia, Augusta developed into an important center, and with the cession of Florida and eastern Louisiana, Mobile became the "grand magazine" of the English in the southwest.

The policies of the British in attempting to regulate the Indian trade have already been traced.[151] Here it is necessary only to repeat that the regulations laid down in the Proclamation of 1763, the Plan of 1764, the treaties with the various tribes, and the provincial Indian trade act of 1769 were never adequately enforced and that the Indians were constantly being cheated by unscrupulous traders who usually carried a plentiful supply of rum. The Indians on their part were frequently sullen and resentful and did not scruple to plunder a trader if the opportunity offered itself. The insidious feature of this trade was that the Indians, though originally self-sufficing, could not exist without the wares of the white man, once they had become accustomed to them.

The commerce was conducted by traders who loaded their goods on pack-horses and made their way into the Indian country. The streams which extended far inland were doubtless utilized by the traders, though specific references are lacking in regard to this particular means of transportation. The articles most acceptable to the Indians were rum (the exchange of which for skins was strictly prohibited by both British and colonial regulations), guns, ammunition, and articles of clothing and dry goods of British manufacture, which the Indians prized with childish delight and which brought the traders a handsome profit. The prices of all articles were established at

150. V. W. Crane, *The Southern Frontier,* pp. 111–112.
151. See Chaps. I, II, and III above.

Indian congresses and values were reckoned in terms of pounds of half-dressed deerskins.[152]

It is difficult to estimate accurately the volume of the Indian trade. Durnford, who on the whole is a rather conservative and reliable source, said that a vessel of two hundred tons made annual trips to Mobile for the purpose of bringing British merchandise and transporting peltry to England.[153] Hutchins estimated that the value of the skins and furs annually exported from Mobile was between twelve and fifteen thousand pounds sterling.[154] This did not include the furs which came down the Mississippi. There was no customs house in the western part of the province, no records were kept there, and the trade was irregular and frequently illegal. In a memorial of 1779 against Governor Chester it was stated that the value of the exports of West Florida—peltry, tobacco, indigo, and staves—was at least £200,000 annually,[155] but petitioners and memorialists are notorious for exaggeration.

With the failure of the Spanish trade to materialize, the establishment of Spanish administration in Louisiana, and the influx of settlers to the western part of the colony, the English and colonial merchants developed a thriving trade on the Mississippi. Several circumstances contributed to the growth of this commerce. The French, who had formerly enjoyed the trade of Louisiana, were at this time almost excluded. Spain, anxious to profit from the possession of the province, forbade the inhabitants to trade with other Spanish colonies, but was not able to supply the wants of the people nor to offer adequate markets for the skins and indigo which were the principal articles of export.[156] The English, with the privilege of free navigation of the Mississippi River, were in a position to sell supplies to the French of Louisiana and to buy their surplus prod-

152. See H. L. Shaw, *British Administration of the Southern Indians*, pp. 195–197, for a copy of prices and a typical set of regulations.
153. C.O.5: 591, pp. 9–32, Miss. Trans.
154. Hutchins, *Louisiana and West Florida*, p. 70.
155. C.O.5: 595, pp. 13–16.
156. Alcée Fortier, *History of Louisiana*, II, 10–11, 37.

ucts. The difficulties of ascending the river, which made progress slow and intermittent and gave ample opportunity for the ship captain to trade with inhabitants on both sides of the stream, were peculiarly favorable to the development of such a commerce. The Spanish authorities in Louisiana were experiencing so much trouble establishing themselves that they did not have the resources to cope effectively with the evasions of their mercantile regulations. This illegal intercourse with Louisiana was supplemented by trade with the settlers on the British side of the river and by the interception of the fur trade which came down the river from the Illinois country and from northern Louisiana.

In 1776 a memoir on Louisiana was prepared by Don Francisco Bouligny, a member of the military establishment of that province. He had come to Louisiana in 1769 as aide-de-camp to the governor, General O'Reilly, and wrote with appreciation and discernment of the possibilities and needs of the colony. His account of commercial conditions throws much light on the activities of the English on the Mississippi. The commerce of Louisiana amounted to about six hundred thousand dollars annually, he said. Of this amount the Spanish and the French (who were allowed by the crown to carry two shiploads of products to France yearly) received only about fifteen thousand dollars. All the remainder went to the English, who always had on the Mississippi ten or twelve boats not counting one or two floating stores. The English furnished the planters what they needed, receiving their products in payment. To stop this practice would have been almost impossible, as it would have necessitated placing a guard at every house. The articles which the merchants could not dispose of directly to the inhabitants were sold to the owners of the floating stores, or were sent to Manchac to form there a depository from which goods might be furnished to any who applied. The English engaged in this commerce with the greatest profit and without any risk, as it was the buyer and not the seller who incurred the danger of trouble in landing the goods.[157]

From other sources it is possible to check the statements of Bouligny.[158] Richard Nichols, master of a small vessel, complained to Lieutenant Governor Browne of the uncivil conduct of General O'Reilly as his boat proceeded up the Mississippi "warping trading etc.," as was the "general custom." The Spanish governor had ordered him to leave the Mississippi and allowed him to dispose of only two of the twenty Negroes that he had for sale.[159] In 1774 the *Two Pollies*, a sloop from Rhode Island, was seized in the Mississippi, two miles above New Orleans, on the charge of illegal trading, and the vessel and cargo, valued by the

157. Bouligny's memoir is quoted in *ibid.*, pp. 25–53.

158. See *Documents Relating to the Commercial Policy of Spain in the Floridas,* edited and translated by A. P. Whitaker. In a summary of a representation of 1778 by Manuel de las Heras, Spanish consul at Bordeaux, relative to the decline of commerce in Louisiana, the following paragraph is found (p. 5):

"In order to realize the profits which foreigners derive from Louisiana it is necessary only to regard its *location* and that *of the English colonies which are separated from it by the Mississippi alone.* This propinquity makes it easy to inquire into the articles which are most needed there and to introduce them without risk; for, *as the* British *ships go upstream from the mouth to New Orleans,* a distance of more than thirty leagues, *they have an opportunity to unload as they go whatever is desired by the inhabitants of the houses on the banks of the river. Nor is it possible to find any means of preventing them,* if we consider on the one hand, the great distance, and, on the other, that their progress upstream is necessarily very slow since the densely wooded forests do not give free access to the winds."

In a summary of a report of the same year by Governor Galvez a similar statement is found (p. 17). After remarking on the failure of the Spaniards to supply the wants of Louisiana the report continued: "In these circumstances it is impossible to attain the object of excluding foreigners, for, as the consul says, *English ships stocked with necessary articles* idle along the river and, *according to the treaties of peace, they cannot be prevented from anchoring or mooring wherever they see fit.* And what inhabitant having what he needs at the door of his house will fail to take advantage of the opportunity to obtain it, since there are no witnesses to accuse him of fraud? *What vigilance, what force, or what body of customs officers would be able to keep watch and prevent this abuse over a distance of a hundred leagues of river whose banks are fringed with habitations?"*

159. Nichols to Browne, Oct. 14, 1769, C.O.5: 577, pp. 225–227.

owner, Joseph Nash, at 9,000 dollars, were immediately
sold for 3,500 dollars. When Nash was eventually tried
and acquitted and the latter amount returned to him he
claimed that he had sustained a loss of 5,500 dollars. When
Governor Chester protested to the Spanish governor, the
reply was a curt statement that Nash had been suspected
of illegal trading and that when he had been acquitted,
restoration had been made.[160] The remarkable points in
this case are that Nash was molested at all, and that after
he had been arrested he was able to clear himself. Durnford, in his account of the province, said that the indigo
and skins of Louisiana were "a great part bought by our
settlers and merchants trading to those parts," and paid
for in goods.[161]

John Fitzpatrick, the Manchac merchant to whom
casual reference has already been made, kept a letterbook
which, having happily been preserved, bears to the commerce of the western part of the province the same relation that Dunbar's diary has to agriculture and plantation
life. Fitzpatrick was both a retailer and a middleman. He
bought British manufactured goods from importers of
Pensacola, Mobile, and even New Orleans and disposed of
them to settlers and planters in his own neighborhood,
Baton Rouge, Point Coupée, and Natchez, and to merchants and Indian traders who operated along the river
and in upper Louisiana and the Illinois country. Fitzpatrick's business amounted to thousands of dollars annually and was carried on largely without benefit of
specie. For the goods that he sold he received carrots of
tobacco, indigo, corn, and other agricultural produce, and
deerskins (all meticulously valued in dollars and reals),
and bills of exchange or promises to pay; and with these
articles and notes he reimbursed his creditors. In 1772
he mentioned having 4,548 skins ready for shipment to

160. Chester to Dartmouth, Sept. 10, 1774 (enclosing correspondence,
affidavits, etc.), C.O.5: 591, pp. 367–428, Miss. Trans.; also Minutes of
Council, April 20, 1774, C.O.5: 630.
161. C.O.5: 591, pp. 9–32, Miss. Trans.

McGillivray and Struthers of Mobile. The position of affluence which Fitzpatrick reached is suggested by the losses which he claimed to have suffered as a result of the disorders preceding and accompanying the conquest of the Mississippi region by Spain. These, he said, amounted to more than fifteen thousand dollars.[162]

The French, deprived of trading rights by the cession of Louisiana and denied admission to the Mississippi, except as mentioned above, attempted to continue their commerce with Louisiana by using the British flag to bring their ships into the forbidden region. The English were not content to enjoy their illicit trade without effective interference from the Spanish authorities and deeply resented the competition of the French in their unlawful activities. In 1773 the West Florida council requested Admiral Rodney of the Jamaica base to station an armed vessel at the mouth of the Mississippi to prevent French vessels from going up the river under the protection of British colors. Chester wrote in a similar vein to Dartmouth.[163] The British secretary of state replied immediately that he had communicated to the Lords of the Admiralty the king's command that a vigilant watch be kept to prevent fraudulent and illegal commerce, meaning of course the fraudulent and illegal commerce of the French and not that of the British.[164] France, however, was by race, ruling dynasty, and political and colonial interests, the natural ally of Spain. Her merchants received special privileges in Louisiana and it was impossible entirely to exclude them from this trade.[165]

The British enjoyment of commercial supremacy along the Mississippi was short-lived. The accession, in Febru-

162. The Fitzpatrick letterbook is in the New York Public Library. For a more complete description of this letterbook, see Bibliographical Note.

163. Chester to Dartmouth, Feb. 19, 1773 (enclosing Council Minutes), C.O.5: 590, pp. 127–138.

164. Dartmouth to Chester, June 10, 1773, *ibid.*, pp. 155–158.

165. John W. Caughey, *Bernardo de Galvez in Louisiana, 1776-1783,* p. 70.

ary, 1777, of the brilliant young Don Bernardo de Galvez to the governorship of Louisiana put new vigor into the whole administration of the province. His popularity with the French was in sharp contrast to the lack of popularity of his predecessors and put him in a position to deal drastically with smugglers.

It is well to remember in this connection that France was about to go to war with Great Britain, that Spain sympathized with France and eventually entered the war on her side. The international situation was reflected in the relations of Louisiana and West Florida. The first intimation that the English had of a radical change of Spanish policy was the sudden seizure, on the night of April 17, of eleven vessels on the Mississippi, with their cargoes valued at 70,000 dollars, on the charge of illegal trading. These were sold at auction for 54,475 dollars. This occurrence naturally caused great consternation and two members of the West Florida council, Lieutenant Colonel Andrew Dickson, of the military establishment, and John Stephenson, a merchant, were sent to investigate the seizures. They remained in New Orleans for almost a month, July 31 to August 26, and this period was marked by a sharp exchange of correspondence between them and Galvez. The Spanish governor did not give them much satisfaction, claiming that the vessels had been engaged in illegal trading. Dickson and Stephenson argued that this trade had been allowed by previous Spanish governors and that Galvez had interrupted it without warning. They argued further that the French were allowed to participate in this trade and that the English, therefore, likewise had the right to participate, under the most-favored-nation clause of the treaty of 1667, which had been confirmed by the Treaty of Paris. The English emissaries denied not so much the illegal trading as the right of the Spanish authorities to seize English vessels in the Mississippi River, the free navigation of which had been guaranteed to the British by the Treaty of Paris. Galvez, however, was unmoved by the arguments. He was able to put Dickson and

Stephenson on the defensive, because of carelessly worded statements in their first letters, and he refused to make restitution.[166]

On their return to Pensacola the envoys made a report of their trip which sheds some light on the Mississippi trade. Galvez, soon after his arrival, had issued a proclamation allowing French vessels from the French West Indies to come in ballast and purchase the products of Louisiana. Two commissioners were appointed by the French government to reside at New Orleans for the purpose of purchasing supplies for the French islands.[167] As a matter of fact, both French and English vessels brought in goods which they disposed of without interference. It was thought for a while that Spain intended to allow free trade on the Mississippi. The thing that brought down the wrath of Galvez upon the English traders, the report said, was the seizure by British authorities on Lake Pontchartrain of several small Spanish vessels which were carrying naval stores from West Florida to Louisiana.[168]

This was the beginning of the end of English participation in the Mississippi River trade. The next year saw the disastrous Willing raid. Furthermore, the Americans began to use the Mississippi as a means of communication with New Orleans, where they were received with increasing friendliness. To them an English vessel was fair prey. In 1778 the schooner *Dispatch*, belonging to David Ross and Company, with fifty Negroes and one hundred barrels of flour was captured by the Americans. A request for the restoration of the vessel and the arrest of the prize crew

166. Copies of this correspondence are in Minutes of Council, Sept. 29, 1777, C.O.5: 631.

167. See also Fortier, *Louisiana,* II, 56–57, for a discussion of this point, and Caughey, *Galvez,* p. 70.

168. See also letter from Harry Alexander to Lord George Germain, April 25, 1777, for confirmation of this point. James Bruce, collector of customs at Pensacola, wrote John Pownall, secretary of the Board of Trade, an interesting account of the situation on the Mississippi, Oct. 16, 1777. These letters are in C.O.5: 155, Florida State Historical Society photostats. This episode is also treated in Caughey, *Galvez,* pp. 71–76 and in James A. James, *Oliver Pollock,* p. 79.

was made in vain to Galvez.[169] The outbreak of actual
hostilities between England and Spain in 1779 meant, of
course, that the English were entirely excluded from the
Mississippi.

Vessels engaging in the Mississippi River trade came
from various parts of the British empire. Jamaica, Rhode
Island, and London are places specifically mentioned. In
view of this commerce, it is rather difficult to explain why
the British government did not establish a customs house
on the Mississippi. The advisability of such a step was
suggested several times. Perhaps the difficulties which
were experienced in the seaboard colonies in the decade
after 1770 prevented the mother country from expanding
the customs service.

The question of the monetary medium of the province
is closely connected with the study of the commerce. The
parliamentary support fund was reckoned in English currency—pounds, shillings, and pence sterling. Duties and
taxes, levied by the assembly, as well as most fees, formally
prescribed by the council for provincial officers, were also
designated in sterling. The proximity of the Spanish
colonies and the West Indies accounted for the circulation
of Spanish money. The Spanish milled dollar is the most
frequently mentioned coin and it would seem from bills of
sales and conveyances that many of these found their way
to West Florida. Indeed, it seems probable that Spanish
money almost replaced English in ordinary commercial
transactions. A bill of sale of October 17, 1767, contains
the phrase, "Spanish milled dollars being current money
of the province." [170] The real—or "ryal" as it was usually
spelled—worth one-eighth of a dollar, was sometimes used.
The French livre is rarely mentioned. Rates of exchange
varied, but five livres were usually valued at a dollar, and
four dollars and two reals were worth slightly less than a
pound sterling; or, in other words, a dollar was worth

169. David Ross and Company to Galvez, April 11, 1778, in Minutes
of Council, April 25, 1778, C.O.5: 631.
170. C.O.5: 601, pp. 77–81.

about four shillings, sixpence.[171] There are occasional references to other coins. In 1772 the council ordered the clerk to prepare an advertisement warning the people against light-weight half-johannes, a large number of which were said to have been lately brought into Pensacola.[172]

From this survey of social, religious, intellectual, and commercial life it is apparent that West Florida was back country. The institutions of government were indifferently developed and functioned inefficiently; officials were frequently more interested in private gain than in public duties. Social life was primitive; there were few amusements and few community gatherings because of the sparsity of population and of the exigencies of frontier existence. Religion was slighted; Anglican ministers were poorly paid and those of other denominations rarely appeared. About half of the time Pensacola was without a rector, and apparently a Protestant church building was not erected in the colony during the British period. Education was neglected, for the province would not coöperate with the home government in its feeble effort to establish schools. Indeed, few of the inhabitants were themselves cultured. Commerce with the Indians, with the Spanish colonies, and with other parts of the British Empire, was hampered by the lack of intelligent and efficient regulation. Despite marked resemblances to her sister colonies on the Atlantic seaboard, West Florida was quite patently a frontier colony.

171. The pound was usually reckoned in sterling, though there are references to "York currency," probably paper money issued by the colony of New York.

172. Minutes of Council, Oct. 22, 1772, C.O.5: 630. A half-johannes was a Portuguese coin worth approximately a pound sterling.

VIII

THE CONQUEST OF THE PROVINCE [1]

THE relations between the authorities of British West Florida and Spanish Louisiana were never friendly, and the reasons for lack of goodwill are not hard to find. There was the natural feeling of hostility resulting from the traditional enmity of the mother countries and the recent war, not to mention the fact that West Florida had been formed in part at the expense of Spain. Furthermore, the Spaniards resented the attempts of the British to encourage the dissatisfied subjects of Louisiana to immigrate to West Florida. The Mississippi River and the trade thereon was another cause of friction, for the Spaniards did not wish to see the English monopolize this profitable commerce, yet the English considered the occasional seizure of one of their vessels as a contravention of their right to navigate the river as guaranteed by the Treaty of Paris. The Indians in the two provinces and in the regions adjacent were numerous and warlike, with great possibilities for good or for evil in time of war. The English accused the Spanish of tampering with the Indians east of the Mississippi, and countercharges were

1. There are a number of articles and books by competent historians which relate to the subject of this chapter and the present writer has not hesitated to use them, though in many cases he has been able to check the correctness of facts by his own investigations. The articles referred to are found in the *Mississippi Valley Historical Review*. They are as follows: James A. James, "Spanish Influence in the West during the American Revolution," IV, 193–208, and "Oliver Pollock, Financier of the Revolution in the West," XVI, 67–80; W. H. Siebert, "The Loyalists in West Florida and the Natchez District," II, 465–483; Kathryn Abbey, "Efforts of Spain to Maintain Sources of Information in the British Colonies before 1779," XV, 56–68. Books which should be mentioned are P. C. Phillips, *The West in the Diplomacy of the Revolution;* John Walton Caughey, *Bernardo de Galvez in Louisiana, 1776–1783;* and James A. James, *Oliver Pollock.*

made that the Pensacola authorities were attempting to disaffect the natives who were under the protection of Spain. Lastly, neither party regarded the settlement of 1763 as satisfactory or final. The English looked upon New Orleans with covetous eyes and said bitterly that free navigation of the Mississippi was a joke as long as this city was not in their possession. Consequently, they planned campaigns against New Orleans and looked forward to the next war when these plans might be executed. To the Spanish the right of the English to navigate the Mississippi was a fundamental difficulty in the control of the Louisiana trade, and they looked forward to the expulsion of the British from the Mississippi and the Gulf of Mexico, the gaining of eastern Louisiana, and the recovery of Florida.

The period before 1777, however, was not a propitious time for either party to execute these ambitious projects. In West Florida the authorities were occupied with the problems of establishing civil government and making the necessary adjustments between the civil and the military, fostering the will-o'-the-wisp Spanish commerce, and putting into operation a workable Indian policy; besides, the province was very sparsely populated. In Louisiana the Spanish were experiencing great difficulty in establishing their authority over the French. One governor was actually expelled and it was necessary for the next to come with an army at his back in order to exact obedience and respect. Then, too, Europe was attempting to recuperate from the exhausting Seven Years' War and the mother countries were willing to let matters rest for a while.

The situation was rapidly changing in 1777. Civil government had been established in West Florida and disputes with the military, though still occurring, were at least less frequent and better concealed. The Indians were under control and friendly, immigration to the province was brisk, and the vacant lands on the Mississippi were rapidly being occupied. In Louisiana the French were becoming reconciled to the idea of Spanish rule and the arrival of

Bernardo de Galvez as governor in the early part of 1777 put a vigor and confidence into the administration which had not been present before. His standing with the people was such that an English official remarked that the conquest of Louisiana, which would have been a comparatively easy task before his arrival because of the disaffection of the French, would at this time be a matter of greatest effort because of the popularity of the new governor.

Even before 1777, the imperialistic policies of Great Britain had come into violent conflict with the spirit of independence which had developed in her colonies on the Atlantic seaboard and they were in rebellion. In the unequal contest with Great Britain the refractory provinces sought aid wherever it might be found. France, the ancient rival of England, still suffering from the humiliation of the loss of her colonial empire and international prestige in the Seven Years' War, lent a sympathetic ear to American appeals and delayed support only long enough to make sure that the rebels had a reasonable chance of success. In the meantime, the colonies and France made overtures to Spain. As early as December, 1776, the Continental Congress in seeking an alliance with Spain had offered to aid in the conquest of Pensacola on condition that ships of the United States be allowed free use of that port and harbor and free navigation of the Mississippi River.[2] In the early part of 1777 this offer was informally made to Spain in an interview held at Turgos between Arthur Lee, representing Congress, and Grimaldo, Spanish minister of foreign affairs. Throughout this year, Vergennes, the French secretary of state, exerted vigorous efforts to convince Florida Blanca, Grimaldo's successor, of the advisability of a Franco-Spanish alliance with the colonies against England.[3]

2. *Journals of the Continental Congress* (Ford ed.), Dec. 30, 1776, VI, 1057.

3. Phillips, *The West in the Revolution*, p. 69. See S. F. Bemis, *Diplomacy of the American Revolution*, Chaps. VI–VIII for the diplomatic

To Spain, however, the question of any alliance which would involve her in a war with Great Britain was very complicated. Unlike France she still possessed a large colonial empire, which in case of hostilities would suffer from attacks of the British navy and thus might be lost. The acquisition of the Floridas without exclusive control of the Mississippi and the Gulf would not be satisfactory, as the existing arrangement between Spain and England proved. Then, too, if Spain rendered active aid to the rebelling provinces of Great Britain, such a policy would put her in an equivocal position in regard to her own colonies. Since the ambitions of both England and the colonies in the west were inimical to the interests of Spain, would it not be a better plan, Florida Blanca pondered, to foster the struggle between the contending parties and thus weaken both? Besides, Spain had designs on Gibraltar and Minorca. So Spain dallied and played with the proposition of an alliance with France and aid to America without definitely committing herself. Governor Galvez allowed American ships to enter New Orleans and permitted the rebellious colonists to purchase supplies in Louisiana.[4] He sent a secret agent to Pensacola and two confidential agents were dispatched by the Spanish government to the English colonies.[5] The Spanish foreign minister and Vergennes conducted continuous negotiations without positive results. "At times Florida Blanca would talk in terms of undoubted belligerency; but when he had almost committed himself he would find some pretext on which to draw back."[6]

The news of the surrender of Burgoyne, reaching Paris early in December, 1777, forced the hand of Vergennes. The Americans had proved that they were able to offer

background of Spain's entrance into and participation in the Revolutionary War.

4. James, "Spanish Influence in the West," *Mississippi Valley Historical Review*, IV, 197.

5. Abbey, "Efforts of Spain to Maintain Sources of Information," *Mississippi Valley Historical Review*, XV, 63–68.

6. Phillips, *The West in the Revolution*, p. 72.

formidable resistance to England. Now, if ever, was the time for France to come out openly on the side of the colonies. Failure to make a decisive move would probably result in a reconciliation between the mother country and her wayward daughters, a step which would deprive France of her opportunity to humiliate England. Vergennes made another determined effort to secure the aid of Spain, but failing in this succeeded in committing his government to an alliance with the Americans in the hope and expectation that Spain would adhere at a later time. The treaties of the Franco-American alliance were signed on February 6, 1778. Spain, however, continued to pursue a vacillating policy inspired in part by reluctance to cast her lot with the Americans, whose interests in regard to the West in general and the navigation of the Mississippi in particular were incompatible with hers, and in part by the hope that by acting as mediator she might secure for herself the Floridas, and perhaps additional territory on the Mississippi and Ohio rivers, without the expense and danger of entering the struggle. Disappointed in her effort to play the rôle of mediator, Spain eventually came into the war in 1779 as an ally of France on the promise of "the recovery of Gibraltar, the possession of Mobile and the restitution of Pensacola, . . . the expulsion of the English from Honduras and Campeche, and the restitution of the isle of Minorca." [7] Because they were unable to agree over the navigation of the Mississippi, Spain and the United States did not form an alliance, though both were the enemies of Great Britain.

Meanwhile the unsettled condition of European politics had been reflected in the relations of Louisiana and West Florida. The latter province had been practically untouched by the revolutionary agitation that had thrown her sister provinces on the Atlantic seaboard into such turmoil. The failure of this agitation to penetrate West Florida was probably due to the isolation of the colony; to the fact that the legislature, that popular organ of dis-

7. *Ibid.*, p. 106.

content, had not been in session since 1771; and to the
lack of effort on the part of "patriot" leaders to foster a
rebellious spirit in the people. Indeed, on October 22,
1774, the Continental Congress, sitting at Philadelphia,
had addressed to the speaker of the West Florida assembly
a communication advising certain measures, and the letter,
ironically enough, had been delivered to Attorney General
Wegg, who had·presided over the assembly of 1771. This
royal official discreetly turned the message over to Chester,
and the governor was careful to prevent its publication.[8]
Two positive circumstances tended to keep West Florida
decidedly loyalist in character. One was the designation
of the province as an asylum for the friends of the king,
with provisions made for pecuniary aid and liberal grants
of land to those taking advantage of this opportunity.
This action, as has already been noted, resulted in the
influx of a large number of loyalists. The second was the
Willing raid of 1778 which caused a decidedly unfavorable
reaction against the Americans.[9]

Even before the arrival of Galvez in 1777, Chester had
reason to be suspicious of the friendly attitude of the
Louisiana authorities toward the rebellious colonies. Oliver
Pollock, an influential merchant living in New Orleans,
was active in behalf of the Americans and later became the
agent of the Continental Congress and the state of Virginia. By virtue of having placed a cargo of flour at the
disposal of Governor O'Reilly during a crisis in 1768,
when this commodity was selling at a great premium,
Pollock had won the confidence of the Spanish authorities
and had been awarded freedom of trade in the province.
In August, 1776, Captain George Gibson, with a few
followers, came down the river to New Orleans bearing a
dispatch from General Charles Lee, American commander

8. Chester to Lord George Germain, Nov. 24, 1778, C.O.5: 595, pp.
393–424, Miss. Trans. The letter is printed in *Journals of the Continental
Congress* (Ford ed.), Oct. 22, 1774, I, 102–103.
9. See Chap. IX for a fuller discussion of the reasons why West
Florida remained loyal.

of the southern district, for the Spanish governor, Don
Luis de Unzaga. The purpose of this expedition was to
secure for the American army such necessary supplies
as guns, blankets, and medicines. It was through the influence of Pollock that Gibson was received and that ten
thousand pounds of powder was purchased for the use of
the Americans. Most of this was immediately sent up the
river in the charge of Lieutenant William Linn and
eventually reached Fort Pitt in the following spring. Gibson, himself, was temporarily imprisoned as a blind to the
British authorities, but was later sent to Philadelphia by
sea.[10] That Chester was not ignorant of the expedition
of Gibson and its purpose is indicated by his correspondence with the home government.[11]

Under Galvez the Louisiana administration was even
more hostile to the British and even more friendly to the
Americans. The opening of trade with the French islands
and the sudden seizure of eleven British ships have already
been discussed. Galvez declared the port of New Orleans
free and open to American commerce and to the admission
and sale of prizes captured by American cruisers. He
corresponded with Colonel George Morgan regarding the
conduct of operations in the west in case France and Spain
combined in an attack on Great Britain and Portugal.[12]
By July, 1777, two thousand barrels of gunpowder, a
quantity of lead, and a large amount of clothing had been
deposited at New Orleans subject to the order of Virginia.
And by the end of the year the Americans had been
aided by arms, ammunition, and provisions valued by one
authority at seventy thousand dollars.[13] During this time,
the protests of Governor Chester were unheeded.

10. James, "Oliver Pollock," *Mississippi Valley Historical Review*,
XVI, 67–71; also *Oliver Pollock*, pp. 61–73, by the same writer.
11. Chester to Germain, Dec. 26, 1776, C.O.5: 593, pp. 105–112, Miss.
Trans.; also [Chester] to [General Howe], Nov. 21, 1776, Carleton
Papers.
12. James, "Spanish Influence in the West," *Mississippi Valley Historical Review*, IV, 197–198.
13. *Ibid.*, pp. 201–202 (figures from Charles Gayarré, *History of
Louisiana*, III, 313).

On July 10, 1777, the Board of War of the Continental Congress recommended that one thousand men under the command of General Edward Hand be sent down the Mississippi against Mobile and Pensacola and that Colonel Morgan be sent to New Orleans to confer with Galvez on arrangements for the expedition. The proposition was considered in Congress on July 19, 24, and 25. It was argued that such a campaign would result in the gaining of vast stores of merchandise and supplies, the interruption of trade between West Florida and England and the British West Indies, the probable acquisition of a fourteenth state for the confederacy, and the gaining of glory and lustre for American arms. Henry Laurens, who had just taken his seat, vigorously opposed the plan as too expensive and too precarious of success, and on the further ground that the troops required for it could be used to a better advantage in Georgia and South Carolina.[14] Though Congress eventually voted to postpone the matter, a similar plan on a smaller and more informal scale came to fruition in the Willing expedition of the following year.

The exposed and unprotected condition of the Mississippi region of West Florida had for some time been a cause of anxiety to the inhabitants. On February 4, 1778, the grand jury at a court of general sessions held at Manchac requested Chester to inform the home government of the defenseless state of this section of the province and to make clear the need of militia for protection from a slave insurrection and for defense in case of a rupture with Spain.[15] In the latter part of this month occurred the Willing raid which came with dramatic suddenness to Natchez and Manchac and left in its wake destruction, fear, and bitter feeling.

14. *Journals of the Continental Congress* (Ford ed.), VIII, 576–577, 578, 579. Edmund C. Burnett (ed.), *Letters of Members of the Continental Congress,* II, 445–449, Laurens to the President of South Carolina [John Rutledge], Aug. 12, 1777; James, *Oliver Pollock,* pp. 107–108. James' citations on these pages to the *Journals of the Continental Congress* should be to *Letters of Members of the Continental Congress.*
15. C.O.5: 580, pp. 309–311.

James Willing was a younger brother of Thomas Willing of the well-known Philadelphia firm of Willing and Morris, which participated so actively in financing the Revolution. In 1774, James settled at Natchez where he led a dissipated life for several years, though he apparently stood rather well in the community. In 1777, he returned to Philadelphia, and received authorization from the Commerce Committee of the Continental Congress to lead a small expedition down the Mississippi. The instructions of this Committee to Willing have not been found, so it is impossible to make a complete statement as to the purposes of his excursion, but it is apparent that one aim was to secure supplies from New Orleans. It may be that he was also directed to seize the property of those attached to the British cause who lived along the east bank of the river and to secure a pledge of neutrality from others. At any rate, he enlisted a company and set out from Pittsburgh on January 10, 1778, in the armed boat, *Rattletrap*.[16]

The conduct of Willing was ill-calculated to win supporters for the colonies. As his expedition proceeded down the river it gathered recruits who added to the numbers if not to the quality of the personnel. The village of Natchez was taken by surprise on February 21, and an agreement of neutrality was forced upon the inhabitants. Anthony Hutchins, one of the leading settlers of the district, was held as prisoner. The expedition continued on its way to Manchac, burning and pillaging some of the settlements where Willing had been entertained during his residence in the colony. Some of the plantation owners, among them William Dunbar, heard of the approach of the marauders in time to flee with their slaves and valuables to the Spanish side of the river, but others saw their slaves and their movable property carried away. Arriving at Manchac on February 28, Willing and his followers made the inhabi-

16. R. G. Thwaites and L. P. Kellogg, *Frontier Defense on the Upper Ohio, 1778–1779*, pp. 191–192n. Also Burnett, *Letters of Members of the Continental Congress*, II, 565n, and the Commercial Committee to Robert Morris, Feb. 21, 1778, *ibid.*, III, 95–96.

tants prisoners on their parole, and captured a British armed vessel. They then proceeded with their spoils to New Orleans where they were hospitably received by Galvez and allowed to dispose of the booty.[17]

The entire province was thrown into great excitement and apprehension by this occurrence. Chester authorized the raising of a troop of twenty-five officers and two hundred and fifty enlisted men under the command of John McGillivray. Captain Francis Miller, formerly of the Massachusetts provincial troops, was directed to raise an independent company.[18] Chester protested vigorously to Galvez for receiving the Willing forces and for allowing them to dispose of their plunder in New Orleans.[19] He sent a small force to Manchac in order to protect the Mississippi region. He appealed to General Dalling, governor of Jamaica, who sent a force of one hundred men, and to Sir Peter Parker, in command of the Jamaica naval base, who responded by sending the frigate *Active* and the armed schooner *Florida* to the mouth of the Mississippi.[20] A resolution of the council required that all strangers appear before a justice of the peace within five days of their arrival in the province and give account of themselves, testifying of their disapprobation of the rebels and taking the oath of allegiance if required; tavern-keepers were instructed to report to the council the arrival of strangers.[21] The British government itself was aroused and determined to send reënforcements to the province and to occupy again the post at Manchac.[22] Chester reported that the

17. Dunbar placed a full account of this expedition in his diary (Rowland, *William Dunbar,* pp. 60–63); see also Anthony Hutchins to Germain, May 21, 1778, C.O.5: 594, pp. 475–483. The best modern accounts are in Caughey, *Galvez,* pp. 102–134, and James, *Oliver Pollock,* pp. 117–130.

18. Chester to Germain, April 14, 1778, C.O.5: 594, pp. 365–372, Miss. Trans.

19. Same to Galvez, May 28, 1778, *ibid.,* pp. 629–641.

20. Same to Germain, June 2, 1778, *ibid.,* pp. 621–624.

21. Minutes of Council, March 10, 1778, C.O.5: 631.

22. Germain to general officer commanding in West Florida, July 1, 1778, C.O.5: 594, pp. 463–474, Miss. Trans. General Sir Henry Clinton to Brigadier General John Campbell, Oct. 27, 1778, Carleton Papers.

presence of ships at the mouth of the Mississippi and the troops at Manchac caused Galvez to assume a more civil air toward West Florida authorities.

The results of the Willing raid were, on the whole, quite unfavorable to the American cause. Manchac and Natchez were soon in British possession again after counter attacks led by Adam Chrystie and Anthony Hutchins. Military posts at these places were reëstablished and strengthened to such an extent that the sending of supplies from New Orleans up the river to the Americans became uncertain and hazardous. The settlers along the Mississippi, far from being won over, were alienated by the excesses and indiscretions of Willing. This leader was soon at odds with Galvez over an alleged infringement of Spanish sovereignty, and with Oliver Pollock, commercial agent of the Continental Congress, over the division of the plunder and other matters relating to finance. Not surprisingly, he soon wore out his welcome in New Orleans. Attempting to return to Philadelphia by sea, Willing was taken prisoner when the sloop on which he took passage was captured. After an uncomfortable confinement he was eventually exchanged or released.[23]

Willing, Pollock, and Galvez evidently discussed at length the question of the conquest of West Florida. On October 10, 1778, the Board of War reported to the Continental Congress that the papers referred to it had been taken into consideration. These papers were letters and extracts of letters from the governor of New Orleans, from Pollock, and from Willing, on the situation of affairs on the Mississippi. The report recommended: that because of the numerous operations under way at the time, it was impracticable for the States to undertake an enterprise of the

23. Caughey, *Galvez,* pp. 129–134. Early historians carried a story to the effect that Willing was captured while on a reconnaissance near Mobile, and narrowly missed being hanged. Peter J. Hamilton, *Colonial Mobile,* p. 251, and J. A. Pickett, *History of Alabama,* p. 348. After the disturbance that Willing had caused, however, it seems highly improbable that Governor Chester would have failed to mention such an episode in his correspondence with the home government.

magnitude recommended by Governor Galvez; that probably Congress would be enabled to turn its attention to operations in that quarter in the near future; and, finally, that Galvez be requested to accept the thanks of Congress for his spirited and disinterested conduct toward the States and be assured that Congress would take every opportunity of evincing the favorable and friendly sentiments which were entertained toward him.[24]

The need for protecting the province against further depredations moved Chester to summon the assembly for the purpose of passing a militia act. The governor, it will be recalled, had quarrelled with the commons house in 1772 over the question of privilege and no assembly had been called since that time. The members of the lower chamber of the assembly of 1778 were jealous of their rights, and Chester was no more willing to compromise than he had been in 1772. A disagreement occurred over the representation in the assembly of the town of Mobile. The commons house was not willing to proceed with the business at hand until Mobile had been given representation. Chester, on his part, claimed that the apportionment of seats was part of the royal prerogative which was delegated to the governor and he refused to make any concessions. After a fruitless session of six weeks the assembly was indefinitely prorogued.

The Willing raid impressed upon the British government the defenseless condition of West Florida. The military and naval reënforcements from Jamaica have already been mentioned. In the latter part of 1778, Brigadier General John Campbell was on his way to Pensacola with reenforcements of about 1,200 men, including 700 Waldeckers[25] and 475 Pennsylvania and Maryland loyalists.[26]

---

24. *Journals of the Continental Congress* (Ford ed.), Oct. 31, 1778, XII, 1083–1084.
25. Waldeckers were German mercenary troops from the principality of Waldeck.
26. Campbell to Germain from Kingston, Jamaica, Dec. 26, 1778, C.O.5: 597, pp. 1–9, Miss. Trans.

He had orders to establish a post on the Mississippi near old Fort Bute (Manchac) and was instructed to give all proper protection to the subjects of the king in their efforts to carry on lawful commerce and to improve and cultivate their land. He was warned, however, not to offend the Spaniards or the Indians in alliance with the British.[27] Campbell reached Pensacola on January 17, 1779. He was impressed by the poor repair in which he found the fortifications of the province and was handicapped in carrying out his orders by the lack of supplies and equipment. In a letter to Sir Henry Clinton, British commander at New York, he said, "And last of all I have to set forth to your Excellency the total impossibility of beginning the fortifications to be erected on the Mississippi for want of materials, for want of tools, for want of artificers, for want of proper vessels for the navigation to transport troops and provisions, and even for want of provisions. In short for a thousand reasons it cannot possibly be begun until next fall." [28] Nevertheless, by midsummer he had not only dispatched troops to Manchac, but had ordered the establishment of a small post at Natchez, site of the old French Fort Panmure.[29]

In the meantime, Spain having at last come into the war as an ally of France (June 15, 1779), the authorities in England planned to capture New Orleans. In a secret and confidential dispatch of June 25, 1779, Campbell was ordered to coöperate with Admiral Sir Peter Parker in the execution of this design. On receiving this order Campbell wrote Clinton that a surprise attack on New Orleans was impossible because of the lack of naval transports, intrenching tools, and artillery, and because of the condition of his troops as a result of desertion and sickness.[30] Ger-

27. Germain to general officer commanding in West Florida, July 1, 1778, C.O.5: 594, pp. 463–474, Miss. Trans.

28. Feb. 10, 1779, C.O.5: 597, pp. 41–98.

29. Campbell to Germain, July 14, 1779, Miss. Trans., vol. X. This is a volume of miscellaneous manuscripts from the Public Record Office.

30. Sept. 11, 1779, *ibid.*

main advised a similar expedition against New Orleans in the latter part of 1780.[31]

The news of the entrance of Spain into the war reached Pensacola on September 9, and Campbell immediately dispatched communications to Colonel Alexander Dickson and Captain Anthony Forster, commanding at Manchac and Natchez, respectively, apprising them of this fact and ordering them to make all possible preparations for hostilities.[32] But the news had reached New Orleans earlier, at least by August 20, and the energetic Galvez had proceeded immediately up the Mississippi with a large force. Dickson, retiring from Manchac, fell back to a stronger position at Baton Rouge, twelve miles up the river. Galvez pressed on, attacked him there, and on September 21, Dickson agreed to articles of capitulation whereby all British forces on the Mississippi were surrendered with full honors of war.[33]

In the face of this emergency the old quarrel between the civil and the military authorities flared up again, and the colony was torn once more by internal dissensions. The prorogation of the assembly of 1778 had by no means settled the question at issue. Several members of the body, led by Adam Chrystie, the speaker, forwarded a memorial of protest to Samuel Hannay, legislative agent of the province in London, with the request that it be placed before the king.[34] In the spring of 1779 a petition signed by 136 "Gentlemen, Freeholders and Principal Inhabitants"

31. Germain to Campbell, Nov. 1, 1780, C.O.5: 597, pp. 465–468, Miss. Trans.

32. Letters of this date from James Campbell (secretary to General Campbell) to Dickson and Forster, Miss. Trans., vol. X.

33. Campbell to Germain, Dec. 5, 1779, C.O.5: 597, pp. 229–254, Miss. Trans. Also Campbell to Clinton, Sept. 14, 1779, and Nov. 7, 1779 in Carleton Papers. For a Spanish account of the campaign, see Bernardo de Galvez to José de Galvez, Oct. 16, 1779, translated transcripts in Howard Memorial Library in New Orleans. Good secondary accounts are Caughey, *Galvez*, pp. 149–170, and James, *Oliver Pollock*, pp. 191–198.

34. Minutes of a meeting held at the Carolina Coffee Shop, March 10, 1779, C.O.5: 595, pp. 473–476, Miss. Trans.

of West Florida was sent to the king charging Chester and his private secretary, Philip Livingston, Junior, with misappropriations of public funds and other grave irregularities.[35] So intense was the feeling against the governor that it was not until 1782, a year after the fall of the province, that the agitation against him was finally dropped.[36] On September 10, 1779, Campbell suggested to Chester, in view of the danger which threatened the colony and the lack of a militia law, that martial law be established for a period of not less than six months.[37] Accordingly, Chester placed the matter before the council. Lieutenant Governor Durnford, Lieutenant Colonel Stiell, Captain Rainsford, and Captain Johnstone, who might be said to represent the military point of view, favored such an action, but Chief Justice Clifton, Customs Collector Bruce, and Messrs. Stephenson and Hodge, local merchants, agreed with the governor that such a step would be illegal and unconstitutional. As a possible compromise, Chester suggested to Campbell that he was willing to issue a proclamation requiring that all inhabitants take the oath of allegiance before magistrates and enroll in military companies under officers of their own selection.[38]

Chester, furthermore, declined to act on a suggestion from Campbell that the assembly be called together for the purpose of passing a militia law, on the ground that in the preceding year it had been given ample opportunity to act on this matter and had failed to do so. Besides, he pointed out, eight of the members were in Manchac and Natchez, by this time under Spanish control, and two others had left the province; a quorum, therefore, could not be obtained. The governor criticized the general severely for his failure

35. *Ibid.*, pp. 785–816. A manuscript copy of Chester's defense has been printed by James A. Padgett in the *Louisiana Historical Quarterly*, XXII, 31–46.
36. Albany Wallis to one Cumberland, April 28, 1782, C.O.5: 581, p. 28. *Journal of the Commissioners of Trade and Plantations*, May 1, 1782, XIV, 472.
37. Campbell to Chester, Miss. Trans, vol. X.
38. Chester to Campbell, Sept. 11, 1779, *ibid.*

to protect the Mississippi region, saying that though Campbell had been in the province since January 18, he had made no attempt to fortify the western part of the colony.[39] Campbell on his part spoke feelingly in regard to the inhabitants, the Indians, and the governor. "I find the inhabitants in general," he said, "self-interested and without public spirit, whose minds are only attached to gain and their private concerns; in short nothing can be had from them even in this emergency but at an enormous and extravagant price, and personal service on the general principles of national defense is too generous and exalted for their conceptions."[40] The Indians, he said "are a mercenary race, and are the purchase and slaves of the highest bidder, without gratitude or affection. However, my lord, I'm afraid the Europeans themselves have taught them these principles." His characterization of Chester in the same letter was equally unflattering: "The governor, too, perseveres cold, phlegmatic, and indifferent, in his conduct, and, would not proceed one tittle beyond the strict and most limited construction of the law, to save West Florida."[41]

With such mutual distrust and lack of coöperation between the civil and military heads of West Florida, and with Great Britain pressed by the active hostility of half of Europe and the armed neutrality of most of the other half, it is not surprising that a leader of the ability and determination of Galvez should have been successful in his operations against the colony. In early February, 1780, the Spanish governor set out from the Balise, at the mouth of the Mississippi, for Mobile with an expedition of twelve small vessels and 750 men. Though the fleet was damaged by a hurricane, it eventually reached its destination and was joined by five ships with reënforcements from Havana.

39. Same to Germain with enclosure, Nov. 15, 1779, C.O.5: 595, pp. 821–824, Miss. Trans.
40. Campbell to Germain, Sept. 14, 1779, C.O.5: 597, pp. 393–404, Miss. Trans.
41. Same to same, Dec. 15, 1779, *ibid.*, pp. 229–254.

On March 1, Galvez demanded the surrender of Fort Charlotte, but Lieutenant Governor Durnford, the commandant, refused although his forces were greatly inferior in number. The Spanish therefore made preparations for an attack. Meanwhile, General Campbell, at last persuaded that an appeal for help from Mobile was not just a ruse to draw him from Pensacola, rushed reënforcements to the beleaguered town. The bombardment of the fort began on the morning of March 12 and by sunset the Spanish cannonading had made such a breach in the walls of the fort that Durnford was forced to ask for terms of surrender. The arrangements eventually agreed upon were with minor variations similar to those made with Dickson. General Campbell's reënforcements arrived a few hours too late.[42]

Galvez prepared to capture Pensacola and complete the conquest of the province by using Mobile as a base and obtaining aid from Havana. The English prepared for a final stand; friendly Indians were summoned to Pensacola; naval and military reënforcements were sent from Jamaica.[43] Spanish authorities at Havana made at least two gestures toward an attack on Pensacola but were deterred by timidity and by reports of British ships of war in the vicinity.[44] In August Galvez himself went to Havana and after numerous *junta de guerra* a formidable expedition sailed on October 16 for the West Florida capital. But Pensacola was saved for the time being by a hurricane which scattered the fleet and necessitated the temporary abandonment of the project.[45] In January, 1781, Campbell sent a force overland to make a counter-attack on

42. Same to same, March 24, 1780, *ibid.*, pp. 331–340; Chester to Germain, May 17, 1780, with Articles of Capitulation, C.O.5: 595, pp. 935–938, Miss. Trans. Hamilton, *Colonial Mobile*, pp. 250–257. Caughey, *Galvez*, pp. 171–186.

43. Governor Dalling to Chester, Feb. 16, 1781, C.O.5: 137, vol. 80, Florida State Historical Society photostats.

44. Campbell to Germain, May 15, 1780, C.O.5: 597, pp. 405–412; Caughey, *Galvez*, pp. 187–190.

45. Campbell to Germain, Jan. 5, 1781, C.O.5: 597, pp. 573–576; Caughey, *Galvez*, pp. 192–193.

Mobile, but the expedition was repulsed with heavy losses. An additional negative effect, from the English point of view, was the fact that this incident served to strengthen Galvez's hand in his endeavor to convince the officials at Havana of the necessity of bringing Pensacola under Spanish control.[46]

The dangers threatening to overwhelm West Florida did not cause cessation of internal friction. In July, 1780, Campbell wrote Germain setting forth his view of the merits of the dispute over jurisdiction in which he was engaged with Chester.[47] In the following January, he complained of the indifference of the governor in encouraging civilians to aid in the defense of the colony: "In short, my lord, (with regret I say) there is no civil authority in this province only what is sufficient from the nature of the constitution to prevent the establishment of the military." [48]

During the winter of 1780–81, Galvez had reassembled and reorganized his expedition and on the last day of February the small armada set sail from Havana. Ten days later the fleet arrived before the Pensacola harbor and after a brief delay a landing was effected. This maneuver was the more easily accomplished because of the inadequacy of the harbor defenses and the lack of naval protection. Soon reënforcements of 2,300 men arrived from Mobile and New Orleans, and on April 19 a combined Spanish and French squadron with another 2,300 appeared unexpectedly. Galvez now had more than 7,000 men under his command and besieged the town by land and by sea. Campbell had a force of about 2,500, including about a thousand Indians, with which to oppose him. Despite this disparity in numbers the British put up a stubborn resistance and the issue was long in doubt; but the explosion, on May 8, of an English powder magazine, re-

46. Campbell to Germain, Jan. 11, 1781, C.O.5: 597, pp. 581–585 Miss. Trans.; Caughey, *Galvez*, pp. 194–195.
47. Campbell to Germain, July 27, 1780, C.O.5: 597, pp. 369–372, Miss. Trans.
48. Same to same, Jan. 5, 1781, *ibid.*, pp. 573–576.

sulted in the surrender of the town and garrison on the following day. It was agreed by the two commanders and Governor Chester that the British soldiers should be transported to some part of North America where the British were still in control and that the ultimate fate of the province should be left to the respective courts.[49]

A tragic phase of the conquest of West Florida was the rebellion against Spanish authority which broke out in the Natchez district during the latter part of April. The uprising had been sanctioned by Campbell and though successful at first, it naturally collapsed on the arrival of the news of the Spanish success at Pensacola. Some of the leaders were seized and imprisoned for a while and others fled with their families to the seaboard states. Though their property was confiscated it is to the credit of Galvez that there were no executions.[50]

As has already been pointed out, Spain's objectives in the war were the Floridas (especially Pensacola, Mobile, and the Mississippi region), Gibraltar, and Minorca. After winning West Florida she sent an expedition against Gibraltar, the possession of which was necessary to her security and self-respect and the desire to gain which was the key to all of her diplomatic maneuvering. England on her part was unwilling to give up the Floridas without a struggle, and the provisional treaty between England and

49. Chester to Germain (from Charles Town), July 2, 1781, C.O.5: 596 (not paged). Two letters with enclosures, Campbell to Germain, May 7 and 12, 1781, C.O.5: 597, pp. 619–630, Miss. Trans. Campbell to Clinton, May 12, 1781, and May 21, 1781, and Articles of Capitulation, May 9, 1781, in Carleton Papers. Two interesting maps of the siege, one depicting the land and the other the water operations are in the William L. Clements Library of the University of Michigan. They were made by Captain-Lieutenant Henry Heldring of the Third Waldeck Regiment who was acting engineer at Pensacola. The best secondary account is found in Caughey, *Galvez,* pp. 187–214.

50. Campbell to Germain (from New York), July 21, 1781, C.O.5: 597, pp. 751–755, Miss. Trans. Campbell to Clinton (from New York), July 17, 1781, and acrimonious correspondence on the subject between Galvez and Campbell in the Carleton Papers. Good secondary accounts are Siebert, "Loyalists in West Florida," *Mississippi Valley Historical Review,* II, 465–483, and Caughey, *Galvez,* pp. 215–242.

the United States provided a northern boundary of thirty-one degrees for West Florida in case the province remained in the hands of Spain (this was the boundary prescribed by the Proclamation of 1763). But in the event that England was able to regain possession, the boundary was to be thirty-two degrees and twenty-eight minutes[51] (the boundary as established by the additional commission to Governor Johnstone in 1764). Spain's hopes for Gibraltar, however, were crushed by the victory of England's relief expedition in 1782. By the terms of the treaty negotiated between England and Spain in Paris, in 1783, the Floridas with boundaries undefined, and Minorca were formally ceded to the latter power; nothing was said of Gibraltar except that the Treaty of Utrecht was confirmed, meaning of course that the fortress was to remain in the possession of England.[52] The discrepancy between the northern limit of West Florida, as defined in the preliminary treaty between England and the United States and as interpreted by Spain, was to be the fruitful cause of much controversy between the United States and Spain.[53]

51. W. M. Malloy (compiler), *Treaties, Conventions,* etc., I, 580–584 (Senate Documents, 61st Congress, 2nd Session, vol. 47). Also Hunter Miller (ed.), *Treaties and Other International Acts of the United States of America,* II, 101n.
52. Charles Jenkinson, *A Collection of Treaties,* III, 392–400. See also Bemis, *Diplomacy of the American Revolution,* Chaps. XVII and XVIII.
53. I. J. Cox, *The West Florida Controversy,* Chap. I, and S. F. Bemis, *Pinckney's Treaty,* Chap. I.

IX

THE PLACE OF WEST FLORIDA IN THE BRITISH COLONIAL SCHEME

URING the first one hundred and twenty-five
years of English colonization, the policies
adopted by the mother country in dealing with
overseas possessions were inspired by the postulates of
mercantilism, which valued such possessions in proportion
to their part in making the mother country self-sufficing
and prosperous. Any colony which made no contributions
to these ends was without value in the eyes of the mercantilists. Not only this, but every effort was exerted to make
the plantations self-supporting. Near the middle of the
eighteenth century, however, the colonies had increased to
such an extent in population and area of settlement that
they had become an important factor in the struggle which
was being intermittently waged by Great Britain and
France for commerce and world leadership, and the British government was forced to put into operation certain
policies which were not in accord with the tenets of mercantilism. These policies, calculated to strengthen the
British colonial position in an international way and to
tighten the reins of control which the mother country had
hitherto allowed to hang rather loosely, sometimes called
for expenditures which did not promise an immediate return, and sometimes portended results which the mercantilists thought would be detrimental to their schemes.
These policies were usually denominated imperialism. By
the time of the conclusion of the French and Indian War
the imperialists were strong enough to force England to
take Canada rather than Guadeloupe from France,
though the island, with its tropical products, would have
been of infinitely more value from the mercantilist point
of view.

The motives which prompted the establishment of the province of West Florida were apparently both imperialistic and mercantilistic in character. To the imperialists, it was necessary that some steps be taken to occupy Pensacola and Mobile, which were of strategic importance in view of their proximity to the Mississippi River and New Orleans. Then, too, these settlements were a valuable key in the management of Indian affairs and it would be dangerous to leave the populous Creeks, Choctaws, and Chickasaws open to the tampering of the authorities in Louisiana. Finally, it was essential that the stream of land-hungry emigrants from the colonies on the Atlantic seaboard be diverted from the land which the Indians claimed between the Appalachians and the Mississippi. The Indians felt so strongly about encroachments on their hunting grounds that it was necessary to conciliate and reassure them while, on the other hand, the colonists who had aided in the winning of the war felt that the broad territories which had come into the undisputed possession of Great Britain as a result of a victory they had helped to win should be open to them for settlement. The creation of the provinces of East and West Florida with the promise of liberal government and cheap land would, to some extent at least, relieve the pressure on the Indian lands. The settlement of the regions on the Gulf of Mexico would strengthen the position of the English in the newly acquired territory and make it more difficult for the Louisiana authorities (French or Spanish) to tamper with the Indians, who by virtue of their location ought to be dependent on the English crown.

The establishing of West Florida would fit into mercantilist plans also. Pensacola with its fine harbor was very favorably located for commercial intercourse with the Spanish colonies, a trade involving the exchange of English manufactured goods for gold and silver, and tropical products which did not compete with the commodities of the British possessions. Such an exchange, though illegal, was in thorough accord with mercantilist principles. The ports of Mobile and Pensacola would furnish convenient bases for the Indian trade and give the English merchants a monopoly on this commerce in the territory east of the Mississippi. That the province was valued by the mercantilists is strongly suggested by the memorials of protest from merchants of London and Liverpool on the occasion of the withdrawal of the troops in 1768.

West Florida met to a large extent the expectations and requirements of the imperialists. The occupation of Pensacola and Mobile established British authority in a region of great strategic importance, for West Florida and Louisiana were points of contact between two great colonial empires. North of West Florida lay the colonies of England, south of Louisiana lay the vice-royalties of Spain. These provinces therefore were of importance from an international standpoint. British authorities were not slow to use West Florida as a point of vantage from which they could view the activities of their Spanish rivals. And as the value of New Orleans became more apparent, plans were laid for the capture of this city in case of war with Spain. The Louisiana authorities entertained similar designs toward the English settlements in West Florida and were more able in executing them. West Florida was found to be very convenient in the management of Indian affairs. John Stuart, superintendent for the southern district of North America, was frequently there and his deputy, Charles Stuart, resided at Mobile. Important congresses were held at Pensacola with the Creeks and at Mobile with the Choctaws and Chickasaws. Immigration before 1769 was not very rapid, but in this year settlers began to come into the Natchez country and the population of this district increased rapidly. With the outbreak of the Revolution and the designation of West Florida as a place of refuge for loyalists the stream of immigrants grew larger and continued to flow until the conquest of the province.

At the same time the expectations of the mercantilists were realized only in part. The Spanish trade of which so much had been expected flourished for a brief period and

then died away, carrying with it the commercial importance of Pensacola. The trade with the Indians was more
satisfactory. Each year the Indians bought large quantities of British merchandise and paid for it in half-dressed
deerskins which were exported to the mother country.
Mobile was the center of this commerce but there were also
warehouses at Manchac. The trade along the Mississippi,
which had doubtless not been a factor in the establishing of
the province, soon reached large proportions as a result of
the instability of the Spanish government in Louisiana;
it was participated in by ships from different parts of the
empire. But it was seriously checked in 1777 by the strict
policy of Galvez and passed completely out of British
control with the fall of the western part of the province in
1779.

The government established in West Florida was that
of the usual royal province, a form which had been in the
process of development since the annulment of the Virginia
Company's charter in 1624. The governor was an appointee of the crown. His commission was in the usual
form; his general instructions were similar to those issued
to other governors, save in a few particulars (such as the
boundaries of the province) where local conditions necessitated variations; and his trade instructions were identical
with those issued to other governors. He was advised by a
council whose members owed their appointment to the
crown; this body also acted as the upper house of the provincial legislature and, with the governor, as a court of
appeal. The chief justice, the attorney general, the provincial secretary, the provost marshal, the clerk of the
council, and the receiver general were appointed directly
from England by royal patents; but the governor appointed justices of the peace, masters in chancery, rangers
of the woods, and other minor officers, and temporarily
filled vacancies in patent offices, by commissions under the
great seal of the province or under "his hand and seal at
arms." The lower house of the legislature, usually called
the commons house, was elected by the freeholders. A bill

passed by this house and concurred in by the council when sitting in a legislative capacity, and signed by the governor, became a law immediately unless it contained a suspending clause, in which case it did not go into effect until approved by the Privy Council. All laws enacted in the colony were subject to disallowance in England. The judicial system of West Florida, as in other royal colonies, was based on that of England. Justices of the peace were named in a blanket commission and these in groups of three to five handled minor cases. Appeals might be made from the justices of the peace to a court presided over by the chief justice; this same court exercised original jurisdiction in cases of major importance. Appeals in civil cases might be made from this court to the governor in council and under certain conditions from there to the Privy Council. The new province had thus a thoroughly normal frame of government.

Even in less important respects West Florida gave evidence of being an integral part of the British colonial empire. Jacob Blackwell was the agent appointed for the sale of stamps under the law of 1765 [1] and Governor Johnstone claimed that the attempt to enforce this act was one of the causes of the troubles of his administration, though the evidence does not indicate that an appreciable quantity of stamps was sold. In 1765 Charles Saunders, treasurer of the Royal Hospital for disabled sailors at Greenwich, made James Bruce, collector of customs at Pensacola, his agent and deputy in West Florida.[2] As a result, the six-penny duty was evidently collected to a certain extent, at least, for twelve years later when Bruce was on the point of leaving the province he made George Urquhart his deputy for this office.[3] The memorial in 1775 of Arthur Neil, keeper of the ordnance in West Florida, against Governor Chester for dismissing a bill in chancery,

1. His bond, C.O.5: 602, pp. 26–30.
2. Deputation dated May 20, 1765, *ibid.*, pp. 68–70.
3. Deputation dated March 21, 1777, C.O.5: 612, pp. 70–73.

is evidence of the operation of a court of this kind.[4] The
material in regard to the vice-admiralty court is scanty but
of sufficient interest to justify a fuller discussion later. In
1770 the Rev. Robert Cholmondeley, surveyor and auditor
general of his Majesty's revenues arising in America,
authorized John Lorimer to act as his deputy in West
Florida. The customs service at Pensacola and Mobile was
supervised by surveyors general and inspectors general
who visited the colony from time to time.[5]

In one particular, however, West Florida differed
sharply from the typical royal province. The parliamentary support fund for the maintenance of civil government was found only in Nova Scotia, Georgia, and the
Floridas, colonies which were important primarily for
strategic and military purposes.[6] It is this support fund
which illustrates the imperialistic motives in the minds of
those who brought the province into being, for government aid to a province unable to support itself cannot be
said to have been a mercantilist principle. The amount appropriated annually for West Florida varied from £3,900
to £7,200 according to the needs of the province and
the liberality of Parliament. It was doubtless intended that
this appropriation be only a temporary expedient, ceasing
when the colony became populous enough to support itself. Be that as it may, the appropriation continued during the entire period of British occupation and the funds
raised by the provincial assembly were never more than
negligible in comparison. The constitutional importance
of the parliamentary fund, in freeing the executive from
legislative control, has already been emphasized. It did
not, however, serve to avert the struggle between the gov-

4. Memorial to Dartmouth, Jan. 20, 1775, C.O.5: 115, pp. 131–132.

5. Record of His Majesty's Sign Manuals, Patents, Commissions, and
Other Papers Passed under the Broad Seal of His Majesty's Province
of West Florida, hereafter cited as West Florida Commissions, pp. 44,
74, 125.

6. L. W. Labaree, *Royal Government in America*, p. 334.

ernor and assembly which, at one period or another, occurred in practically all of the crown colonies.[7]

There were several interesting aspects of administration in West Florida which suggest the character of the colony and its place in the British system. Because of its outlying position and the constant presence of troops, the military had an important part in the civil administration. Indeed, at least one of the older writers assumed, probably because of Governor Johnstone's previous connection with the navy, that the government was entirely military. While this assumption is far from true, military officers were frequently found on the council, sometimes filled civil positions, and were used by the governors on diplomatic missions to New Orleans. It is interesting, if not significant, that four of the five men who filled the office of governor— Johnstone, Browne, Durnford, and Chester—had served as military or naval officers before coming to the colony. This may or may not have influenced them in their attitudes toward the local commanders, but the mutual hostility and jealousy of the civil and military heads of the province was one of the characteristic features of its history. Bloodshed was narrowly averted in the time of Johnstone. Chester was chronically complaining that his rights were being infringed upon, and, with the Spaniards daily expected at Pensacola, he and General Campbell were engaged in sending criminations and recriminations about each other to the home government.

Pluralism and absenteeism, those twin evils so characteristic of colonial administration in the eighteenth century, were not lacking in West Florida.[8] As early as 1767 Lieutenant Governor Browne complained to the Board of Trade of the inconveniences suffered by the colony because patent officers resided in England while they sent irresponsible deputies to West Florida.[9] Several examples of ab-

7. See Chap. I above, for a fuller account of the parliamentary support fund.
8. Cecil Johnson, "A Note on Absenteeism and Pluralism in British West Florida," *Louisiana Historical Quarterly*, XIX, 196–198.
9. Sept. 27, 1767, C.O.5: 575, pp. 301–302.

senteeism are available. On January 24, 1766, a royal warrant was issued directing that Samuel Hannay, who later served as legislative agent of the colony, be appointed provost marshal. In London on March 30, he appointed John Hannay to act as his deputy. John went to West Florida but did not long exercise the duties of the office, for on August 7 he authorized James Johnstone to act in his place.[10] In the same year two royal warrants directed that Alexander Duncan be appointed clerk of the crown and clerk of the common pleas in West Florida,[11] and by a commission under the great seal of the High Court of Admiralty he was made judge of the vice-admiralty court.[12] By a deputation, executed at London, June 30, 1767, Alexander McPherson was delegated to act for Duncan in these offices. McPherson, it is interesting to note, was register and scribe of the court of vice-admiralty in his own right. He proceeded to the colony where he held these offices until his death in 1774.[13]

The case of James McPherson (celebrated or notorious, according to the point of view, for his famous *Fingal*) is also worthy of note.[14] Under letters patent from the crown he held the offices of provincial secretary, clerk of the council, and register. His rather cavalier conception of the obligations imposed by the offices is indicated by his actions. He went to West Florida, but remained only a short while. In 1767 he sent a deputation which authorized Daniel Clark to act in his place; and in case Clark refused to accept the deputation or died after accepting it, Jeremiah Terry was designated as next choice.[15] In 1770 McPherson made Philip Livingston, Junior, who was on the point of

10. C.O.5: 602, pp. 60–65.
11. C.O.324: 51, pp. 285–286, Florida State Historical Society photostats.
12. West Florida Commissions, pp. 122–131. Duncan was empowered by his commission to have a deputy.
13. *Ibid.*, pp. 197–198.
14. *South Carolina Gazette,* July 13–20, 1765. See article on McPherson in the *Dictionary of National Biography* for an account of controversy in regard to the authenticity of *Fingal.*
15. West Florida Commissions, p. 38.

going to the colony as Governor Chester's private secretary, his deputy for the offices. According to the terms of the agreement between the two, McPherson reserved to himself the salaries granted by Parliament and Livingston was to have the fees collected in the colony.[16] In 1775 the arrangement was renewed with the additional provision that Livingston might select a deputy to aid him.[17] Richard Combould served for a while as deputy clerk of the council,[18] but in 1778 Livingston delegated all of the offices which he held of McPherson to Elihu Hall Bay. In 1780 Bay deputized John Bay (probably his son) to act for him.[19] There was thus an interesting chain: McPherson held of the king, Livingston held of McPherson, Elihu Hall Bay held of Livingston, and John Bay held of Elihu Hall Bay.

Philip Livingston, Junior, was a speculator in offices as well as in lands. In addition to the offices already mentioned, he was at various times during his decade of residence in the colony, a member of the council, receiver general, collector of the customs at Mobile, and assistant judge. A petition of 1779 against Chester asserted that Livingston at that time held, either directly or indirectly, nine provincial offices and that the governor and his secretary had greatly increased the number and amounts of the fees exacted.[20] The secretary's account book indicates that these charges were not without some foundation.[21]

The vice-admiralty court is another interesting phase of the colonial administration, though the evidence for the study of this subject is very fragmentary. Soon after the creation of the province by the Proclamation of 1763 a royal warrant was issued authorizing the appointment of vice-admirals, judges, and other officers requisite for courts of vice-admiralty in East and West Florida, Que-

16. *Ibid.*, pp. 109–111.
17. *Ibid.*, pp. 214–217.
18. *Ibid.*, pp. 282–283.
19. *Ibid.*, pp. 351–353.
20. C.O.5: 595, pp. 785–815, Miss. Trans.
21. Two manuscript volumes in Library of Congress.

bec, and Grenada.[22] Accordingly commissions as vice-admirals were issued to Johnstone and his successors. It was customary for such commissions to be issued to the governors of the royal colonies. The first court of vice-admiralty which operated in the colony was established by Johnstone in February 1765, a few months after his arrival. It was of an informal character and set up apparently for the purpose of condemning a small vessel belonging to Major Robert Farmar, which had been seized for importing a small amount of wine from New Orleans.[23] Edmund Rush Wegg, the attorney-general, was appointed judge; Arthur Gordon was made advocate general; Samuel Fontinello was selected as register of the court; James Johnstone, a nephew of the governor, was made marshal. All of these officers were selected and commissioned by Governor Johnstone. Their commissions, with the exception of the one to James Johnstone, were similar in form to those issued to other provincial officers and did not mention the vice-admiralty powers of the governor. The commission to James Johnstone did recall these powers.[24]

Probably in the early part of 1768, Alexander McPherson appeared in the province bearing a deputation from Alexander Duncan, who had been commissioned judge of the West Florida vice-admiralty court by the High Court of Admiralty. McPherson held a commission as register and scribe, as has already been indicated, in his own right. He acted as judge and register until his death in 1774 when Governor Chester appointed Elihu Hall Bay until the pleasure of the patentee was known, and Andrew Rainsford, register, until the will of Lord Dartmouth had

22. C.O.324: 40, pp. 302–304, Florida State Historical Society photo-stats.

23. The enmity between Johnstone and Farmar has already been discussed in Chap. II. In this particular case the court ordered the restoration of the boat to Farmar and the payment of costs by the plaintiff. However, the deputy customs collector appealed the case to the Privy Council and on April 14, 1769, an order in council was issued which completely reversed the decision of the West Florida court. *Acts of the Privy Council, Colonial Series*, IV, 754.

24. West Florida Commissions, pp. 16–19.

been ascertained.[25] The appointments were apparently agreeable to all concerned for these officers continued to serve almost until the end of the provincial period. The marshals were regularly appointed by the governors. No additional mention was made of the advocate general.

The records of the vice-admiralty court of West Florida evidently have not been preserved, but from other sources one finds interesting bits which pique the curiosity and suggest something of the character of the work of the court. In 1772 Evan Jones, a merchant, complained to the council of the refusal of McPherson and James Ferguson, marshal of the court, to give him a clear title to a brig which had been condemned by the court, and bought by him at public auction. In the course of the petition he remarked, "That the said court of vice-admiralty, as it is now managed by the present officers of it, is become more pernicious in its consequences than a Roman Catholic Inquisition; and the abuses daily practised in it, to the prejudice of the subjects, call loudly for redress." [26] The council after an investigation, which did not reflect much merit upon Jones, refused to intervene in his favor.

In 1772 John Campbell of Pensacola sued Samuel Thomas and Phillips Comyn, owners of the brig *Africa,* for the loss of a trunk which had been shipped on the said brig from London but which never arrived at Pensacola. A decree was rendered in favor of the plaintiff but the defendants appealed to the Privy Council. This appeal was dismissed on December 21, 1773, because of the failure of the defendants to prosecute it. In the meantime, the situation was further complicated by the fact that Chief Justice Clifton of West Florida had issued a writ of prohibition against all concerned in carrying out the decree of the vice-admiralty court on the ground that it did not have jurisdiction in the case. The matter came before the Privy Council again in December, 1774, and in January of the following year it ordered that the governor enforce the

25. Chester to Dartmouth, Sept. 22, 1774, C.O.5: 592, Miss. Trans.
26. Minutes of Council, July 28, 1772, C.O.5: 630.

original sentence of the vice-admiralty court. From a later entry in the council records it seems probable that this order was never sent.[27]

One other case, which was tried in January, 1781, is of more than passing interest because it is illustrative of a rather common type of cause. John Buttermire, master of the *Nelly*, though he did not have a commission of marque and reprisal, seized the Spanish schooner *El Poder de Dios*. When he reached Pensacola the prize was taken over by the authorities of a man-of-war which was stationed in the harbor, on the ground that Buttermire's seizure had been unauthorized and illegal. The vessel was condemned in the court of vice-admiralty. Buttermire brought suit in behalf of himself and his crew for the money realized or to be realized from the sale of the prize. Elihu Hall Bay, who was acting as judge at this time, refused to render a decision, doubtless feeling that the law was on one side and justice on the other. He referred the matter to the king with the recommendation that a decision be made in favor of Buttermire and his crew.[28] The *Acts of the Privy Council* fail to show that this case was ever considered in England and it is possible that at the capture of Pensacola a few months later the vessel again fell into the hands of the Spanish and a decision became unnecessary.

The failure of West Florida to join in revolt against the mother country is not surprising. The province was remote from the scene of action. Pensacola was eighteen days by sea from Charles Town and the journey by land was so dangerous that it was not frequently made. Communication with the seaboard colonies by way of the Mississippi was equally slow, the trip up the river requiring about seventy days. Dunbar, whose diary covers the period from 1776 to 1780, made no reference to the revolt of the colonies until the Willing raid in 1778 brought the matter to

27. *Acts of the Privy Council, Colonial Series*, V, 378–379; Dartmouth to Chester, March 2, 1774, and memorial, Clifton to Chester, Aug. 30, 1774, C.O.5: 591, pp. 339–350, Miss. Trans.

28. C.O.5: 596, pp. 35–54, Miss. Trans.

his attention in a disagreeable way. Then, too, the province was sparsely settled and the local officials, who owed their livelihood and hopes of promotion to the British government, formed an influential element in the population. Such men as Chester, Durnford, Chief Justice Clifton, Attorney General Wegg, Bruce and Blackwell, customs collectors, and others were unwavering in their loyalty to Great Britain. Little pressure was brought to bear on them to enlist their support for the revolting colonies because the people had few real grievances. The colony was young and there was little local tradition and background upon which claims to complete self-government could be based. It is true that many of the inhabitants of West Florida had come from the older colonies, but most of these came from the back country of the Atlantic provinces and settled in the region around the Mississippi. They were too much involved in the exigencies of establishing themselves on the frontier to take a great interest in politics which did not affect them. Their sympathies, if with the Americans, were dormant. The civil establishment of the colony was entirely supported by Parliament; the taxes actually collected were used largely to pay the expenses of the assembly (the largest item being the salaries of members) and the amount collected was not large. There is little evidence that the Stamp Act and the Townshend Acts were effectively administered. The support of expensive civil and military establishments in West Florida, it is significant to notice, was a part of the imperial scheme which made these taxes necessary. Good land was easily available at a low quit-rent which was never collected. Why should the people have been disaffected? As if to make assurance doubly sure no assembly was summoned during the turbulent years from 1772 to 1778. And when the body, summoned in the latter year because of the crisis precipitated by the Willing raid, tended to become unruly over the questions of privilege and the apportionment of representatives, it was adjourned and not reassembled. Somewhat ironically, a communication from the Continental Congress in 1774 advising certain measures for arousing public sentiment in favor of the revolting colonies, fell into the hands of Chester and was not made public.

West Florida, adjacent as it was to Louisiana, was strategically important and the presence of garrisons at Mobile and Pensacola possibly exercised a stabilizing effect. The designation of the province as a place of refuge for loyalists, the appropriation by Parliament of a sum to aid those in distress, and the subsequent arrival of a large number of people who had suffered becaused of their loyalty to the crown, made the colony less inclined than ever to join her rebellious sisters. Any enthusiasm for revolution which might have existed was dampened by the action of James Willing, a former resident of the Natchez district, in coming down the Mississippi in 1778, in the name of the Continental Congress, at the head of an expedition which seized and destroyed much property.[29] The reaction of the people on the Mississippi to the ill-considered conduct of Willing is suggested by the successful counter-attacks which were led by Anthony Hutchins and Adam Chrystie on the American forces left at Natchez and Manchac.

When one considers the remoteness of the colony from the scene of disaffection, the sparsity of the population, the loyalty of the official group, the favors which the province received from the home government, the absence of grievances, the stabilizing effect of the presence of troops,

29. See Chap. VIII above. William Dunbar, one of the despoiled planters, recorded his feelings emphatically in his diary: "The party was commanded by James Willing of Philadelphia, a young man who had left this country the year before; perfectly and intimately acquainted with all the gentlemen upon the river at whose houses he had been entertained in the most hospitable manner and frequently indulged his natural propensity of getting drunk—this was the gentleman, our friend and acquaintance, who had frequently lived for his own conveniency for a length of time at our houses, I say this was the man who it seems had solicited a commission by which he might have the opportunity of demonstrating his gratitude to his old friends." Rowland, *Life, Letters, and Papers of William Dunbar,* pp. 60–61.

the coming of the loyalists, and the effects of the Willing raid, one is not surprised that West Florida remained loyal; an opposite attitude would have been unreasonable.

The study of West Florida in the British period is of more than local interest, for the province was an integral part of the British colonial scheme. It has already been suggested that the colony was brought into existence in 1763 in order to meet imperialistic needs, and that its favorable location for the Spanish commerce and the Indian trade doubtless caused it to be of value also in the eyes of the mercantilists. Save in the matter of the parliamentary support fund, the administration was, in all particulars, that of a typical royal province. The royal governor with his commission and instructions; the usual set of royal officers, who often remained in England and conferred their authority on deputies; the appointed council which acted as the upper house of the legislature; the assembly elected by the freeholders which was in frequent disagreement with the executive; the royal disallowance, which was freely exercised; the vice-admiralty court with its unpopular decrees; appeals to the Privy Council, which caused long delays—all of these proclaimed West Florida a royal province of the standard type.

British occupation did not leave a permanent impress upon the region. There was little in the English system of administering a royal province which would conform to the Spanish ideal of colonial government. Two important activities, however, which began in the period from 1763 to 1781 were destined to exert an important influence on the future development of the section. The people in the back country began to use the Mississippi as a highway of commerce; and the inhabitants of the older colonies learned of the value of land in West Florida and a stream of immigration began. These two movements presaged the eventual annexation of the region to the new nation whose independence was acknowledged in 1783.

BIBLIOGRAPHICAL NOTE

THIS study is based in large part on documents the originals of which are in the Public Record Office at London. To the student of English colonial history the careful charting of this field of sources by Professor Charles M. Andrews is a work of basic importance. "His *Guide to the Materials for American History, to 1783, in the Public Record Office of Great Britain*, vol. I, *The State Papers* (Washington, 1912); vol. II, *Departmental and Miscellaneous Papers* (Washington, 1914), and the *Guide to the Manuscript Materials for the History of the United States to 1783, in the British Museum, in Minor London Archives, and in the Libraries of Oxford and Cambridge* (Washington, 1908), by Professor Andrews and Miss Frances G. Davenport, are invaluable to the worker in these collections or in transcripts therefrom." Usable bibliographies of colonial history are found in the first volume of *The Cambridge History of the British Empire*, under the general editorship of E. A. Benians, J. Holland Rose, and A. P. Newton (Cambridge, 1929), and in Leonard Woods Labaree, *Royal Government in America* (New Haven, 1930). Professor Labaree has carefully annotated the works on his list and it is especially valuable for the crown colonies. Oliver Perry Chitwood, *A History of Colonial America* (New York and London, 1931), contains a bibliography which is extensive and critical.

MANUSCRIPTS

PHOTOSTATS and transcripts relative to West Florida from the Public Record Office are found in important quantities in the collections of several research institutions. The Mississippi Department of Archives and History, at Jackson, has transcripts of C.O.5:582–597, and occasional documents from other volumes. A small part of these, edited by Dunbar Rowland, has been published as volume I of the *Mississippi Provincial Archives, English Dominion* (Nashville, Tennessee, 1911). The Alabama Department of Archives and History, at Montgomery, possesses transcripts of the provincial laws and an incomplete set of legislative journals and council minutes. The Florida State Historical Society has many valuable photostats and a large

number of maps. By far the most important collection of manuscript material on West Florida is in the Manuscripts Division
of the Library of Congress. Here one finds practically a complete
set of transcripts or photostats from C.O.5:574–635. These records contain correspondence of the Board of Trade and the
secretary of state with West Florida governors, the minutes of
the council, journals of the assembly, laws, warrants for surveys,
returns of surveys, grants of land, bills of sale, indentures, and
other legal documents. In addition to these there are several
volumes of original manuscript material which came to the Library by way of the General Land Office. The most interesting
of these is a Record of His Majesty's Sign Manuals, Patents,
Commissions, and Other Papers Passed under the Broad Seal
of His Majesty's Province of West Florida. This contains full
copies of some one hundred and sixty warrants, commissions,
and deputations of various kinds and is very useful for the study
of constitutional history. Other manuscript volumes contain
conveyances and grants of land, warrants for pardons, minutes
of certain meetings of the council, and journals of some of the
sessions of the assembly. Most if not all of the gaps in council
and assembly records are filled in by photostats from the Public
Record Office. Two volumes of the Secretary's Account Book
throw light on the fees of the colony.

The military history of West Florida is best followed through
documents which have only in recent years been made available.
In the William L. Clements Library of the University of Michigan is the correspondence of General Thomas Gage, British
commander-in-chief for North America, and the military commanders of West Florida. These letters with enclosures run into
the thousands and are concerned largely with the routine of
military administration and the disputes between the civil and
the military which characterized the history of the province.
Perhaps the most important letters in this collection from the
standpoint of West Florida are those of Brigadier General Frederick Haldimand, who was on terms of intimacy with General
Gage. These are for the most part calendared in the *Canadian
Archives*, 1890 (Ottawa, 1891). Selected letters from this collection have been compiled and edited by Clarence E. Carter, *The
Correspondence of General Thomas Gage*, 2 vols. (New Haven
and London, 1931 and 1933).

The Carleton Papers which contain the correspondence of
General Sir William Howe and General Sir Henry Clinton with

the West Florida commanders are in the possession of Colonial Williamsburg, Incorporated, and are available to the investigator in photostat form. These papers compare in importance, character, and volume with those referred to in the Clements Library but cover a later period. They give the British picture of the fall of the province. They have been calendared in "Report on American Manuscripts in the Royal Institution of Great Britain," *Historical Manuscripts Commission* (vol. I, London, 1904; vol. II, Dublin, 1906; vols. III and IV, Hereford, 1907 and 1909).

Less important materials are in other archives. The Howard Memorial Library in New Orleans has transcripts and translations of pertinent Spanish letters including Despatches of the Spanish Governors of Louisiana and Confidential Despatches of Don Bernardo Galvez to his uncle Don José de Galvez, secretary of state and ranking official of the Council of the Indies. The translations were made as a part of the Survey of Federal Archives in Louisiana Project under the direction of Stanley C. Arthur.

In the office of the Chancery Clerk at Natchez, Mississippi, there are a few volumes of local Spanish records beginning July 30, 1781. Some of these, containing as they do inventories of estates confiscated as a result of the outbreak of 1781, help to give an understanding of the standard of living maintained by Natchez planters. Translations are available.

The New York Public Library contains the letter book of John Fitzpatrick, a trader who resided variously at New Orleans, Mobile, and Manchac. Here is found a mine of information in regard to commerce on the Mississippi in the West Florida period. It has been occasionally referred to by historians but apparently has never been used to an appreciable extent.

There are maps in various collections that relate to this area in this period. In the Clements Library there are many, including one in detail by Bernard Romans to which is attached a description of the province. Interestingly enough no maps were found in the corresponding collections in Williamsburg. The Library of Congress has many photostats of maps from the Crown Collection of Great Britain. The Howard Memorial Library has a number of contemporary maps. In the Archives of the Mississippi River Commission at Vicksburg there has recently been discovered a contemporary manuscript map of the Mississippi region by William Wilton, assistant provincial surveyor, which

gives the location of some three hundred grants of land and by
an attached key names the grantees. Stanley C. Arthur has
made it available, in photostatic form and with brief editorial
comment, to the Howard Memorial Library and several other
institutions. A portion of the Stuart-Purcell Map of 1778, showing the road from Pensacola to St. Augustine, has been reproduced by Mark Boyd in the *Florida Historical Quarterly*, XVII
(1938–39), 15–24.

PRINTED DOCUMENTS

VERY little of the documentary source material for West Florida
has been published. The single volume of *Mississippi Provincial
Archives* has already been mentioned. Selections from the correspondence of Governor Peter Chester are found in volume V of
Publications of the Mississippi Historical Society, Centenary
Series (Jackson, 1925). The *Louisiana Historical Quarterly* has
published, with occasional introductions and brief annota-
tions by James A. Padgett: "Commission, Orders and Instructions Issued to George Johnstone, British Governor of West
Florida, 1763–1767," which includes the regular, the supple-
mentary, and the vice-admiralty commissions of Governor
Johnstone along with his instructions in regard to trade, XXI
(1938), 1021–1068; Minutes of the Assembly [title varies from
instalment to instalment], November 3, 1766, to June 29, 1769,
XXII (1939), 311–384, 943–1011, and XXIII (1940), 5–77;
"Minutes of the Council of West Florida," April 3 to July 22,
1769, XXIII (1940), 353–404; "The Reply of Peter Chester,
Governor of West Florida to Complaints Made Against His
Administration," XXII (1939), 31–46.

Several published collections include individual documents
which relate to West Florida. Among these are the following:
Acts of the Privy Council of England, Colonial Series, vols. IV–VI
(London, 1911–1912), edited by W. L. Grant and James Munro,
and *Journal of the Commissioners for Trade and Plantations*,
vols. XI–XIV (London, 1935–1938), contain many references
to West Florida and throw light on the history of the colony
from the standpoint of the mother country; *Documents Relating
to the Constitutional History of Canada, 1759–1791*, vol. I (Second and Revised Edition, Ottawa, 1918), edited and annotated
by Adam Shortt and A. G. Doughty, contains several papers
informative on the origin of West Florida; *Collections* of the
Illinois State Historical Library, vols. X, XI, and XVI (Spring-

field, 1915–1921), edited by Charles Walworth Alvord and Clarence Edwin Carter, contain documents which show Great Britain's plans for the West from 1763 until 1769; *The Correspondence of General Thomas Gage*, 2 vols. (New Haven and London, 1931 and 1933), compiled and edited by Clarence Edwin Carter, gives interesting sidelights on West Florida from the military point of view; Arthur Preston Whitaker's "Documents Relating to the Commercial Policy of Spain in the Floridas," in *Publications* of the Florida State Historical Society, vol. X (Deland, Florida, 1931), includes two reports which are of exceptional importance in explaining the English trade on the Mississippi River.

CONTEMPORARY ACCOUNTS

SEVERAL individuals have left valuable accounts of the provinces Captain Bernard Romans was in the colony for several years before the outbreak of the Revolution and was aided in his researches and map-making by grants from the British government. He wrote *A Concise Natural History of East and West Florida* (New York, 1775). This useful volume is very rare and a reprint would be most welcome. The Florida State Historical Society has already brought out a reprint of Romans' Map of 1774 with an explanatory volume, "Notes on the Life and Works of Bernard Romans," by P. Lee Phillips (Deland, Florida, 1924), *Publications*, vol. II. William Bartram's *Travels Through North and South Carolina, Georgia, East and West Florida* (Philadelphia, 1791), is valuable though the author's reliability may be open to question on occasion. It has been reprinted. *The History of the American Indians, Particularly of the Nations Adjoining the Mississippi, East and West Florida, Georgia, South and North Carolina, and Virginia* (London, 1775), by James Adair, is well-known and its value is probably not marred to any great extent by the endeavor of the author to identify the Indians as the descendants of the lost tribes of Israel. Captain Philip Pittman's *The Present State of the European Settlements on the Mississippi* (London, 1770), is an officer's sketch of the region described in the title. *An Historical Narrative and Topographical Description of Louisiana and West Florida*, by Thomas Hutchins, "Geographer to the United States" (Philadelphia, 1784), is a very informing account of the country. Hutchins was thoroughly familiar with the colony because of his work in West Florida as an engineer and he wrote with a sure touch. For a view of the conditions of agriculture and planting, the diary of William Dunbar in *Life, Letters, and Papers of William Dunbar*, by Mrs. Dunbar Rowland (Jackson, Mississippi, 1930), is not surpassed. Dunbar's plantation was on the Mississippi not far from Manchac and the owner kept a careful record of his activities between the years 1776 and 1780. Later he was to become, on the recommendation of Thomas Jefferson, a member of the American Philosophical Society and was to make numerous contributions to its volumes. *Memoirs and Adventures of Captain Matthew Phelps*, by Anthony Haswell (Bennington, Vermont, 1802), is an account of the sad experiences which befell an inhabitant of Connecticut when he attempted to take up land on the Mississippi during the period of the Revolution. It is significant in suggesting the flow of emigrants from the New England colonies to West Florida in the 1770's. The journals of Israel and Rufus Putnam, New Englanders who made a trip to the Mississippi in the interest of the Company of Military Adventurers, have been edited by A. C. Bates and published by the Connecticut Historical Society (Hartford, 1931). *An Account of the First Discovery and Natural History of Florida* (London, 1763), by William Roberts with maps and plans by Thomas Jefferys, "Geographer to His Majesty," was probably written to meet the demand of the English for information about the newly-acquired territory and is of value largely because of the maps by the famous cartographer.

CONTEMPORARY MAGAZINES AND NEWSPAPERS

No papers or magazines were published in West Florida during the British period but contemporary issues of *Scots Magazine* (Edinburgh), *The Gentleman's Magazine* (London), *The Political Magazine* (London), and the *South Carolina Gazette* (Charles Town) contain numbers of references to West Florida which, if not of great historical value, at least indicate the current interest in the new province.

SECONDARY AUTHORITIES

SEVERAL of the older state histories contain interesting accounts of West Florida but the student must guard carefully against errors when using them. Among the best are the following: *History of Alabama and Incidentally of Georgia and Mississippi, from the Earliest Period*, by James A. Pickett (Sheffield, Alabama, 1896; the first edition is dated 1851); *Mississippi as a Province, Territory, and State* (Jackson, 1880), by John Francis Hamtramck Claiborne; *History of the Discovery and Settlement of the Valley of the Mississippi*, in two volumes, by John W. Monette (New York, 1846). The first two volumes of Alcée Fortier's *A History of Louisiana* (New York, 1904), touch on this period and contain liberal excerpts from valuable documents. Richard L. Campbell, *Historical Sketches of Colonial Florida* (Cleveland, 1892) devotes a number of chapters to British West Florida and gives many intimate touches.

Modern historians have touched lightly but with increasing frequency upon the province. Charles Walworth Alvord's *The Mississippi Valley in British Politics* (2 vols., Cleveland, 1917), and an article, "The Genesis of the Proclamation of 1763," in *Michigan Pioneer and Historical Collections*, XXXVI, 20–52 (Lansing, 1908), are very helpful in indicating the policy of the British government in the West after 1763. Clarence Edwin Carter has made four contributions of importance. These are *Great Britain and the Illinois Country, 1763–1774* (Washington, 1910); "British Policy towards the American Indians in the South, 1763–8," in the *English Historical Review*, XXXIII, 37–56 (London, 1918); "Some Aspects of British Administration in West Florida," in the *Mississippi Valley Historical Review*, I (1914–15), 364–375; and "The Beginnings of British West Florida," *ibid.*, IV (1917–18), 314–341.

C. N. Howard has published a series of articles that relate to various aspects of the history of the colony. Apparently these are chapters from a doctoral dissertation presented at the University of California. Most of them have appeared in the *Florida Historical Quarterly:* "The Military Occupation of British West Florida," XVII (1938–39), 181–197; "Governor Johnstone in West Florida," *ibid.*, pp. 281–303; "Colonial Pensacola: The British Period," XIX (1940–41), 109–127, 246–269, 368–398. In the *Louisiana Historical Quarterly* is "The Interval of Military Government in West Florida," XXI (1938), 18–30. The *Journal of Southern History* contains "Some Economic Aspects of British West Florida, 1763–1768," VI (1940), 201–221. Dr. Howard writes with erudition and discernment. Apparently he has not had at his disposal important sources which might have added light in various places. He leans heavily upon the Minutes of the Council, uses the correspondence of the governors sparingly, depends largely on published materials for military matters, and seemingly has not used a complete collection of the laws of the province.

Additional articles in the *Mississippi Valley Historical Review* should be mentioned: "Spanish Influence in the West during the American Revolution," IV (1917–18), 193–208, and "Oliver Pollock, Financier of the Revolution in the West," XVI (1929–30), 67–80, by James Alton James; "The Loyalists in West Florida and the Natchez District," II (1915–16), 465–483, by Wilbur Henry Siebert; and "Efforts of Spain to Maintain Sources of Information in the Colonies before 1779," XV (1928–29), 56–68, and "Peter Chester's Defense of the Mississippi after the Willing Raid," XXII (1935–36), 17–32, by Kathryn Abbey.

Two recent biographies relate in part to the history of West Florida. James Alton James, *Oliver Pollock: The Life and Times of an Unknown Patriot* (New York and London, 1937), reveals clearly the interest of the Continental Congress in the province and the relations between the revolting colonies and Spanish Louisiana. Dr. James' interesting and valuable study might have been more complete had he used all the materials available in the Library of Congress for the British side of the picture. John W. Caughey, "Bernardo de Galvez," in *Publications* of the University of California at Los Angeles in Social Sciences, vol. IV (Berkeley, 1934), gives a full account of the conquest of the province by Spain. Dr. Caughey's strength is that he has utilized fully available Spanish accounts. He has used British accounts less fully. Both Dr. James and Dr. Caughey have incorporated in their books the findings reported in earlier articles which they have published.

A valuable monograph is "The West in the Diplomacy of the Revolution," by Paul Crisler Phillips, in the *University of Illinois Studies in Social Science*, vol. II (Urbana, 1913). A Bryn Mawr doctoral dissertation, *British Administration of the Southern Indians, 1756–1783* (Lancaster, Pennsylvania, 1931), by Helen Louise Shaw, touches on West Florida. Arthur Preston Whitaker's *The Spanish American Frontier: 1783–1795* (Cambridge, 1927) treats adequately the subject covered by its title. Peter Joseph Hamilton's *Colonial Mobile* (New York and Boston, 1898), is a delightful volume and his "British West Florida," in *Publications* of the Mississippi Historical Society, VII, 399–426 (Oxford, Mississippi, 1903), is a good brief treatment of the subject.

INDEX

Absenteeism, prevalence of, in colony, 226–228

Acts of Trade, 187

Acts, provincial. *See* Laws

Admiralty, Lords of the, 44

Agent, colonial (fiscal), 97n

Agent, colonial (legislative), 97

Agriculture, products of, 169–172

Aird, William, house of, rented for government purposes, 96

Alexander, Harry, urges moving seat of government to Mississippi region, 146; writes Germain on seizures in Mississippi River, 197n

Alliance, Franco-Spanish, 1779, 204

Alliance, Franco-American, 204

Alsopp, Andrew and wife, Sarah Forward apprenticed to, 181

Ames, John, carpenter, 181

Amory, Simon, appointed register of grants, patents, and records, and clerk of naval office, 27–28; death of, 28n

Amoss, James, unable to serve in assembly, 94

Apprentices, terms of indentures, 181

Artisans, scarcity of, 181

Assembly, composition and procedure as prescribed by governor's instructions, 16–18; urges opening of Spanish trade, 45; election and first session of, 47, 85–91; laws enacted, 48, 110–112; protests removal of troops, 66; full discussion of, 83–114; circumstances relating to first meeting of, 84–85; rules of order, 87–90; committees of, 91–92; procedure in, 92–94; personnel of, 98–99; relations of Johnstone with, 100–101; of Browne with, 101–105; dissolved by Eliot, 105; relations of Durnford with, 105–106; Chester has trouble with, 106–110; laws disallowed by Privy Council, 113–114; significance of, 114; abortive session in 1778, 211; Continental Congress writes to, 205

Atkin, Edmund, first Indian agent for southern district, 37

Augston, Thomas, sells Negro, 177

Augusta, 190

Baird, James, immigrant from North Carolina, 148

Barnaby, Sir William, attends Indian congress, 41

Bartram, William, describes Mobile, 156; describes inhabitants of Point Coupée, 158; mentions road to Manchac, 185

Bassett, immigrant from Georgia, 147

Baton Rouge, neighborhood of plantations, 157

Bay, Elihu Hall, member of provincial bureaucracy, 99, 228; town lots sold to, 146; presides in vice-admiralty case, 231

Bay, John, holds several offices by deputation, 228

Beverages, alcoholic, 160

Biloxi, settled by French, 1699, 151; occupied by only a few families, 158

Blackwell, Jacob, appointed to council, stamp tax distributor, 26, 224; receives mandamus for grant of land, 131; sells ten slaves, 177

Blackwell, Rebecca, wife of Jacob,

Crips, a producer of naval stores, 184

Crofton, Fort, 158

Crook, Robert, appointed to council, 26

Cuba, returned to Spain, 1

Culture. *See* Blommart, John; Education; Religion

D'Abbadie, Monsieur, ranking French officer in Louisiana, contends with Farmar regarding government property in Mobile, 13

Dalling, General John, governor of Jamaica, sends force to defend West Florida, 209

Dartmouth, Earl of, frowns on western expansion, 124; informed regarding immigration, 140; warns against improvident grants of land, 141; designates province as asylum for loyalists, 144; requested to send armed vessel to mouth of Mississippi, 195

Dartmouth, town of, ordered laid out, 145; lots sold in, 146

Dawson, Rev. William, Anglican minister at Pensacola, 164

Debts and debtors, 112, 162

Deerskins. *See* Fitzpatrick, John; Trade, Indian

Delaware, unicameral legislature in, 83

Dickson, Lieutenant Colonel Alexander, sent on mission to New Orleans, 196; in discussion with Galvez, 196; reports to council, 197; attacked by Galvez and surrenders Mississippi region, 213

Dispatch, schooner, captured by Americans, 197

Disputes, civil *vs.* military. *See* Campbell, John; Chester, Peter; Farmar, Robert; Johnstone, George

Dobbins, Thomas, apprenticed to Samuel Carr, 181

Dominica, ceded to England, 1;

two ports in opened to Spanish trade, 44

Donald, James and Robert, immigrants from Virginia, 147

Driscoll, Henry, part owner of saw mill, 182

Dunbar, William, comes to West Florida, 148; buys supplies at Point Coupée, 159; clothes allowed slaves, 159; slaves sickly from cold, 160; describes a social occasion, 160; life on his plantation, 171–173; agricultural products, 171; treatment of slaves, 172–173; prices received for slaves, 177; mentions mulatto child, 178; employs carpenter and blacksmith, 181; interested in stave-making, 184; imports oxen from Point Coupée, 185; mentions Natchez road, 185; flees Willing raiders, 208; describes Willing raid, 233n

Duncan, Alexander, clerk of crown, clerk of common pleas, judge of vice-admiralty, 227

Duncan, William, confined by order of assembly, 91

Durnford, Elias, lieutenant governor and surveyor general, appropriations made to, for fortifications, 22; admitted to council, 26; goes to England, 70; appointed lieutenant governor, 71; assumes government, 72; sketch of, 72n; relations with assembly, 105–106; receives mandamus for grant of land, 131; activities in Mississippi region, 135; tells of immigration to Mississippi region, 136; sends vessel to Vera Cruz, 136; estimates population, 149, 152; lays out Campbell Town, 152; herd of cattle, 170; comments on Spanish and skin trades, 189, 191; favors proclamation of martial law, 214; in command at fall of Mobile, 216

Durnford, Rebecca, wife of Elias, petitions for grant of land, 131

Gage, General Thomas, informed of visit of Spanish ship to Pensacola, 13; urges friendliness to The Mortar, 41; comments on dispute between civil and military, 53; receives satirical letter from Johnstone, 54; replies in kind, 54n; transmits orders for removal of troops, 65; low opinion of worth of colony, 67n; comments on policy of setting one Indian tribe against another, 78n; explains reluctance of Indians to cede lands, 81n; comments on Spanish trade, 188

Galvez, Bernardo de, comments on English trade in Mississippi River, 193n; strengthens Spanish administration in Louisiana, 196; seizes English ships in Mississippi, 196; refuses to have Americans surrender seized schooner, 197; extends favors to Americans, 203, 206; corresponds with Colonel George Morgan, 206; conquers Mississippi region, 213; leads expedition against Mobile, 215–216; visits Havana, 216; besieges Pensacola and receives surrender, 217

Georgia, West Florida laws similar to those of, 111; immigrants from, 147; has parliamentary support fund, 225

Germain, Lord George, urged to move seat of government to Mississippi region, 146; gives permission to apply fines on church building, 166; advises expedition against New Orleans, 211

Germans, in Louisiana, 32, 32n; brought in by Jeremiah Terry, 152-153

Germany, James, frees slave, 178

Gibson, Captain George, brings dispatch to Governor Unzaga, 205

Gillies, Rev. David, appointment as

Anglican minister at Pensacola opposed, 165

Gin, cotton, mentioned, 183

Gordon, Arthur, advocate general of vice-admiralty court, 27; records proceedings of Indian congress, 39

Gordon, Captain Harry, comments on production of naval stores, 184

Gordon, John, immigrant from Virginia, 147

Gordon, Rev. William, Anglican minister at Mobile, 163, 166

Gospel, Society for Propagation of, to aid in erection of church at Mobile, 29

Governor, part in administration of colony, 15–20; forbidden to leave colony for Europe, 16; attempt to build home for, 96n See also Chester, Peter; Johnstone, George

Grand Jury, calls attention to need for militia, 207

Grant, Francis, governor of East Florida, 3

Grayden, Alexander, immigrant from South Carolina, 147

Grenada, island of, ceded to England, 1; government recommended for, 3; government of, erected by Proclamation of 1763, 5; immigrants from, 148

Grenadines, ceded to England, 1

Grimaldi, Jerónimo, Spanish foreign minister, urged to aid Americans, 202

Haldimand, Brigadier General Frederick, commands southern district, 65; unfavorable report on colony, 67; house rented for government purposes, 96

Halifax, Earl of, succeeds Egremont as secretary of state for southern department, gives directions regarding proposed proclamation, 4; memorialized by French in Mobile, 31; allows

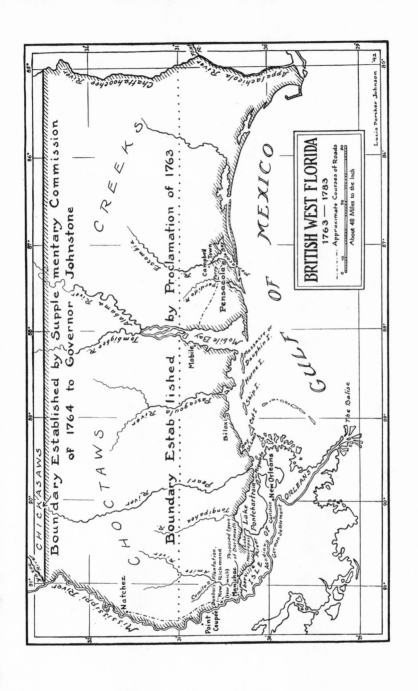

BRITISH WEST FLORIDA
1763 — 1783
------ Approximate Courses of Roads
About 48 Miles to the Inch

Lucia Porcher Johnson '42